Literary
Interpretations
of Biblical
Narratives

The Bible in Literature Courses

Literary Interpretations of Biblical Narratives

Edited by Kenneth R. R. Gros Louis
with James S. Ackerman
and Thayer S. Warshaw

Nashville   Abingdon Press   New York

LITERARY INTERPRETATIONS OF BIBLICAL NARRATIVES

Copyright © 1974 by Abingdon Press

Library of Congress Cataloging in Publication Data

GROS LOUIS, KENNETH R. R. 1936-   Literary in-
terpretations of Biblical narratives. (Bible in litera-
ture courses). Based on lectures presented at the
Indiana University Institute on Teaching Bible in
Secondary English in the summer of 1970-73. Bib-
liography: p. 1. Bible as literature. I. Ackerman,
James Stokes. II. Warshaw, Thayer S., 1915-
III. Title. IV. Series.
BS535.G76   809'.935'22   74-12400

ISBN 0-687-22131-5

MANUFACTURED   BY   PARTHENON   PRESS   AT
NASHVILLE, TENNESSEE, UNITED STATES OF AMERICA

Contents

16851

Preface

In 1969 the Indiana University Department of Religious Studies received the first of three grants from the Lilly Endowment, Incorporated, to conduct a series of summer institutes for secondary school teachers of English who wanted to develop or improve courses or units using the Bible in their literature classes. There were three favorable conditions: increasing student interest in the Bible, the trend toward elective courses, and the 1963 U. S. Supreme Court decision banning devotional Bible reading in public schools and its accompanying opinion that encouraged study of the Bible as part of the academic curriculum. We have been overwhelmed by the interest shown by professional educators and by the flood of applications at the secondary school and, more recently, college levels.

Although we hope that what we have begun will be continued in the modified form of a regular summer school course at Indiana University, the series of intensive institutes officially ended with the summer of 1974. We have worked with over three hundred outstanding secondary school and college teachers from forty-eight states (besides the District of Columbia, Canada, and Great Britain) and helped them develop syllabi, curricular units, and teaching materials appropriate to the specific needs and interests of their own classes. The institutes focused on four main areas: historical and critical study of Scripture, sensitivity to problems of teaching the Bible in the public schools (and colleges) of an open society, critical analyses of literature that depends on the Bible (the Bible *in* literature), and the Bible *as* literature—the concern of this book.

As we (one a university biblical scholar, the other a high school teacher of English) prepared ourselves for this new enterprise, one disheartening fact became immediately apparent: literary analyses of the Bible are virtually nonexistent. There is a vast corpus of commentaries on the various books of the Bible, which often provide background information but little direct help for the literature teacher's main interest. The dominant interest of biblical scholarship is historical, linguistic, and theological—not literary.

We turned, therefore, to the Indiana University Department of English for help in providing original critical analyses of the literary craftsmanship of the Bible. We have found a rich abundance of resources. Kenneth R. R. Gros Louis, chairman of the department and editor of this volume, produced an excellent series of lectures on the literary aspects of several portions of the Bible. The results of his lectures form the nucleus of this book. Fifteen of the seventeen essays collected here were first given as lectures in our institute; fourteen were written by scholars primarily trained in literary criticism. The major thrust, then, is literary rather than religious or sectarian. Although it is not an important factor and quite accidental, the odd fact is that of the nine contributors, three come from within the Jewish tradition, three from the Roman Catholic, and three from the Protestant.

Unfortunately, our institutes have been unique and limited in capacity and duration. We have been uncomfortably aware that the 300 participants we selected are only a small percentage of the thousands of literature teachers whose schools have introduced or are introducing the Bible into their curriculum. We feel an obligation to make our innovative lectures, which our alumni found so useful, available to other teachers.

This book is a pioneering venture into relatively uncharted territory: we are not presenting biblical scholarship nor are we merely exploring the superficial esthetic surface of biblical literature. We feel strongly that we are opening up a new and very fruitful way of examining Scripture which will benefit both disciplines on the one hand, enrich the insights gained from other existing interpretive methodologies and, on the other, offer to literature teachers ways of approaching the Bible within the usual categories of their discipline. We realize that this volume represents only a first step and hope that others will be encouraged to make further contributions in this area.

Thanks are in order, not only to Lilly Endowment, Incorporated, for sponsoring the five years of institutes and providing partial subsidy for publishing the results, but also to the editors of Abingdon Press for nonsectarian service to public education by agreeing to publish this book, which is the first in a series of resources for teachers of literature. Other volumes in the series will soon follow: (1) a teacher's guide for using the Bible in secondary school, with practical suggestions for curriculum and methods and for ways of dealing with issues arising from the special nature of the subject; (2) a book giving scholarly background on the literature of the New Testament, as a companion to the 1973 *Teaching the Old Testament in English Classes*, written by James S. Ackerman et al., and published by Indiana University Press; (3) an anthology of analyses of contemporary literature strongly dependent on biblical stories—the Bible *in* literature; (4) bibliographies of suitable materials for use by teachers and by students.

A final word of gratitude for help with this publishing project: to Jo Ann Carlton, our administrative assistant, for her charm, efficiency, intelligence, and energy in seeing the wide variety of projects undertaken by our institute program, including this book, through to completion; to Amy Hazelrigg, Donna Hearn, Connie Neuenschwander, and Jo Ellen Legg for the long hours they have put in typing and retyping manuscripts; and to our patient wives, Alexandra and Bernice.

James S. Ackerman
Thayer S. Warshaw

Introduction

This collection may at first glance seem superfluous or redundant. More studies are in print about the Bible than about any other book in Western culture; indeed, with the exception of Shakespeare's plays, no stories originally intended for a particular national audience have been as internationally assimilated as biblical narratives. A significant gap exists in biblical scholarship, however, which this volume would begin to fill.

Biblical scholarship pursues a wide variety of interests: (1) establishing accurate texts and translations, which involves analyzing the linguistic relationships between Hebrew and other languages; (2) understanding the cultural milieu and historical circumstances in which biblical literature developed and about which it is principally concerned; (3) searching for possible sources and analogues of Bible stories; (4) explicating biblical theology—the idea of God and man, the concept of salvation, and so on; (5) determining the explicit or implicit religious attitudes of various sources in the Bible, particularly as they reflect the changing attitudes of the Hebrew people; (6) seeking the earliest form of individual stories by peeling away their layers and explaining how they gradually developed. These interests are either specifically identified—form criticism, redaction criticism, *Literaturgeschichte*—or fall under the more traditional classifications of literary scholarship.

The major preoccupations of biblical scholars, in other words, have involved in some form or another the quest for historical reality. Scholarship on the Moses birth and youth story (Exodus 1-2), for example, has been concerned with analogies in other ancient Near Eastern heroes' birth stories, the Egyptian background of Moses' name, Egyptian culture and the pharaoh's court, the enslavement of the Hebrews during the New Kingdom period (especially the construction of Raamses and Pithon during the 18th and 19th Egyptian dynasties). The quest has also turned to literary analysis, and identified a priestly source in Exodus 1:1-7, 13-14; 2:23-25, and two narrative sources which can be characterized according to certain criteria. The motivation for this source division, however, is historical; the extrapolated theologies of the sources provide insights into the various religious viewpoints which developed over the centuries. These approaches to the text may be necessary and important, but they must be consigned to the realm of "background information" for the student of literature who would interpret the text as a whole, regardless of the historical event described in the story and the historical circumstances which brought the text into its present form.

Shakespearian scholarship is, of course, also characterized by most of the scholarly interests loosely defined above (they are by no means mutually exclusive). But the scales are not weighted on the side of textual, historical, and theological studies. The world of the play—of the narrative of *Hamlet*, for example—is acknowledged as existing on its own, too. We may want to know when *Hamlet* was written down and by whom, what the audience was like, what sources were used, what historical circumstances contributed to the play, how the play was performed, how its philosophical or religious tendencies reflect Shakespeare's age, and how accurate the text is. Similar concerns have characterized scholarship on the Bible. With *Hamlet*, however, we also recognize that we can read and analyze the play without knowing any of this information; the play itself gives us everything we need. Studies exist, therefore, often without reference to Shakespeare's cultural and historical milieu, of the characters in the play, the atmosphere at the court of Denmark, the images which help us define Hamlet's world, the significance of individual soliloquies, even of brief asides. Scholarly baggage is left at the station and the critical train moves out anyway. (Obviously I exaggerate somewhat; the ride is more enjoyable if we have not lost all our baggage.) A balance has been achieved, for us as readers and students, between historical reality and literary reality. In biblical studies, on the other hand, there is no balance between the two. Only a few articles and a few chapters in books analyze biblical literature without recourse to highly specialized scholarly apparatus. The effect is to keep most modern readers of biblical criticism at a considerable distance from the marvelous literature of the Bible. We remain awed. Literary analysis of the Bible and its hypothesized authors or compilers will in no way detract from the magnificence of the stories or the astonishing achievements of the tellers. On the contrary, the study of the Bible as literature, without regard to its textual and historical background, its religious and cultural foundations, is likely to enlarge its already considerable empire in our minds.

As students of literature we have several options or strategies which we might call upon in a literary study of the Bible. We can concentrate on the hypothetical writers' biographies, if we can deduce them, and analyze how they influence the creative work. We can study the historical circumstances of these writings—the social, political, religious, economic backgrounds—and ask how the narratives reflect and comment on these conditions. (We should recognize that these and the following options are considerably more of a problem with the Bible than with other literature. With no other literature does belief in the existence of a creative author or compiler involve the salvation or damnation of the reader's soul.) We can consider the genres or modes of the writing—does it slavishly follow tradition or is it innovative? We can seek out sources; compile them; compare them with the biblical narrative; note the deletions, changes, and additions. We can examine the stories as they might relate to myths and legends, to archetypal characters and situations. We can, if we are adherents of a specific school of criticism, if we read literature narrowly as reflecting a political or ethical philosophy, apply to the narratives limiting interpretations in terms of Freudian psychology, Marxism, existentialism, Christianity, and so on. We might analyze the narratives in relation to other narratives of the same epoch, in the same region or in other parts of the world. Or, finally, we can study the biblical narratives as worlds of their own apart from all of these concerns—analyze internal dynamics, ironies and paradoxes, interaction among characters and among scenes, narrational intrusion, settings, development of thematic and imagistic patterns, transformations of character, formal structures.

As students of literature we have all of these options or strategies, any offshoot of one, or any combination of all, available to us. But as teachers of literature, I believe that our emphasis should be on the last option—on biblical narratives as worlds of their own. This does not mean that we should be ignorant of biographical, bibliographical, historical, and generic information, sources and religious interpretations, or various critical approaches. Our emphasis in the classroom, however, should not be on these kinds of knowledge. Teaching the Bible can be controversial. We should avoid playing a biblical text off against an underlying historical reality. The text itself affirms a reality, one which is obscured when the text is divided into sources or when questions of historical validity are raised. The text is best understood when taken as a whole and when the questions raised center on literary craftsmanship.

This is the assumption which underlies the following essays. The collection is obviously not exhaustive. In moving into a relatively new territory for biblical studies (and not without considerable fear and trembling), an attempt has been made to include essays on popular narratives and some not so popular, on prose narratives and poetry, on entire books of the Bible and on individual sections of books. The essays, constant in their assumption, are not constant in their literary method and approach. My own essays are shamelessly formalistic and tend to let the biblical narratives do most of the work. The essays on the Rabbinic method,

Moses, and Jonah, on the other hand, make more use of historical and scholarly knowledge, but only when it contributes naturally to literary analysis of the text being considered. The essays on Joseph and Matthew take particular critical stances and develop theses which open up further study of these and similar texts. D. F. Rauber's essay on Ruth deserves special mention because it represents one of the earliest attempts at literary analysis of the Bible (as Professor Rauber clearly recognizes in his introduction). The essay also demonstrates the loss which Professor Rauber's premature death meant for literary study of the Bible. For the most part the essays follow the order of the Bible; several changes have been made in order to group essays on similar biblical passages (individual characters, poetry, statements of pessimism) together.

Despite the observations made about biblical scholarship at the opening of this introduction, these essays owe a significant debt to a number of historical studies and source analyses of biblical narratives. Scholarly approaches to the Bible have produced remarkable results and added immeasurably to our understanding of Israel's historical and religious development within her cultural environment. Some of the important studies are cited in the essays themselves; others, equally important, influenced a number of the essays. The matter of indebtedness in any collection of this kind goes well beyond secondary sources. In this instance, my greatest personal debt is to the participants of the Indiana University Institute on Teaching the Bible in Secondary English in the summers of 1970-73. The seventy teachers each summer who made up the audience which first heard my lectures constituted the best audience I have ever had. They were not students, but colleagues; and their response to my venture into little-known territory made me feel like a native. Their enthusiasm for the study of the Bible as literature must, by now, have affected many classes of students, as it potently affected me. Jim Ackerman and Thayer Warshaw, co-directors of the Institute, have been remarkable in the accuracy and justness of their criticisms of my drafts. It is customary to thank one's wife and children in introductions; I thank Dee, Amy, and Julie for slowing down the writing enough to give me ample time to come to the drafts of the essays with a fresh view.

Kenneth R. R. Gros Louis

I The Rabbinic Method and Literary Criticism

KALMAN P. BLAND, *Department of Religion, Duke University*

A medieval Jewish mystic once compared the Bible to a "beautiful and stately maiden, who is secluded in an isolated chamber of a palace." Her lover "passes by her gate unceasingly, and turns his eyes in all directions to discover her." What does she do? "She thrusts open a door in her secret chamber, for a moment reveals her face to her lover, giving him a signal of love, then quickly retreats back to her hiding place." Catching her message, the lover "is drawn to her with his whole heart and soul, and with all his being." The face of the maiden, her signal of love, and her invitation to ever greater intimacy are "the words of the Torah." This beguiling allegory teaches that to appreciate the meaning and beauty of Scripture in its fullness we must not dismiss a single word as mere rhetorical embellishment or as unnecessary verbiage. Only our attentiveness to the latent significance of each and every word and to their contextual relationships will permit us, like the mystics and the rabbis before them, to know the Bible. Let me share with you several examples of this method for reading Scripture inspired by the traditional Jewish way of biblical study known as *midrash aggadah*.[1]

When Noah is described as a "righteous man, blameless in his generation" (Gen. 6:9), does it not strike the careful reader that the phrase "in his generation" is superfluous? Can anyone imagine Noah, or any man for that matter, living in an age not his own? That phrase and the question it raises are a "signal of love" from the Torah[2] which beckons intellect and imagination to participate with this verse in the creation of its meaning or meanings. Perhaps "in his generation" comes to praise Noah, for despite the wickedness of his evil contemporaries, Noah remained steadfast in his refusal to sink to their corruption. Or perhaps "in his generation" comes to criticize Noah. Judged against the moral standards and practices of his day, he was righteous; but had he lived in an age blessed with truly good men, Noah would not appear to be blameless. When we recall his drunkenness and the events connected with it (Gen. 9:20-27), this latter interpretation seems more plausible and satisfying.

Consider: Do we not know that Abraham is the father and that Isaac is the son? Why then does Genesis 22 find it necessary to repeat again and again the words "father" and "son" (vv. 2, 3, 6-10, 12, 13) in a chapter which uses only nineteen verses to record with unsurpassed economy the story of Abraham's greatest trial? And is it not Isaac's greatest trial as well? The redundancy becomes all the more irritating when we search in vain for a single explicit comment describing the emotional and psychological state of either Abraham or Isaac. Our irritation here is the effect of having received a scriptural "signal of love." By means of what it does say and what it does not say the Bible arouses us to share with it in the creation of its meaning. To read the Bible in a passive way, expecting everything to be explicit, demanding that everything be presented in a finished form, is to transfer to the study of biblical literature habits and postures acquired through overexposure to our visual media. We are accustomed to being observers, not participants in the creative act which produces art. Yet this is precisely what is called for in reading Scripture as literature. Without our involvement and engagement in this process, the Bible will forever remain "in her secret chamber, in her hiding place." As for Genesis 22, does not the disproportionate use of "father" and "son" heighten the drama, underscore the tension, and cause our souls to shudder sympathetically with Abraham and Isaac? Even the reader cannot escape sensing the enormity of what is transpiring between a father and "[his] son, [his] only son, whom [he] love[s]." And does not the twice-uttered phrase "they went both of them together" (vv. 6, 8) suggest a mutuality of spirit as well as a physical walking side-by-side?

Here is a more complicated example. Having been informed by the omniscient narrator that "Isaac was old and his eyes were dim so that he could not see" (Gen. 27:1), is not Jacob's concern and Rebekah's hastily conceived ruse in the matter of the blessing misdirected? Haunted by the oracle that Esau would serve Jacob (Gen. 25:23) and blinded by her love of Jacob, she overlooks the obvious. Overeager to receive his father's blessing, Jacob's fear of discovery by touch also overlooks the obvious. Ironically it is their vision and not Isaac's which is truly impaired. Are not their eyes "dim so that [they] could not see" that a blind man compensates for his handicap by listening more carefully than the sighted, and that a blind father will recognize his son the moment he hears his voice? No porridge, no matter how tasty, and no disguise, no matter how ingenious, could ever fool a blind father. Yet mother and son fail to foresee that despite his eyes, Isaac will see the truth. "The voice is Jacob's voice, but the hands are the hands of Esau." Since he proceeds, nevertheless, to bless the impostor, may we not infer that Isaac is fully aware of the deception, that he is permitting himself to be fooled for reasons the Bible has not made explicit? Here is Jacob standing in place of Esau disguised in an animal's skin, "the skins of the kids." Touching that skin, Isaac's memory flashes images of that fateful moment when his own father Abraham

lifted up his eyes and looked, and behold, behind him was a ram, caught in a thicket by his horns; and Abraham went and took the ram, and offered it up as a burnt offering instead of his son. So Abraham called the name of that place The LORD will provide; as it is said to this day, "On the mount of the LORD it shall be provided." And the angel . . . said, "By myself I have sworn, says the Lord, because you have done this, and have not withheld your son, your only son, I will indeed bless you. . . . And your descendants shall possess the gate of their enemies." (Gen. 22:13-17)

Then it was Isaac's physical survival, now it is his spiritual destiny that is guaranteed in precisely the same way: by an act of one standing in the place of another. Isaac senses the imperative that he must join wholeheartedly with mother and son to conspire in denying the rights of primogeniture to

Esau, just as his own mother, Sarah, had done when she banished his older brother, Ishmael (Gen. 16). Whether or not these were the kinds of thoughts echoing in Isaac's mind is of little importance. Whatever the truth might be, our analysis does suggest the depth of aesthetic enjoyment—and dare we say it, the edification—waiting for the careful student of Scripture.

Before leaving Genesis 27, we should not ignore what lies hidden in "Jacob's voice." To be sure, it means the sound of, the physical properties of Jacob's voice. But listen to how Jacob betrays himself by his language when contrasted with the words of Esau: "I have done as you told me. Now sit up and eat . . . because the LORD your God granted me success." Is Esau the kind of son who ever said to his father: "I have done as you told me"? Look to Genesis 26:34-35. When before has Isaac ever heard Esau, the "skilful hunter, a man of the field" (Gen. 25:27), attribute his success to God?

Neither should we overlook the device of redundant identification used in exactly the same way as it is used in chapter 22. Esau, described from Isaac's perspective, is "his older son" (27:1); from Rebekah's perspective merely "his son" (v. 5). Is not the missing "older" an important signal? Speaking to Jacob in verse 6, Rebekah calls Esau "your brother." But in verse 15, Esau is now "her older son." In this subtle shift, Scripture reveals a mother's agony when finally she realizes that what she is doing on behalf of her child is done only at the expense of her other child, her firstborn son. The possibilities for interpretation here seem limitless.

Jacob, however, is spared the pain which comes with realizing what this loss means to his brother. At least he is spared any immediate sense of guilt, any immediate suffering. But consider Jacob's life after the deception. "Measure for measure" the ancient rabbis would say. Enchanted by the younger Rachel, he is deceived into marrying Leah, the elder (Gen. 29:15-27). Leah *in place of* Rachel! Will Jacob see the weak eyes of Leah and not be plagued with memories of a trick played against an aged father whose "eyes were dim"? Does he not know the anguish of Esau when Laban states: "It

19

is not so done in our country, to give the younger before the first-born." Will not Jacob be punished for his deception in taking precedence over his older brother by the very same instruments he used when he deceived?

Years later, Jacob and Rachel have two sons and the elder, the seventeen-year-old Joseph, is sold into slavery by his ten brothers. To deceive Jacob, his ten sons

> took Joseph's robe, and killed a goat, and dipped the robe in the blood; and they sent the long robe with sleeves and brought it to their father, and said, "This we have found; see now whether it is your son's robe or not." And he recognized it, and said, "It is my son's robe; a wild beast has devoured him; Joseph is without doubt torn to pieces." Then Jacob rent his garments, and put sackcloth upon his loins, and mourned for his son many days. All his sons and all his daughters rose up to comfort him; but he refused to be comforted, and said, "No, I shall go down to Sheol to my son, mourning." Thus his father wept for him. (Gen. 37:31-35)

Sunk in a bitter, inconsolable mourning, the once encouraging but now empty assurances of his mother ring mockingly in his memory: "Upon me be your curse, my son," Rebekah had said. First the deception and trickery of Laban, then an interminable series of family crises, and now the loss of Joseph—what is left for Jacob to suffer? "No, I shall go down to Sheol to my son, mourning."

Not until Jacob sees Joseph dressed in the royal robes of Egypt will his grief come to an end. And not until Joseph's brothers turn dreams into reality, thereby consummating the oracle of Rebekah that the older shall serve the younger, will the Bible relax, however briefly, the ever-increasing dramatic tension with which it narrates the eventual liberation of Israel at Sinai. But in Genesis 37 Jacob is a broken man, shattered by the intensity of his loss. The reader, however, knows what Jacob cannot know, that Joseph is alive and well: "Meanwhile the Midianites had sold him in Egypt to Potiphar, an officer of Pharaoh, the captain of the guard" (v. 36). What better way to make us feel Jacob's agony than to juxtapose the high-pitched description of his mourning with a laconic, objective, neutral statement of historical fact?

But how explain the placement of chapter 38, the episode of Tamar and Judah, which so rudely interrupts the natural continuity of 37:36 and 39:1, breaking as it does the unity of thematic, dramatic, and chronological development? Why this sudden shift from Jacob's grief, ironically unfounded in fact, and from Joseph's career in Egypt to the story of a man, three sons, and his daughter-in-law?

Before undertaking to answer this question, a restatement of the method for reading Scripture described here is in order. The art of biblical narrative consists of signals addressed to the sensitive reader. These signals function as agents which stimulate our intellect, our imagination, and our capacity for empathy in order to engage us in a mutual act of literary creation with Scripture itself. These signals take many forms. We have already discovered irony, ambiguity, superfluity, understatement, and the echo effect which accompanies the consistent development of a literary conceit; e.g., the garment and the disguise. In the discussion so far, we have exhausted neither the examples analyzed nor the repertory of signals employed by the Bible. Careful readers will delight in discovering and unraveling the significance of the contradictions, inconsistencies, and repetitions which abound in Scripture. The apparent misplacement of the Judah/Tamar episode illustrates another of the biblical signals, one which belongs to a family of structural rather than linguistic devices.

The Bible can describe Jacob's grief at the moment he sees Joseph's bloodied tunic. It can heighten our emotional involvement by contrasting the intensity of verse 35 with the dispassionate tone of an understated fact in verse 36. But how can it make us feel the reality of Joseph's death as it was felt by Jacob? Looking at the tunic, Jacob knows that Joseph is gone. Reading 38:1, "It happened at that time that Judah went down from his brothers, and turned to a certain Adullamite, whose name was Hirah," we like Judah are forced to forget, however briefly, the existence of Joseph. Joseph might just as well be dead; for all intents and purposes he is dead the moment our attention is shifted to Judah, whose "voice" of moderation at the pit prepared us for learning more about him.

The disappearance of Joseph, the illusion created by the interruption of his story, is insufficient to drive him entirely out of our mind. The episode with Potiphar's wife anticipated by 37:36 is a tale too highly charged, too well known to the reader to be forgotten. The effectiveness of the illusion struggles with the known reality of Joseph's situation, thereby creating in the reader's mind a sense of being suspended between what was and what will be, a state of mind reinforced by the relatively long and detailed chapter 38 in which time itself seems to be poised between past and future.

A close look at chapter 38 will show how Scripture constructs, then exploits the apparent collapse of temporality. Lest we forget what is about to happen to Joseph with Potiphar's wife, the theme of this chapter is explicitly sexual. To foreshadow Joseph's demand for a pledge against fulfillment of a promise (Gen. 42:18-20, 44:32), Tamar demands a pledge from Judah (38:17-18). When Judah recognizes the signet, cord, and staff (v. 26), we recall Jacob in Genesis 37:33 recognizing his son's robe, and Isaac in 27:23 not recognizing his son Jacob. Tamar gives birth to twins (v. 27), and Genesis 25:24—"there were twins in her womb"—rises to consciousness. The crimson thread of 38:28 reverberates with the birth of Esau who "came forth red" (Gen. 25:25). Tamar tricks Judah with a disguise, then uses his own garments to trap him, a pattern of events with which we are familiar. To read this chapter, therefore, is to review the past and to preview the future. Through the variety and richness of its literary devices Genesis 38 integrates the entire patriarchal narrative into an organic entity in which each part suggests and interprets simultaneously any other part or the whole of the narrative. Other foci which function in the same way throughout the patriarchal narrative are such terms as "feeling" (Gen. 27:22, 31:37) and "stealing" (Gen. 30:33, 31:19, 40:15). "The acts of the fathers are a sign for the sons" is the classical, rabbinic formulation of this fundamental principle underlying biblical historiography.

Finally, we come to Genesis 39—Joseph in Potiphar's service. "After a time his master's wife cast her eyes upon Joseph" (v. 7). After what time? Only after Joseph "found favor in Potiphar's sight, and attended him, and he made him overseer of his house and put him in charge of *all* that he had"; only after Joseph recovered from the ordeal of traveling to Egypt, with plenty of food to eat and time to care for his personal appearance—after all this, "now Joseph was handsome and good-looking." Then and only then did "*his* master's wife cast her eyes upon Joseph." Is Joseph as high-minded as Scripture seems to suggest? Or is he perhaps guilty of behaving in a provocative, teasing fashion? (cf. Gen. 37:5-11) "When his master heard the words which his wife spoke . . . his anger was kindled." With whom was he angry? With Joseph for dallying with his wife? Then why not kill Joseph immediately instead of merely sending him off to prison, and not just to any prison, but to the one "where the king's prisoners were confined." Was Potiphar angry with his wife? Scripture doesn't say he believed her story; it says he "heard" her "words." Should Potiphar have expected a wife who shares intimacies with the servants to have behaved any differently? Once again it is the silent eloquence of a garment which proclaims the truth.

From a medieval Jewish mystic we learned to search the Bible for its meaning by recognizing its "signals of love." The mystics also teach that the Torah has a different face for each man who reads it. From Shalom Spiegel, one of the most brilliant and inspiring twentieth-century scholars of Hebrew literature, we learn that "just as a pearl results from a stimulus in the shell of a mollusk, so also a legend may arise from an irritant in Scripture." [3] Discovering the "irritants" demands reading the Bible with myopic precision; it means hearing the questions which Scripture addresses to us. To invent answers to these questions in a disciplined way demands knowledge, intellect, and imagination. But when the task is done, then a precious pearl is created.

II Literary Criticism of the Bible: Some Fallacies

LELAND RYKEN, *Department of English, Wheaton (Illinois) College*

Literary study of the Bible represents a significant recent trend in literary criticism, especially as conducted in high school and college classrooms. Unfortunately, the resurgence of interest and proliferation of academic courses on the literature of the Bible are frequently characterized by basic confusions as to the exact nature and methodology of literary criticism of the Bible. Ultimately, any practice of criticism will be determined by the theory underlying it. The purpose of this essay is to examine critically some current fallacies in the study of biblical literature and to suggest the form that a truly literary approach to the biblical text might take.[1]

One of the fallacies that is prevalent is the assumption that everything in the Bible is literary in nature and amenable to the ordinary tools of literary criticism. To observe this trend one has only to glance at the syllabi of courses on the literature of the Bible or at the tables of contents of books and anthologies on the subject. One of the commonest failings of books and courses on biblical literature is their lack of a precise and accurate definition of what constitutes literature. Most teachers of literature are much more discriminating in their definition of literature when dealing with nonbiblical writing than they are when studying the Bible. Surely a critic should select his material from the Bible by the same literary principles and criteria that he applies elsewhere.

Although definitions of literature vary from critic to critic, there should be general agreement on two criteria when distinguishing between the literary and nonliterary parts of the Bible. The first is that literature is a presentation of human experience. Its content is human experience, not primarily abstract thought, and its formulation is presentational, to use the term of Suzanne Langer and others. Instead of developing abstract principles or accumulating factual information, the writer of literature presents characters in action or concrete images and sensory descriptions.

When this criterion is applied to the poetry of the Bible, no difficulties arise. Poets think in images. Their medium is concrete and emotive and evocative in its very essence. With historical narrative the issue is much less clear-cut; in fact, the criterion of concreteness of presentation will not always distinguish literary from nonliterary narrative. At the presentational end of the narrative continuum, however, there is an abundance of dialogue, a relative plenty of descriptive detail, a relatively high degree of narrative elaboration of an event, and a minimum of propositional commentary on the meaning of events. If a narrative answers not only the question, "What happened?" but also, "How did it happen?" it is tending toward presentational rather than expository form. A good illustration of presentational narrative is Genesis 1–3, which many readers tend to think very abstract and undetailed, hence nonpresentational. Yet in these chapters there is not a single instance of a theme stated in propositional form. All of the themes and creation ordinances that we might deduce from the story have been incarnated in the actions and the dialogue. With oratory and epistle it becomes very difficult to defend the material as being presentational. The only case that can be made is that the speaker is in a dramatic stance of addressing an audience directly, but this usually turns out to be a rather small claim.

The other criterion of literature is that it is artistic in form. The obviously poetic books easily fit this definition, since poetry is the most consciously formalized kind of discourse. Artistry also becomes a chief criterion for distinguishing between literary and nonliterary narrative. At the consciously artistic end of the narrative spectrum it is possible to discern three things: (1) a story that is carefully unified around one or more controlling literary principles (such as tragedy, comedy, satire, or heroism), (2) a plot that has structural unity and pattern, and (3) a story that makes use of such narrative forms as foreshadowing, dramatic irony, climax, suspense, poetic justice, foils, image patterns, and symbolism. The criterion of artistry also opens the way for stylistic analysis of biblical oratory and epistle.

Although definitions of literature might vary, it is obvious that not everything in print is literary in nature.[2] Regardless of how a critic defines "literature," he needs an accurate and rigorously applied definition when he turns his attention to the Bible.

A second fallacy is the premise that what Bible scholars have traditionally called "literary criticism" of the Bible is, in fact, the kind of literary criticism that teachers of literature perform and constitutes a large body of *bona fide* criticism on biblical literature. Probably all teachers who have faced the prospect of working up a course on biblical literature have gone through a similar process. The process begins at the card catalog or in the library stacks. It leads to a wide range of Bible commentaries, some of which have such promising titles as *Literary Criticism of the Old Testament, Literary Criticism of the New Testament,* and *A Literary Approach to the New Testament.* The process leads to increasing frustration and confusion. Finally the literary critic is faced with the dilemma of abandoning either the existing body of commentary or what he knows as a critic of literature.

All of this leads to the conclusion that the people who are qualified to conduct literary criticism of biblical literature are teachers of literature, not biblical scholars as they have pursued their methods to date. For one thing, biblical scholars do not use the term "literary criticism" in the same way that literary critics do. Klaus Koch, in his excellent guide through the world of form criticism, offers the following biblical scholar's definition of "literary criticism": "The literary critic . . . attempts to discover the original writings, to determine exactly their date of origin, and to grasp the personality of the writer as much as is possible. This means that he approaches the text with, so to say, a dissecting knife in his hand . . . Literary criticism is the analysis of biblical books from the standpoint of lack of continuity, duplications, inconsistencies and different linguistic usage, with the object of discovering what the individual writers and redactors contributed to a text, and also its time and place of origin."[3]

As Amos Wilder has observed, "It is truly a matter of some astonishment that the term 'literary criticism' should have such different connotations for biblical scholars as for students of literature generally."[4] In fact, the biblical scholar's definition is virtually the opposite of the literary critic's definition. Instead of assuming disunity and fragmentation, the literary critic assumes unity and pattern. In an essay published by the Modern Language Association, Northrop Frye gives a definitive statement of the present climate in literary criticism when he writes, "The primary understanding of any work of literature has to be based on an assumption of its unity . . . . Further, every effort should be directed toward understanding the whole of what we read."[5] Similarly, Helen Gardner, a teacher and critic of English literature, has stated, "To concentrate upon the single work, the created whole, is the thing which I feel most called upon to do. The discovery of a work's centre, the source of its life in all its parts, and response to its total movement . . . is to me the purpose of critical activity."[6]

The disagreement over the definition of "literary criticism" affects everything that biblical scholars and literary critics do with biblical literature. Most of all it affects the questions that they ask of the biblical text, and ultimately any criticism depends on how the text is questioned. The biblical scholar asks, What is the date of the work? What are the layers of accretion, and how many redactors worked on the text as it evolved into its present form? What is the historical value of the work? What is the theological import? What religious or moral truth does this text teach, and how can a person apply it in his life?

Biblical scholars tend not to ask the questions that a literary critic asks. Their tendency is to fragmentize the text and to move away from the text to the process of composition behind it. Verse by verse commentary is the staple. A literary critic also looks closely at the details, but not without first discovering the elements of structure and unity in a work. A literary critic approaches a story, for example, by asking, How is the story structured? What are the unifying narrative principles by which the story teller has selected his material? How do the individual episodes relate to these overriding narrative principles? How does the story unfold sequentially, and what is important about this ordering of events? What are the plot conflicts, and how are they resolved? How does the protagonist develop as the story progresses? What archetypal plot motifs are important in the story? How is the thematic meaning of the story embodied in narrative form? It is these narrative questions that biblical scholars seem to find unimportant, yet it is the task of the literary critic to ask them.

The critical performance of biblical scholars has been better in the area of lyric than in the area of narrative. Biblical scholarship has identified literary forms such as the lament psalm and the psalm of praise, for example, with numerous subcategories. Even here, though, some strictures are necessary. There is a tendency to move at once from a given poem to an attempt to trace the supposed historical development of the form. There is a greater interest in the theological or cultic content of the poem than in the reflective or emotional experience that the lyric poet aims to give. In terms of lyric form, biblical scholars are skilled at identifying general types of lyrics, but they are deficient in looking for more specifically artistic elements of form such as balance, contrast, pattern, recurrence, and variation. Finally, biblical scholars are inclined to overlook the questions that a literary critic regards as the essential lyric questions; namely, What is the exact nature of the emotional experience being presented? How is the usual three-part lyric structure of stimulus/response/resolution worked out? What are the meanings of the poet's concrete images and metaphors and allusions? What feelings are communicated by his hyperboles, images, exclamations, apostrophes, and pathetic fallacies? How does the poem fit Robert Frost's definition of a poem as "a performance in words"?

An additional disappointment that the literary critic is likely to find in reading the "higher critics" is their insensitivity to the sheer wonder and delight of literature. Biblical literature asks us to respond with a child's sense of wonder to story, to sensations, to the weather, to elemental emotions such as terror or love or trust, to mystery, to miracle. Biblical literature is replete with adventure, marvelous events, battles, supernatural characters, villains who get their comeuppance, brave heroes, beautiful and courageous heroines, dragons, dungeons, quests, rescue stories, romantic love, boy heroes, and (at the end of it all) a bride and bridegroom who live happily ever after in a glittering palace. Biblical literature is alive. Biblical scholars have too often given the impression that biblical literature is a dry-as-dust document to be cut up and put on display as a relic of ancient cultures.

To put all this into focus, I am not suggesting that the literary critic has nothing to learn from the biblical scholar. I am disputing the common assumption that in dealing with the Bible the literary critic should abandon his usual procedure in deference to biblical scholars. Literary criticism and biblical scholarship are complementary. The literary critic is as authoritative in his sphere as the biblical scholar is in his. The literary critic and the teacher of a course on biblical literature should begin with what they know about their own discipline. Faced with the choice between depending on their own literary theory and experience on the one hand and biblical scholarship on the other, their best procedure by far is to rely on their own methodology for their primary framework and to make use of biblical scholarship in a very secondary way.

There are several good reasons why a literary critic cannot afford simply to move into the existing world of biblical scholarship. That field is enormously specialized and sophisticated. A literary critic's attempts to make pronouncements in that field are bound to be as amateurish and rudimentary as the attempts of biblical scholars to conduct literary criticism. After all, the literary critic usually doesn't even know the original language. In short, a literary critic is far better off operating as an expert in literary criticism than as a low voltage biblical scholar.

Although a literary critic should depend on his own discipline for his primary framework, it is of course essential that he assimilate insights from biblical scholarship. The critic's indebtedness to biblical scholarship falls chiefly into three categories. First, he is dependent on the biblical scholar for his knowledge of the language of the Bible. Acquaintance with biblical scholarship is an obvious prerequisite for explicating the nuances of the words of biblical literature. Secondly, the critic is indebted to biblical scholarship for insights into the cultural milieu presupposed by the biblical writer. And thirdly, the critic is dependent on the scholar for his awareness of literary forms unique to the Bible or the ancient Near East. If left to himself, for example, the literary critic is not likely to recognize that the suzerainty treaty setting influenced the form in which the Ten Commandments are cast, that the beatitude is a literary type falling into two categories in biblical literature, or that Jesus' discourse to his disciples in the upper room adheres to a biblical form known as the farewell discourse.

To summarize this point, literary criticism of the Bible should be performed and judged as literary criticism, not as biblical scholarship. Both endeavors are legitimate. Most literary critics and teachers of literature can attest that for their purposes the reading they have done in Bible commentaries has been a disappointing experience. The practical conclusion is an unwelcome one, namely, that there is no substantial body of literary criticism on biblical literature.

Another common fallacy is the claim that biblical literature is virtually unique and cannot be adequately studied with the familiar tools of literary criticism or compared with Western literature. A typical statement of the case is the following by Amos Wilder: "Arrangements of the Old Testament for modern readers are familiar which use the classifications of epic for its early narratives, oratory for the prophets, drama for

Job, and other terms for other parts, ballad, elegy, short story, etc. . . . A similar approach to the New Testament suggests biography for the Gospels, history for the Book of Acts, formal epistle or treatise for the letters, and other terms for lesser forms: ode, allegory, anecdote, etc. . . . But such procedures are bound to mislead us. Even when we bring such basic categories into play as those of Aristotle we are moving in a different world. . . . This should confirm our discovery in literary criticism today that Western aesthetic norms are often parochial. . . . Our point is that our early Christian literary arts were different from those that ancient paganism produced, and that Greek and traditional humanist categories are inadequate as measuring rods."[7]

Several things are misleading about these statements. The literary forms that Wilder singles out for pejorative comment are far from the best that are available. Furthermore, why limit Western literary criticism to Aristotle, and Western forms to ancient Greek literature? Finally, the usual literary terms will of course be inadequate if we indiscriminately include everything that is written under the heading of "literature."

The objections to the theory of the complete uniqueness of biblical literature go far beyond these strictures on a particular formulation of the theory. We must remember, for example, that the Bible has exerted a strong and formative influence on Western literature from the Middle Ages onward. It is this awareness that leads Northrop Frye to call the Bible "the major informing influence on literary symbolism,"[8] and T. R. Henn to conclude that the Bible "becomes one with the Western tradition, because it is its single greatest source."[9] If the Bible is this central in Western literature, very serious questions should arise in regard to the usual claim from biblical scholars about the uniqueness of biblical forms. If biblical scholars were familiar with literary archetypes, perhaps they would not make claims about the uniqueness of ancient Near Eastern literature. There is good reason to doubt whether biblical scholars have adequately understood the nature and prevalence of literary archetypes.[10] Indeed,

their very preoccupation with ancient Near Eastern literature has minimized their contact with the literature that
would have given them a greater awareness of the archetypal
nature of literature.

Another good reason to question the theory of the uniqueness of biblical literature is that most literary forms belong to
the structure of literature itself. Literary forms tend to have
certain inherent characteristics quite apart from the cultural
situation in which they were written. As Northrop Frye has
written in his well-known essay on "The Archetypes of Literature," "if . . . genre has a historical origin, why does the
genre of drama emerge from medieval religion in a way so
strikingly similar to the way it emerged from Greek religion
centuries before? This is a problem of structure rather than
origin, and suggests that there may be archetypes of genres
as well as of images." [11] There may be archetypes of genres
as well as of images. Exactly. That is why a story obeys
certain narrative principles simply because it is a story. The
same is true of a lyric poem or an epic or a tragedy or a satire.
A metaphor is a metaphor, and a proverb is a proverb. There
is no reason to bury biblical metaphors and proverbs under
the weight of cultural baggage with which biblical scholarship has tended to isolate them. There is no reason, either,
why we should call biblical forms by the esoteric terminology
of biblical scholarship instead of the more familiar terms of
literary criticism.

In the final analysis, any canon of literature is a blend of
the unique and the archetypal, the original and the conventional. Instead of exempting biblical literature from the usual
forms of Western literature, I suggest a critical procedure
that begins by placing biblical literature in the familiar
framework of Western literature and *then* observes where
and how biblical literature breaks out of this framework. Of
course biblical literature is *ancient* literature and will therefore naturally have a different "feel" from English and
American literature. Nor do I wish to minimize the importance of the things that are distinctive to biblical literature—
things such as its pervasive religious identity and theocentric

world view, its tendency to move from the particular event to the spiritual meaning behind the event, its vivid consciousness of values, its historical emphasis, the importance of the spoken word and the speaking voice, its preference for an unembellished narrative style, its indifference to visual detail, and its heavy reliance on story and dialogue.[12] A critic can best discover these distinctive features, however, not by immersing himself in ancient Oriental literature, but simply by being a discerning critic of literature and by reading widely in Western literature.

Moving on to another fallacy, the main effect of the various types of biblical criticism has been to divide the Bible into fragments and to claim that the fragments contradict each other. A glance at Norman Habel's book *Literary Criticism of the Old Testament* will illustrate the typical features of this kind of criticism.[13] The text of Genesis is divided confidently among three different writers. The story of the flood is divided into two separate stories, which are printed side by side in two columns on a page. There are tables listing the contrasts between Genesis 1 and 2 and between the Yahwist and Priestly writers' versions of the flood story. The whole thrust is to set up the individual parts as contrasting and contradictory fragments. A typical summary statement is the following: "This literary contrast is coupled with a theological contrast. The same conflicting approach . . . persists throughout the narrative versions" (p. 37).

As a literary critic I object to both the disunity and the contradictions that this kind of commentary imposes on the Bible. Literary criticism is impossible when a story is divided into different fragments, each of which is claimed to have been written by a different writer living at a different stage in the historical development of biblical religion. It is extremely doubtful that any general reader of any story, biblical or otherwise, can make literary sense of a story thus divided.

It is much more defensible to regard the individual parts of the Bible as being complementary rather than contradictory. Thus, the first two chapters of Genesis present complementary aspects of a central paradox of the God of the Bible, namely, that he is both transcendent and immanent. Applying this principle more generally, the individual parts of the Bible are interdependent. No single work of biblical literature can be regarded as a totally self-contained unit. The meaning of an individual work is deepened and modified by other works. The portrait of God, for example, is built up by a brushstroke here and a brushstroke there, with each story or lyric poem contributing a small part to the total effect. Similarly, no single work is likely to give full scope to the biblical view of man, just as one could not deduce the biblical attitude toward romantic love by reading only the Song of Solomon. A reading of the Bible that regards the individual parts as complementary takes seriously the Bible's status as a story, a progression in which no single moment is self-contained, but is rather part of an overall movement. This way of reading the Bible also does justice to the way in which the Bible preserves the complexities and polarities and paradoxes of human existence. As Roland M. Frye has stated, "The Bible preserves and interprets the mixed texture of human experience, and thus finds it necessary to affirm apparent contradictions as common elements of the ultimate truth."[14]

From a literary point of view, the Bible is a unity.[15] This unity goes far beyond the unity of national authorship, religious subject matter, and didactic purpose. Biblical literature has a unifying plot conflict—the great spiritual conflict between good and evil. Almost every incident in biblical literature turns out to be in some sense a reenactment of this archetypal plot conflict.

The biblical view of history also provides plot unity to the Bible. The subtitle of C. A. Patrides' book *The Grand Design of God: The Literary Form of the Christian View of History* sums it up well.[16] There are at least three ways in which the biblical view of history has the character of a unified narrative. First, it is a patterned story that fits Aristotle's definition of plot as a series of events having a beginning, middle, and end. The beginning is the creation of the world and life before the fall. The fall initiates the middle, which consists of the human pilgrimage through fallen human history. The end is the consummation of history. Further shapeliness stems from the fact that history is spanned at both ends by eternity, and from the fact that the Bible begins with creation and life before the fall and concludes with the consummation of history. Secondly, the biblical view of history is a unified narrative because it has a protagonist, God. In the biblical view, therefore, history is providential, and its record is the record of God's acts of redemption and judgment. Finally, the biblical account of history is, like other stories, a concrete universal. That is, it is a series of particulars that embody general meaning, chiefly that history is providential, redemptive, judgmental, and moving toward a goal.

In addition to having the unifying plot conflict and a patterned movement of history, the Bible has a unity of literary texture based on allusion. Various biblical writers allude to earlier works in the same canon, or to the same historical events, or to the same religious beliefs and experiences, or to the same cultural context. The resulting unity of reference is immediately evident when one consults a modern study Bible containing cross references in the marginal notes. No other anthology of literature possesses the unified texture of allusions that biblical literature displays.

A final element in the literary unity of the Bible is the unified archetypal structure of the Bible. The whole Bible forms a single composite narrative that is best called the monomyth. This composite narrative is cyclic in structure and consists of four phases, corresponding to the four seasons of the year. The literary terms for these phases of the monomyth are romance (ideal experience, wish fulfillment literature); tragedy (a fall from ideal to unideal experience); anti-romance or satire or irony (a world of complete bondage and misery); and comedy (a movement from unideal to ideal experience). Individual parts and image patterns are continual reenactments of the unifying archetypal story of biblical literature, and they become a single literary structure moving from creation to apocalypse.

To conclude this point, a literary approach to the Bible is one that resists the trend of biblical scholarship toward fragmentation. It takes as its province the text of the Bible in its present form, and it sees the Bible as a collection of parts that add up to a total unity.

One of the most serious fallacies in the study of biblical literature is the view that literary criticism of the Bible should be preoccupied with the process that produced the Bible as we know it. This model of criticism comes from biblical scholarship. Its basic assumption, in the words of Koch, is that "no book in the Bible still retains the form it was given when it was first written down. . . . Redaction history therefore follows the work of both the first writer and the subsequent redactors."[17] This procedure underlies most of the work done by "higher critics" of the Bible.

Significantly, it is the literary critics who dispute this preoccupation in biblical scholarship. Helen Gardner, for example, writes, "Form-criticism . . . is not congenial to the temper of mind which regards it as the first duty of the critic to make sense of literary wholes. It . . . is open to the literary objection that it is not dealing with the work itself, but with the materials out of which it was made; and these materials . . . do not exist. . . . When a writer's first drafts, scraps of memoranda, and 'doodles' have been preserved, we may possibly have a limited success in tracing the workings of the creative imagination, though even there the results are highly speculative. To attempt to do this backwards from the finished work is like weaving ropes of sand."[18] Similarly, Northrop Frye has said that "a purely literary criticism . . . would see the Bible, not as the scrapbook of corruptions, glosses, redactions, insertions, conflations, misplacings, and misunderstandings revealed by the analytic critic, but as the typological unity which all these things were originally intended to help construct."[19] C. S. Lewis, speaking both as a literary critic and a writer whose works had been analyzed by critics, records his distrust of critics who presume to explain the process that lies behind a written text, noting that the critics who theorized about the composition of his own works had never once been correct.[20] And Dorothy Sayers channeled her skepticism of higher criticism into parody, writing four essays that applied the methods of higher criticism to the Sherlock Holmes stories.[21]

Most literary critics in the humanities share this disenchantment with the procedure that seems to have been accepted so uncritically by biblical scholars. Few literary critics place much stock, for example, in the attempts to date Milton's *Samson Agonistes* on the basis of internal evidence and the supposed allusions to Milton's life contained in the play. Few would regard the four rival theories as anything other than highly speculative and far removed from the critic's main task of leading the reader to an understanding and enjoyment of the play. Allan Gilbert's elaborate attempts to reconstruct the process by which Milton composed *Paradise Lost* have stood mainly as a curiosity of interesting hypotheses and sometimes erroneous conclusions, such as the theory of two contradictory Satans, the dramatic and the epic.[22] When a Shakespearean critic publishes a book replete with verbal parallels between the works of Shakespeare and Marlowe in an attempt to prove that Shakespeare did not really write the plays attributed to him, it is greeted by members of the clan as a kind of solemn joke. In fact, it has even led to a book length parody entitled *Wasn't Shakespeare Someone Else?*[23] The conclusion is obvious: literary critics are opposed to a critical methodology that devotes its major attention to the process of composition instead of the text itself.

Three remaining fallacies can be treated summarily. There is a lurking and regrettably widespread suspicion that the Bible cannot be taught as literature and should therefore be taught as something else. Several things have contributed to this attitude. The current movement toward the inclusion of religious and moral values as a necessary part of public education has led some teachers to teach the Bible from religious rather than literary motivations. There are other teachers who find the Bible so unfamiliar, or who sense the lack of helpful literary criticism on the subject, that they despair of the possibility of studying the Bible as literature.

There is, of course, a legitimate branch of literary scholarship that treats the Bible as a sourcebook of allusions and an influence on English and American literature. It is obvious, however, that to do no more than this is to curb severely the literary study of the Bible. It is equivalent to regarding the earlier periods of English literature as significant only insofar as the literature of those periods influenced American literature. This disparagement of the literary possibilities of the Bible is illustrated in a statement such as the following: "Analyzing the formal aspects of much Biblical literature is likely to be as disappointingly unproductive as dissecting 'Hickory Dickory Dock' or 'Goldilocks and the Three Bears.' . . . The Bible is not 'literature' in the sense that most works students read in an English classroom are. To insist on the likeness probably distorts the Bible and certainly poses troublesome problems for conscientious teachers. The 'literary values' of the Bible are often slight, and it is difficult to help students see those that are genuinely there."[24] A closer look at the situation will reveal that the literary study of the Bible will yield most if the Bible is studied as literature, not as an appendage to the study of English or American literature. It is also logical to expect that if biblical literature is studied in a literature course, it should be included in the literature curriculum for the same literary reasons that other works are included; namely, because it is of unquestioned importance and worth as literature.

In our century the concept of demythologizing the Bible has become a commonplace. It is a fallacy of literary criticism to regard the supernatural element in biblical literature as something to be discarded. Whether one believes or disbelieves in the supernatural and miraculous is a religious issue, but how a literary critic treats the supernatural is a literary matter. It is the critic's task to make the distinctive features of the "world" of the given literary work come alive for the reader. If the literary world is the realistic world of modern naturalism, for example, the critic's task is to delineate the features of a world devoid of supernatural reality. If, however, the literary world of a work is conceived as one in which supernatural activity is real and constant, the critic's task is to preserve and enhance the reader's response to the miraculous.

Biblical literature is relentlessly supernatural in its orientation. Events are continually related to a divine or spiritual reality beyond the natural world. The curious thing is that many literary critics respond to the transcendental element in biblical literature in a way that they would not consider doing for the *Odyssey* or the *Aeneid* or *The Faerie Queene*. Regardless of a critic's religious beliefs, his literary criticism should reveal rather than discredit the supernatural stance that is one of the most distinctive features of biblical literature.

A final fallacy is the view that it is futile to look for a high degree of literary artistry in the Bible. This belittling of the literary craftsmanship of biblical literature has come from at least two sources. One approach states that the authors of the Bible were not professional authors but religious spokesmen, and that therefore their writing cannot possibly be sophisticated literature. Thus, Martin Dibelius says about the New Testament writers, "The composers of the earliest . . . Christian writings were in reality men without special education. . . . Literary ambition was remote from these simple people who were expecting the end of the world and not thinking of readers in posterity. Readers of contemporary Hellenistic literature did not constitute their public, but rather . . . the unlettered men and women of the first Christian churches. What they wrote down was either completely unliterary . . . or else half-literary and thus unpretentious writing intended for a certain class of people."[25] The other theory destructive of an appreciation of the artistry of the Bible is the theory that works of biblical literature simply happened by an anonymous process of composite authorship and redaction. When a biblical scholar writes that "in one way or another, over a period of more than a thousand years, the whole cultural setting of the ancient world of the Near East and every Israelite in all those centuries had some sort of a hand in the making of the Bible,"[26] he perhaps does not intend to denigrate the artistic accomplishment of biblical literature, but in practice that has been the result.

The literary critic would do well to disregard the theories of the simple minded author and the anonymous process of composition and look instead at the products of biblical literature. If he does so he will find literary artistry of a very high order. It is obvious that biblical authors wrote in well understood literary conventions and with a grasp of literary principles. They knew how to tell stories with well-made plots. They knew how to tell stories that are unified by the principle of tragedy or satire. They knew that a psalm of lament had five main units and that a psalm of praise was expected to have a three-part structure. Biblical poets knew how to invent apt metaphors and how to put statements into parallel form. There was never a group of writers more skilled at the use of allusion. And most of them were masters of style.

A concluding summary will help to put this essay into focus. Biblical literature constitutes a literary achievement of unavoidable importance and indisputable value. Any literary study of the Bible will succeed best if it is based on an adequate theory of literature and literary criticism. This, in turn, is nothing other than a plea for the recognition of the legitimacy of literary criticism, performed by teachers of literature, as a doorway to the understanding and enjoyment of the Bible.

III Genesis I–II

KENNETH R. R. GROS LOUIS, Department of English, Indiana University

To analyze the opening chapters of Genesis as literature we must come as close as possible to performing a very difficult feat. We must attempt to read the accounts of creation as if we had never seen them before. The reason that is so difficult, of course, is that our upbringing, our education, our formal and even our casual contacts with modern culture have developed in us certain associations with Genesis 1 through 3 which are often as much a part of our unconscious thought processes as are the alphabet and the counting of numbers. It does not matter whether we believe in the stories of creation or not. We are simply too familiar with the words and the sentences to enable ourselves to achieve the detachment and objectivity that are so necessary to literary criticism. As literary critics, we are not primarily concerned with where these stories came from or when they were written or who wrote them or how they were compiled and transmitted to the twentieth century. Each of these concerns may be very important to a full appreciation of the Bible, but as critics, we take this to be a literary account of the beginning of the world and of the beginning of man. Our primary concern is not only to see what is said about those beginnings, but also how it is said, what words and images are used, what structural devices are employed. The end of such a study is to attempt to understand what assumptions the narrator or narrators express about God, about the way the world should operate, about man's relation to divine forces, about man himself, and further, to consider the implications of such assumptions. It may be that this kind of investigation will lead us to conclusions that are in conflict with historical and textual research, but even if that happens, we should be prepared to defend our thesis by pointing to the language of the chapters themselves.

A reading of the first and second chapters clearly reveals that the account of creation is divided into two different, complementary segments—each with its own point of view, each concentrating on its own specific interest in the creation process.[1] In chapter 1, creation proceeds according to a very orderly plan, divided into what are called days, and culminates in the statement: "Let us make man in our image, after our likeness. . . ." In the second account, man is created before certain other elements of the created universe which are then created with particular emphasis on their relation and importance to man. To substantiate these differences, we need to examine the opening chapters of Genesis and identify, if possible, the kinds of things we should notice if we could be reading them for the first time and analyzing them as part of a literary document.

The opening sentence, "In the beginning God created the heavens and the earth," is like the topic sentence of an essay in that what follows elaborates on the creation of heaven and earth. Everything is given to us immediately. God created the heaven and the earth; we are then told of the specific creations on each of six days. On the first day God creates light which he then separates from the darkness. On the second day he creates firmament amid the waters and divides the water under the firmament from the waters above the firmament. On the third day he creates land by gathering the waters under the heavens into one place, and he also creates vegetation: plants and fruit trees. On the fourth day he creates lights in the heaven, a greater light and a lesser light that divide the day from the night, to rule over day and night, and to divide the light from the darkness. On the fifth day he creates life within the firmament and gives it the blessing: "Be fruitful and multiply. . . ." And on the sixth day he creates life on land, culminating in the creation of man. On the seventh day God rests. It is clear from this first summary reading that the acts of creation are very carefully patterned in a parallel, systematic way. The creation of light on the first day and God's division of light from darkness is paralleled on the fourth day by the creation of lights, a greater light and a lesser light, which will serve, as it were, as God's heavenly vice-regents and *also* divide the light from the darkness. The creation of the firmament on the second day and God's division of the waters under the firmament from those above the firmament is paralleled on the fifth day by the creation of life *in* the firmament, both in the waters and in the air. The creation of land and vegetation on the third day is paralleled on the sixth day by the creation of life *on* the land and by the explanation of the appropriateness of the vegetation to that life.

And this is only the beginning of the parallel patterns we find in the opening chapter. As the greater and lesser light serve as God's vice-regents, dividing day from night, light from darkness, so man serves as God's vice-regent in having "dominion over the fish of the sea, and over the birds of the air, and over . . . every creeping thing that creeps upon the earth." All the animals are created on the sixth day, but in an ascending pattern culminating in the creation of man, the only animal made in God's image, after his likeness. In a sense God, on the fourth, fifth, and sixth days, puts into motion what he has created on the first three days. Consider what we have after the third day—light, the firmament, the earth and the seas, the vegetation. We can imagine this primeval universe, with its lush forests and green valleys, blue skies and blue-black seas, but without anything in them—an empty magnificent vessel into which God on the last two days pours flying, swimming, walking, and creeping things. The creation of the sun and the moon on the fourth day begins movement as God introduces the cyclical pattern of light and darkness, day and night, into what has been created. Then he populates the earth, air, and seas with fish, birds, animals, including man, and gives them all the blessing: "Be fruitful and multiply." He introduces into earthly existence, in other words, the same kind of pattern he has introduced into the heavens on the fourth day. What God has created will, with his blessing, re-create itself. Time has begun and, the story implies, a time which is presumably moving towards some goal.

It becomes clear that this God knew from the very beginning the order of his creation. He did not begin with light and then experiment on the following days with other creations. He planned from the beginning to have man as his vice-regent, the sun and moon as his vice-regents; he planned to set into motion on the last three days the heavens and earth he created on the first three days; he planned to create living creatures according to a hierarchical ascendancy on the scale of nature. We are awed by this majestic being who creates in such an orderly fashion. At the same time, however, are we not also somewhat uncomfortable with a God who is so distant, so transcendent? We may have difficulty avoiding the feeling that this God is creating a vast machine which will pretty much run by itself after creation is over. "Be fruitful and multiply," he says, and gives man dominion over the living earth. Where does God go after the seventh day when he rests? Why does such an omnipotent God need to rest at all? What is man's relation to this God? Are we no closer to him than in terms of an analogy, one according to which we rule and are creative in earthly affairs as he rules and is creative in the universe? Is this the kind of God we like to imagine? What does it mean to be made in God's image? Theologians will tell us that one possible meaning is that we have the capacity to know and love God, but Genesis 1 does not say that, and can we ever know such an exalted being?

If we look at the language of this chapter our discomfort may grow. Not only is creation classified into segments which are called days, but the pattern for each day is almost the same. "And God said . . . ," "and God saw . . . ," "and God called . . . ," "and God made . . . ." The beginning and close of each day are regulated by stated formulae. By legislative command God creates, then he gives names to his creations, sees that they are good, and a day ends. Consider the verbs that are repeatedly associated with God in the first chapter: *created, said, saw, divided, called, made, blessed.*

These verbs connote a being who operates by immediate command and with complete foreknowledge. They suggest a God whose word is law, whose very sight bestows goodness on what it sees, who gives names to things in order to identify and define them and put them in a certain place in the hierarchy of creation; they suggest the omnipotence of this God, and one verb—only one—the verb *blessed*, invites us to consider the graciousness of a divine being who is concerned for the future of his creation.

These verbs, the overall systematic structure, the lack of metaphors and similes, the descriptions which are both methodical and precise with parallelism in sentence structure and in the narrative—the tone of the whole is that of a narrative, we must remember, that conveys to us a sense of the nature of God. The God who emerges is majestic, but distant; omnipotent and transcendent, a God of order and of pattern and of hierarchy. He projects, in other words, a sense of the structure of the universe and, by analogy, the structure of man's earthly life, a structure which is essentially conservative—one which does not easily admit change, novelty, experimentation. If man is to operate effectively as God's vice-regent, he too must presumably have as his primary concerns the establishment of order, adherence to patterns, acceptance of hierarchies. By deduction as well as by analogy, man, if he is to be in the image of God, must depend heavily on ritual, on ceremony, on tradition, on those elements in man's history in which patterns and hierarchies are predominant. Obviously the political and social implications of this view of God tend also in a conservative direction —perhaps belief in kingship and its divine right, belief in an aristocracy or a ruling elite.

On the basis of this literary interpretation of the first chapter of Genesis, it would appear that this view of God and his creation may have helped leaders to defend traditions and rituals, with their long-established patterns of order, and hierarchy itself, against challenges either from inside or from outside the society. Such a conservative view of God as a God of order and of man in relation to other men is not so necessary in times of prosperity and stability. It is needed, however, when the old ways have to be justified anew, when the time has come to hold together beliefs which seem in danger of being torn apart and discarded.

If we turn to chapter 2, we immediately recognize that we are being given a complementary, and perhaps alternate, account of certain aspects of creation. The beginning of verse 4 seems at first to be merely a summary of what we have already been told: "These are the generations of the heavens and the earth when they were created." But then we read further: "In the day that the Lord God made the earth and the heavens, when no plant of the field was yet in the earth and no herb of the field had yet sprung up—for the Lord God had not caused it to rain upon the earth, and there was no man to till the ground. . . ." When we come to that last phrase, "there was no man to till the ground," we know that we are about to hear a different account of God's creation. And the more we read, the clearer it is that the creations of the fifth and sixth days of chapter 1 are being reformulated, with a different order and with a different emphasis. We are to assume that light, firmament, land, sun, and moon have already been created and that the narrative is here concentrating on the explanation and elaboration of the creation of vegetation and living things. We might even deduce from this that the account shows a greater interest in humanity and in human life and its environment than does the first chapter. The emphasis here is not on creation and the beginning of time; it is rather on creation and the beginning of human history in time; that is why chapter 3 cannot be understood without a full understanding of chapter 2; both chapters describe the origins of human history.

God creates man, then a garden into which man is placed. God then causes to grow "every tree that is pleasant to the sight and good for food" for man, including the tree of life and the tree of the knowledge of good and evil. A river is placed in Eden to water the garden, and four rivers emerge from it. God puts Adam into the garden, gives him a command, then creates the birds and beasts, and finally, woman. Rather than being created the last of the animals and given dominion over other animals, man is in this account created first and then given a social environment in which to live. God creates for him a kind of community that is dominated by social relationships. God creates man, then a place for him to live, then food for him to eat, pleasant sights for him to look on, then animals and birds as companions for him, and finally woman as his special companion. Instead of parallelism and incremental progression on a scale of nature, the pattern of chapter 2 is circular, with various aspects of man on earth and in society emanating from the center of the circle, man himself. The inherent complexities of man's earthly life are suggested in this pattern. First, man is related to his physical environment and required to till it and keep it, to till the ground and care for the garden God has planted for him. Second, man is related to other living creatures and assumes a responsibility towards them by identifying and defining them by giving them names. Third, man is related to other humans and given a special charge relevant to the aid and mutual dependence which characterize human companionship: "Therefore a man leaves his father and his mother and cleaves to his wife, and they become one flesh." This chapter is most concerned with man on earth and implies that that is God's main interest as well.

Such a concern leads us to a different concept of God than we find in the first chapter. Consider not only the phrase "Lord God," which is used throughout chapter 2, but more importantly, the verbs associated with God in this account: *formed, breathed, planted, took,* and *put.* The connotation of each of these verbs leads us to imagine an immanent God who is working with his hands and with his breath to create man and other living creatures. We picture God like a potter working with clay or a gardener or a father who is giving lands to his son; indeed, we picture a very human kind of divine being. So human in fact, that Lord God in this chapter does not seem to possess the foreknowledge of God in the earlier one. The very structure of chapter 1 indicates that God knew from the beginning how his creation would proceed—the plan was set from the first command, "Let there be light." But here, the Lord God seems to be working more experimentally, forming and making new creations as they are needed. After having created man and planted a garden, the Lord God says (and is it an afterthought?): "It is not good that the man should be alone; I will make him a helper fit for him." He forms the animals and birds, but they do not provide the solution: "For the man there was not found a helper fit for him." So God causes a sleep to fall on Adam and, with one of Adam's ribs, he makes woman, who turns out to be the "helper fit" because she is bone of Adam's bones, flesh of his flesh. Again, God is shown to us working with his hands for man, operating on Adam's body, creating anew from it. Both in terms of his imagined physical appearance and his experimental use of his powers, God is manlike in chapter 2. A further indication of this comes at the opening of the next chapter when, after Adam and Eve have eaten of the forbidden fruit and Lord God looks for Adam, he says, "Where are you?" It is hard to imagine the majestic being of chapter 1 asking that question.

The very nature of this God who at times acts as men do affects the relation between man and God and the nature of man himself. God blesses man in chapter 1 and speaks to him, but we do not picture God standing next to man, telling him to be fruitful and multiply. But this Lord God of chapter 2 *takes* Adam and *puts* him in the garden, *brings* him the animals to name, *causes* him to sleep. There is, in other words, a personal relationship between God and man, echoing the concern God shows throughout the second chapter for social relationships in general. The first man and the first woman soon have names, and this serves to underline the personal relationships involved. The command which God gives to Adam, "You may freely eat of every tree of the garden; but of the tree of the knowledge of good and evil you shall not eat, for in the day that you eat of it you shall die," is a personal command, not a general blessing; and it makes clear to us that Adam and Eve have a personal responsibility to this personal God, that they have a part in a dialogue between divinity and humanity. Because of this dialogue man is considerably exalted in chapter 2. He not only has God working for him, helping him, but he also receives from God a personal commandment to obey. He does not have an analogical relation to God, but a direct, even a cozy, one. God reveals his trust in man by letting him name the animals, unlike the God of chapter 1 who did that himself; and this act also gives Adam the opportunity to exercise his intellectual powers and tells us something further about the capacities of God's most intimate creation. The second chapter makes clear the personal relationship between God and man which the previous chapter gives us only by analogy.

For many readers of Genesis, the Lord God is surely more attractive than the God of chapter 1. The very language of chapter 2 suggests the intimacy which is felt towards God. The language is simple and moves in a narrative, storylike fashion from point to point without relying, like chapter 1, on formulae and parallelism in sentence and paragraph structure. Is this the kind of God we would prefer? Or is he too human? Perhaps we should prefer our God to *be* transcendent and majestic and not given to the human need to ask questions and to experiment before finding the right solution to a problem.

If the implications for man of the view of God and creation of chapter 1 are essentially conservative, then it would seem that the implications of the view of the God in chapter 2 are essentially liberal. Here the nature of God is basically philanthropic—he plants a garden for man, gives him trees for pleasure and for food, provides him with water and precious stones, finds him a fit helper. Even after the fall of man, God makes coats of skin for Adam and Eve and clothes them. The political and social implications of this concept of God differ from those which emerge from chapter 1. Man, to imitate this God, must be liberal and philanthropic himself. He must help others, be merciful even under adverse conditions, constantly experiment to improve the life of man in society, work to better the social structure of man's life and of his environment. This means that man might not adhere to traditions, might not adhere to ceremonies or rituals. To change and improve the nature of social life, reform might be necessary, new things might have to be tried. There are commandments which make social life possible, which make civilization possible, as there is a commandment which for a time made paradise possible; but when these commandments, these laws, are broken, mercy and sympathy must accompany punishment, as mercy and sympathy accompanied the Lord God's punishment of Adam and Eve. God's liberality may be noted even in that commandment to Adam; for although God presumably does not want man to sin, he gives him the opportunity to do so, and lets man make of himself what he will. He introduces man to temptation, although he hopes he will shun it. For the Lord God, it is too restricting not to give man choices; men are most free when they can operate virtuously in the face of multiple temptations.

On the basis of this analysis, it would appear that chapter 2 would be more congenial when the various institutions of society were not well defined, at times when men were still in the process of creating ceremonies, patterns, rituals, when experimentation was the order of the day. Times, too, of reasonable prosperity and stability, when man's belief stressed faith in a personal God who recognized man's needs and would help him achieve his new goals.

The two views of God which emerge from the opening chapters of Genesis are by no means incompatible. Indeed, it may be that individuals as well as epochs of man's history have vacillated between seeing God as the transcendent, all-powerful, distant deity of chapter 1 and as the personally concerned, sympathetic, merciful friend of mankind of chapter 2. In the Middle Ages, the transcendent God of order, similar to the God of chapter 1 in Genesis, gives way in literature from the late eleventh to the fifteenth century to the more sympathetic God of chapter 2. In medieval drama, for example, God speaks in a more personal way to man, almost imploring him to concentrate on saving his soul rather than on accumulating worldly goods. Challenges to the medieval world view are repudiated in sermon literature by clerics who point to the God of order who created a universe of patterns and hierarchies, which it was sinful to question, political and social hierarchies which could not be tampered with. But those who were advocating change and reform in medieval Europe talk about a different kind of God, one who has given man the intellectual capacities to create new forms and new ideas, one who approves of man's inquiring into long-established beliefs and traditions and changing them if necessary. Milton and other Renaissance writers who made use of biblical stories and themes have an easy way out of the problem. For Milton, the God of chapter 1 remains as he is; the Lord God of chapter 2, however, becomes Christ. It is Christ, not God, who walks in Milton's garden of Eden, who converses with Adam, and who delivers to him the sentence of his punishment.

Consideration of the concepts of God in the opening chapters of Genesis is as much literary as it is religious, for we are not principally concerned with questions of belief. Our primary concern is rather with investigating man's imaginative perception of a divine being, with answering the question, How do men conceive of divinity? Once we have seen the transcendent and personal aspects of God in these two chapters, we can begin analyzing how these narrators, or indeed any writers, describe such gods, how assumptions about God are revealed in accounts of his activities, what the assumptions about God suggest about the structure of man's political and social life, and about man himself. To put these statements another way, we might say that an analysis of the nature of God in a particular period of man's history, an analysis, that is, of how a significant group of people conceive of divinity in a given time, can reveal to us a great deal about the intellectual concerns of that day, about its political and social interests, its dominant patterns, and its interpretations of man's primary obligations and responsibilities.

IV The Garden of Eden
KENNETH R. R. GROS LOUIS

The third chapter of Genesis begins to suggest to us even more than do the opening chapters the enormous literary potential of biblical stories. The dialogue of relationships begun in chapter 2 is continued and accelerated, with conversations between the serpent and Eve, Adam and Eve, God and Eve, God and Adam, God and the serpent. But because of the particular narrative technique of Genesis, and of much of the Old Testament, we are given only the bare essentials—background information, psychology, and descriptive details are absent. We are left, therefore, with many unanswered questions, questions which have challenged the ingenuity of biblical commentators and the imagination, as well as ingenuity, of countless creative writers. Before looking at this chapter, we need to return to chapter 2 to consider two of these questions: What exactly is the tree of the knowledge of good and evil? What were Adam and Eve like when they were first created? There are no answers to these questions, of course, only alternatives; but how a writer responds to them goes a long way towards determining the kind of biblically inspired work he may write, just as the reader's conscious or unconscious assumptions affect his understanding or appreciation of the Bible stories.

God calls the forbidden tree the "tree of the knowledge of good and evil." Is this a special tree with special powers? Or is it simply a tree which God has forbidden man to eat the fruit of in order to test his obedience? Does man learn anything from the tree itself, or does the act of disobedience teach him the difference for the first time between good and evil? Is there such a thing as forbidden knowledge?

The second question is no more answerable but is perhaps even more important to our reading of Genesis 2 and 3 as literature and to our reading of later literature based on these chapters. How do we imagine Adam and Eve at the time of their creation? What are they like? Are they naïve and innocent? Are they like children? What connotations do these words have for us? Are they appropriate for describing God's special creations, formed with his hands and with his breath? Were Adam and Eve unsophisticated or "primitive"? Are we being patronizing to conceive of them in these ways? If Adam and Eve had not eaten the forbidden fruit, presumably they never would have been old. Why, then, should we think of them as ever having been young, naïve, and unsophisticated? Why not imagine them as being created full-grown and as perfect as they could be? Adam converses with God, he walks with him, he has the intelligence to name all the animals and birds (a feat performed by God in chapter 1). What if we do imagine Adam as full of knowledge as well as great in stature, beautiful and awesome in appearance? And Eve as the queen of the earth, the matriarch of the world? What would such a conception of them do to how we understand the story or to what an artist writes about Adam and Eve and the Garden of Eden?

John Milton offers us a suggestion of our relations to Adam as they would have been if he had not fallen—he would still be alive in Paradise, says Milton, and to that "capital seat" all generations "from all the ends of the Earth" would come periodically to pay him their homage (*Paradise Lost*, XI, 342). The modern critic C. S. Lewis, who argues persuasively for this view of Adam, describes what this might have been like:

To you or to me, once in a lifetime perhaps, would have fallen the almost terrifying honour of coming at last, after long journeys and ritual preparations and slow ceremonial approaches, into the very presence of the great Father, Priest, and Emperor of the planet Tellus; a thing to be remembered all our lives. No useful criticism of the Miltonic Adam is possible until the last trace of the *naif*, simple, childlike Adam has been removed from our imaginations. The task of a Christian poet presenting the unfallen first of men is not that of recovering the freshness and simplicity of mere nature, but of drawing someone who, in his solitude and nakedness, shall *really be* what Solomon and Charlemagne and Haroun-al-Raschid and Louis XIV lamely and unsuccessfully strove to imitate on thrones of ivory between lanes of drawn swords and under jewelled baldachins.[1]

To think of Adam and Eve in this way contributes added richness to the account in chapter 3 of the fall of man. The problem may simply reside in the connotations of the words *innocent, childlike,* and *naïve;* for presumably there was sublime innocence and naïveté in Eden, and yet, how can we recreate it without sounding naïve ourselves, without making Adam and Eve much less than two who were created by God's own hands?

With these alternatives in mind, consider the opening verses of chapter 3.

Now the serpent was more subtle than any other wild creature that the Lord God had made. He said to the woman, "Did God say, 'You shall not eat of any tree of the garden'?" And the woman said to the serpent, "We may eat of the fruit of the trees of the garden; but God said, 'You shall not eat of the fruit of the tree which is in the midst of the garden, neither shall you touch it, lest you die.' " But the serpent said to the woman, "You will not die. For God knows that when you eat of it your eyes will be opened, and you will be like God, knowing good and evil." So when the woman saw that the tree was good for food, and that it was a delight to the eyes, and that the tree was to be desired to make one wise, she took of its fruit and ate; and she also gave some to her husband, and he ate. Then the eyes of both were opened, and they knew that they were naked; and they sewed fig leaves together and made themselves aprons.

And they heard the sound of the Lord God walking in the garden in the cool of the day, and the man and his wife hid themselves from the presence of the Lord God among the trees of the garden (vv. 1-8).

We are left with a great number of questions. Where does the serpent come from? Why is he more subtle than any other wild creature? What motivates him to tempt Eve? By what thought process does Eve arrive at her decision to eat the fruit? How does she reveal her disobedience to Adam? What is his initial response? What then leads him to eat the fruit? What happens when the eyes of both are opened? What goes through their minds as they hide among the trees concealing themselves from the Lord God walking in the garden? How do our answers to these questions affect our attitude toward the story? What would we write, or our students, in answering these questions in a narrative form? As with chapters 1 and 2, it is not necessary to consider whether we believe in this account of the fall of man or not. From a literary point of view, all we need to accept is that we are given a story of temptation and fall. The pattern is clearly a universal one, and raises questions which have nothing to do with the historical validity of chapter 3. How, for example, is a man tempted? What arguments does a tempter use to persuade man to break laws and codes of behavior? What processes does a man go through before making his choice to do the wrong thing? How does he persuade himself that he has no other choice under the circumstances? How does he justify to himself his actions after he has taken them? How does the wrong-doing affect his way of thinking and his attitudes towards those around him?

The opening of chapter 3, while it gives us no answers to these questions, does provide us with many imaginative possibilities. Notice that the serpent's first question implies that there is something unjust about God's command, that God is holding something back. "Did God say, 'You shall not eat of any tree of the garden'?" Eve's answer is straightforward, in response to what she assumes is a straightforward request for information. Eve, we recall, has presumably been told of God's command by Adam—she has no direct knowledge of it. She may also feel that she can exercise her intellectual powers by instructing the serpent. And, we might wonder, has the serpent approached Eve because he knows these things about her? In her answer, she changes the original command slightly (as we are given it in chapter 2) by adding that death will come if they *touch* as well as eat the fruit. Is this a slip in the narrative? Does it suggest that Adam had doubts about Eve and reported the command to her incorrectly to keep her away from the tree entirely? Does it reflect Eve's own doubts about the command? The serpent certainly may see an opening, a weakness.[2] He suggests that God is a liar: "You will not die." He proposes to Eve an explanation for God's withholding of some of his favors, a withholding he has already planted in Eve's mind with his first question: "God knows that when you eat of it your eyes will be opened, and you will be like God, knowing good and evil." In an ironic sense, the serpent is right: their eyes will be opened. The invitation is given to Eve to approach divinity herself and she seizes it. According to the text, her reasons for eating the fruit seem to be these: she is hungry, the fruit looks good, and she wants greater wisdom. She gives the fruit to Adam and he eats it, although we are not told why or what was said during their meeting. They feel shame and guilt and hide themselves from the Lord God.

Adam and Eve had been specifically commanded by God not to eat the fruit of the tree of the knowledge of good and evil; they have sinned, therefore, directly against God. Punishment begins immediately. Adam's internal guilt is suggested not only by his hiding from God, but by his telling God that he was afraid to confront him (v. 10). God perceives what has happened and asks Adam if he has eaten from the forbidden tree. Adam's guilt leads him to shift the blame. "The woman," he says, "whom thou gavest to be with me, she gave me fruit of the tree." The real fault is somehow shared, Adam implies, between God, for giving him Eve in the first place, and Eve, for deceiving him. God questions Eve, and she, like Adam, also seeks to shift the blame. "The serpent beguiled me." By this time, it is clear to God (if it was not clear long before) what has happened. He expands Adam and Eve's punishment from internal guilt and shame to include physical punishments: Eve will suffer pain in childbirth and be under Adam's control; Adam must sweat and toil to raise his food from a disordered nature, "Thorns and thistles it shall bring forth to you." Adam and Eve are physically exiled from the Eden they have already, by their disobedience, metaphorically exiled themselves from. The punishment is severe. At the same time, God demonstrates his mercy—he promises that the serpent will be bruised by Eve's seed; he makes "garments of skins" for Adam and Eve and clothes them.

Chapters 1 and 2 depicted God as both transcendent and immanent—distant, as the creator of the universe, close, as the creator of a garden for man. The universe as a whole is carefully and systematically ordered; man's environment is graciously organized for his well-being. Chapters 3 through 11 of Genesis describe the gradual loss of Edenic possibilities—through the beginnings of evil, we might say, or the beginnings of human misery. These chapters contain numerous genealogical histories, interwoven with and highlighted by events in the lives of individual men. Man's history (the genealogies) and God's purpose in the total movement of history (the selected incidents) seem to coalesce in the narrative, although they do not coalesce in fact—Cain, Noah, and Abraham are separated from the historical process. These chapters are not history, but an interpretation of history.

That interpretation is carefully wrought. Adam and Eve's sin, as we have seen, was directly against God. Their punishment was both internal and external. They were, however, shown mercy by God. The pattern of sin, punishment, mercy also controls the three remaining narratives in these chapters. Cain, in slaying Abel, sins against his own brother and neighbor; he is punished by God: "You shall be a fugitive and a wanderer on the earth" (4:12). But he is treated mercifully; God marks him to forbid revenge against him. In the story of the Flood, man sins against his own nature, "The wickedness of man was great in the earth, . . . every imagination of the thoughts of his heart was only evil continually" (6:5). He is punished through the dissolution of his world; God is merciful in selecting a remnant, Noah and his family, in ordering them to have dominion over a new, but representative, world of creatures, and in saying to them: "Be fruitful and multiply" (9:1). In the story of the tower of Babel, man sins against art, abusing his skills in order to make himself famous, attempting to build a great city to re-create Eden. His punishment is the breakdown of the human community. Mercifully, again, God calls Abraham, "I will . . . make your name great," and invites him and his nation to a different city, whose builder and maker is God.

All four instances of man's disobedience are, of course, against God; but the narrative seems to explore sin in its many manifestations—against God himself, against other humans, against man's own nature, against the ingenuity of his mind and the craftsmanship of his hands. The interpretation of history in Genesis describes the various ways men separate themselves from God and from Eden. Eden increasingly becomes metaphorical—it is harmony and order, it provides a secure sense of place, it is timeless. By contrast, man out of Eden, away from God, is in exile, a wanderer, in darkness, in confusion, in time. Adam and Eve are driven away from God's presence; Cain is driven away from nature ("the ground . . . shall no longer yield to you its strength" [4:12]); Noah's wicked contemporaries are driven off the earth itself; the builders of the tower of Babel are driven from one another. And yet, from this darkness, God, as he had done in creating the heavens and the earth, brings light: man's enemy the serpent will be bruised, Cain shall not be killed, the rainbow will signify the covenant with Noah, Abraham will bless all the families of the earth. Man, because of his potential for sin, will not return to Eden; God, because of his potential for mercy, will return Eden to him.

V Paradox and Symmetry in the Joseph Narrative

DONALD A. SEYBOLD, *Graduate Instructor,*
Department of English, Purdue University

I

The reader is immediately struck by the craft of the Joseph narrative (Gen. 37-50). Rarely in Western literature has form been woven into content, pattern sewn into meaning, structure forged into theme with greater subtlety or success. The result is a narrative of profound paradox that first reveals then resolves itself in absolute symmetry. To look closely at the major patterns of paradox is to discover how the literal level of the narrative fully engenders the meaning and how pattern finally unravels predicament.

The structure is primarily created and controlled by (1) the three sets of dreams which become reality and give us one paradox; (2) the four sets of analogous relationships that Joseph enters into—at home, in Potiphar's household, in prison, and in Pharaoh's household—relationships that provide us with a second paradox; and (3) the variations on the "pit" episode which combine both narrative and symbolic purposes to become the central repositories of paradox as well as provide the links of concatenation through which the other elements combine into the final and deeper significance of the story.

Less central to the main narrative but no less important to its deeper meaning is the Judah/Onan/Tamar story (Gen. 38), which intrudes upon but finally does not disturb the pattern and symmetry of the Joseph narrative. This story within a story presents a paradox which mirrors those of the larger narrative and is essential to the final significance and pattern of the whole.

Another major structuring device is Joseph's clothing. His coats and cloaks operate primarily at the narrative level as symbols of his position and of transition as Joseph moves from the home of Jacob to the household of the Pharaoh.

It is ultimately in the combination of these various recurring elements of the story that its meaning resides —inseparable from them and discoverable only through them. From the surface of narrative pattern emerges a deeper structure of meaning that reveals that the superficially different elements are manifestations of a single theme.

II

The story of Joseph begins (Gen. 37:1-11) with the characteristic sweep and dispatch of the early Hebrew style.[1] In these initial verses we are presented with the first of the dreams and the important relationships that affect Joseph. In the family, he is favored over all his brothers by Jacob and they are resentful. The unnaturalness of a younger son being favored is compounded by the manifestation of Jacob's love, his gift to Joseph of the coat.

Furthermore, the dreams present two sets of "unnatural" relationships that create a kind of double-edged suspense: are the dreams symbolic of Joseph's already "unnatural" relationship with his brothers and his father, or do they reinforce it and portend some further and even more unnatural situation in the future? It seems clear that they are unreal dreams rather than reflections of present reality; even though his brothers are "inferior" to him his father certainly does not bow down to Joseph. Whether the dreams will remain unreal and whether Joseph's present relationship with his family is actually or only apparently unnatural is not yet known. We need to follow these contradictions closely to see whether they are actually paradoxical.

Almost immediately (37:23-4) the dormant tensions of the first twelve verses erupt. The brothers plot to kill Joseph, but instead, at the urging of Reuben, strip him of his coat and cast him into a pit. While these acts are obviously symbolic, the coat is also used as literal evidence to prove to Jacob that Joseph has been devoured by "a wild beast" (37:33). Both functions of the coat become significant through repetition as the narrative progresses.

Joseph is removed from the pit by "some Midianite traders" (Gen. 37:28), sold into slavery, and taken to Egypt. Chapter 37 ends with Joseph being sold to Potiphar, the captain of the Pharaoh's guard.

We should consider the significance of the pit. It certainly points up the unnaturalness of the relationship of Joseph and his brothers by illustrating how such a relationship can lead to an even more unnatural act—one of waste and destruction. The pit is a prison. But the pit is also an alternative to murder—a still more unnatural act. The pit is a refuge which allows Joseph's life to be preserved. In fact, Reuben fully expects to come back later and rescue Joseph (37:22). The merchants, of course, get there first and the brothers believe Joseph to be dead. For the brothers, then, the act of throwing Joseph into the pit is an ambivalent one which ultimately (through subsequent events) becomes a paradox central to the story's outcome and meaning.

At this point the narrative abruptly shifts (Gen. 38) to Judah who leaves his brothers, marries a Canaanite, and fathers three sons. There follows the story of Onan and Tamar; Judah's failure to honor his pledge and his fornication with the temple prostitute, who turns out to be Tamar; and the birth of twins as a result of the union. The story interrupts the orderly flow of the Joseph narrative and seems to have little relationship to it thematically or structurally. From the point of view of literary analysis, however, its placement serves to recast and reinforce some major aspects of the Joseph narrative. Before seeing that, we must return to the major narrative and follow Joseph to Egypt.

At the beginning of Genesis 39 we find that Joseph has been put in charge of Potiphar's household; as a slave, his circumstances and position are quite tolerable. We also are told that Joseph (unlike Judah's oldest two sons of the preceding chapters) has been blessed by the Lord.

The LORD was with Joseph, and he became a successful man; and he was in the house of his master the Egyptian, and his master saw

> that the LORD was with him, and that the LORD caused all that he did to prosper in his hands. . . . From the time that he made him overseer in his house and over all that he had the LORD blessed the Egyptian's house for Joseph's sake; the blessing of the LORD was upon all that he had, in house and field. (39:2-3, 5)

Not only is Joseph blessed, but so is the house of his master. Still, there is a problem—Potiphar's wife. She makes repeated attempts to seduce Joseph which he repeatedly refuses. He explicitly considers such an alliance as both disloyal to his master and a "sin against God" (39:9). Finally, in desperation, she grabs him by his cloak, which is left "in her hands" as he runs out of the house. Potiphar's wife then offers the cloak as evidence of Joseph's alleged attempt at rape, and he is thrown into prison.

> But the LORD was with Joseph and showed him steadfast love, and gave him favor in the sight of the keeper of the prison. And the keeper of the prison committed to Joseph's care all the prisoners who were in the prison; and whatever was done there, he was the doer of it; the keeper of the prison paid no heed to anything that was in Joseph's care, because the LORD was with him; and whatever he did, the LORD made it prosper. (39:21-23)

This passage is startlingly similar to the one describing Joseph's tenure in Potiphar's house (39:2-6). Less obvious, but no less important, is the fact that Joseph's position in both Potiphar's house and the prison is essentially the same as his position at home before being cast into the pit by his brothers. He is a favorite of the head of the household (Jacob, Potiphar, prison-keeper) over others like himself, whether brothers, slaves, or prisoners; and he is in a position of dominance over the others, whether he is checking on his brothers for his father (37:12-14), presiding over the other slaves for Potiphar (39:4-5), or overseeing the other prisoners (39:21-23).

The pit itself prefigures his enslavement in Potiphar's household and his incarceration in the prison. Both the enslavement and the incarceration, like the pit, are first ambiguous and finally paradoxical events. Each step is a movement downward in the relative fortunes of Joseph; it is better to be the favored son than the favored slave, better to be the favored slave than the favored prisoner. While being a slave or a prisoner is destructive to the individual, each is finally less destructive than the alternative of death which Joseph faces from his brothers and from Potiphar.

The coat and cloak have served as emblems of his favor and dominance, then as evidence of his downfall through deceit, and finally as symbols of transition. The robe that his father gave him indicates his favored position over his brothers and is finally used by them to make Jacob think Joseph has been killed by a wild beast (37:31-35). Similarly the cloak representing his dominant position among the servants is used by Potiphar's wife to fool her husband into thinking that Joseph is guilty (39:12-29).

Schematically, the Joseph narrative, through Chapter 39, looks like this:

Head of Household	Jacob		Potiphar		Prison Keeper
Position of Dominance	Joseph		Joseph		Joseph
Position of Subservience	Brothers		Servants		Prisoners
Symbol of Dominance and Transition		Long, Sleeved Robe		Cloak	
Symbols of Ambiguity and Paradox		The Pit		The Prison	

The pattern of the narrative is quite obvious at this point. Joseph has managed to gain dominance in every situation he had encountered even though his progress has been marked by diminishing freedom from that of favorite son, to trusted servant, to favored prisoner. His relative position is identical in each context even though the context itself is increasingly restrictive. The robe and cloak have served symbolically to indicate first his elevation and then a stripping away, a transition downward into a pit, into servitude, and into prison.

That the pit/prison which stood ambiguously between freedom and death is operating paradoxically is also clear: it is the place where Joseph is both condemned and saved —however else this paradox may relate to the other elements of the pattern. That the relationships in the various households are analogous is obvious, but that they are paradoxical in any profound way is not. And, of course, the dreams have yet to become reality, in fact they seem to suggest conditions quite antithetical to those that have transpired thus far.

III

Chapter 40 opens as the Pharaoh's baker and butler are cast into jail with Joseph. He is appointed their attendant (40:4). After a time, they dream, and Joseph offers to interpret their dreams. First, the butler's dream:

There was a vine before me, and on the vine there were three branches; as soon as it budded, its blossoms shot forth, and the clusters ripened into grapes. Pharaoh's cup was in my hand; and I took the grapes and pressed them into Pharaoh's cup, and placed the cup in Pharaoh's hand. (40:9-11)

Then the baker's:

There were three cake baskets on my head, and in the uppermost basket there were all sorts of baked food for Pharaoh, but the birds were eating it out of the basket on my head. (40:16-17)

Joseph interprets the dreams, telling the butler that he will be restored to his post, and the baker that he will be hanged. And this is exactly what happens to each.

These dreams recall those of Joseph. How do these compare and contrast with his? We are dealing with a pair of dreams in each case; yet while Joseph's were dreamed by one man and were similar to each other, the second pair were dreamed by two men and seem quite different from each other. Indeed, the outcome of the baker's and the butler's dreams are radically different. We should also note that in the second set Joseph is not dreamer, but interpreter, and that his interpretations come true. Dreams become reality. This strongly suggests that Joseph's dreams may also come true. If they do come true, however, they will create a seemingly unnatural and untenable situation: his brothers and his father will bow down before him. If such an unnatural situation can somehow be simultaneously natural, we will have a paradox as compelling and necessary as that inherent in the pit/prison. (Further significance in the content of the prisoners' dreams, not immediately apparent, emerges later in the narrative.)

Nearly two years pass and Joseph is still in prison; but as chapter 41 opens, we are told that the Pharaoh has also had two dreams, in which seven fat cows are devoured by seven lean ones and seven full and ripe ears of corn are eaten by seven which are thin and shrivelled (41:1-7). No one is able to interpret the dreams until the butler tells Pharaoh of Joseph and his ability to interpret dreams (41:9-13). Joseph is brought out of the dungeon, and "he had shaved himself and changed his clothes" (41:14). This detail is significant in terms of the previous stripping of his cloaks and subsequent events in this chapter. The Pharaoh repeats his dreams to Joseph who in turn interprets them, saying:

The dream of Pharaoh is one; God has revealed to Pharaoh what he is about to do. . . . There will come seven years of great plenty throughout all the land of Egypt, but after them there will arise seven years of famine. . . . And the doubling of Pharaoh's dream means that the thing is fixed by God, and God will shortly bring it to pass. Now therefore let Pharaoh select a man discreet and wise, and set him over the land of Egypt. (41:25, 29-30, 32-33)

Of course, who is more "discreet and wise" than Joseph? He immediately explains exactly how to prevent the country from being devastated by the famine (41:34-45).

The plan pleases Pharaoh, who says to Joseph, "Behold, I have set you over all the land of Egypt" (41:41). Significantly, the Pharaoh "took his signet ring from his hand and put it on Joseph's hand, and arrayed him in garments of fine linen, and put a gold chain about his neck (41:42). Joseph administers wisely and well, prospers, marries, has children; and after the seven years of plenty, the famine comes and "all the earth came to Egypt to Joseph to buy grain, because the famine was severe over all the earth" (41:57).

At this point some obvious parallels present themselves. First, and most obvious, is the direct correspondence between the Pharaoh's dual dreams and Joseph's earlier dreams. Joseph's are identical in the same sense that the Pharaoh's two dreams are identical. Joseph's two dreams are one: the younger son is dominant over his brothers and his parents. Pharaoh's two dreams are one: the weaker destroys the stronger. Joseph's pair of dreams and Pharaoh's pair are one: the weaker *unnaturally* dominates the stronger. Further, in contrast to the prisoners' dreams, each pair is dreamed by one man and point to only one conclusion. Finally, the doubling of Joseph's dreams, like that of Pharaoh's, means that God had "already resolved to do this." (Had Joseph been able to interpret his own youthful dreams as he has come to understand those of others, what might that have meant to the boy in the pit?)

Pharaoh's dreams and the prisoners' dreams are alike in that Joseph interprets them correctly and they come true. They are unlike in that the prisoners' dreams are contrasting, while Pharaoh's are not, and in that Joseph has some control over the outcome of Pharaoh's dreams, but not those of the prisoners.

Since Pharaoh's dreams are more like Joseph's dreams than those of the prisoners' we might wonder whether the outcome of Joseph's will be more like that of Pharaoh's. That is, Joseph will have some control over the outcome and the outcome will be good. But if this is so then it means we do have a paradox—an unnatural situation is good, therefore presumably natural, especially since it is what God wants.

Other parallels are less striking but significant. For those, we have to return to the Judah/Onan/Tamar story (Gen. 38). At a fairly obvious level we can contrast Joseph's attention to duty and unquestioning allegiance to God with the implied disobedience of Er and the deliberate disobedience of Onan, and contrast Judah's illicit alliance with Tamar with Joseph's refusal of an alliance with Potiphar's wife. All these have implications in the context of the larger story.

A long discussion of endogamy and exogamy is out of place here,[2] but suffice it to say that the obvious and accepted interpretation of the Onan episode is the necessity of preserving the continuity of the family through the eldest male. Onan is bound by law and tradition to insure the survival of his oldest brother's line. This he doesn't do and it is his sin. Furthermore, Judah does not keep his pledge to provide his younger son for Tamar. Her seduction of Judah, her trickery and incest, are therefore more acceptable than Onan's spilling of his seed or Judah's failure to keep his pledge. Judah for his part readily admits this: "She is more righteous than I, inasmuch as I did not give her to my son Shelah" (38:26).

The message seems quite clear. Preservation of the family and propagation of the tribe are natural, and wasting the human seed or failing to impregnate the woman is unnatural. Incest is paradoxically natural under such a compelling natural law.

If the unnatural can in some cases be natural, if such a paradox can hold in this case, it can very possibly hold in the case of Joseph's dreams. If they come true, it is not necessarily a contradiction of natural family relationships, but may be a paradox, hence natural.

Further points which connect the Judah story with the main narrative can best be seen by returning to the dreams of the butler and baker. In the butler's dream we see him capturing, preserving, and then offering the grape nectar to Pharaoh. As metaphor this is a kind of symbolic fertilization of the Egyptian god—an act not unlike the literal fertilization of Tamar by Judah. The baker's dream, on the other hand, shows him being careless with the grain as he allows it to be eaten by the birds—at the metaphorical level an act not unlike that of Onan in wasting the human seed. Both kinds of seed are necessary to life. The butler who has not wasted it survives, as does Judah; the baker who has, is killed by his god, Pharaoh, as Onan is by his. The real significance becomes clearer when we recognize how Joseph is linked with the butler and opposed to the baker: Joseph has indeed preserved and conserved the Pharaoh's grain. This raises the more important question: Will Joseph also in some way be linked with Judah and Tamar and somehow be responsible for preserving or conserving the human seed or will he be linked with Onan and be responsible for wasting it? The paradox as well as the connection seems clear—he will need to commit an unnatural act (make his brothers and parents subservient) in order to do the natural thing (keep his family from being destroyed). Out of his "death" has come the continued life of Egypt; will his "death" mean the life of his family?

Here, let us schematize the narrative once again:

Ruler	Jacob		Potiphar		Prison-keeper		Pharaoh
Deputy	Joseph		Joseph		Joseph		Joseph
Other "Subjects"	Brothers		Servants		Prisoners		Citizens
Symbols of Position and Transition		Long Sleeved Robe		Cloak		Shaved and Changed Clothes	
Symbols of Ambiguity and Paradox		Pit		Prison		Egypt	

Underlying, controlling, and uniting the diverse narrative elements of the story and forming the deep structure of the

surface pattern are the themes of preservation and conservation. The entire tension of the narrative is between acts of
waste (Joseph's various imprisonments, seed spilled by Onan
and the baker) and acts of preservation (Joseph's talents
being used, Judah's impregnation of Tamar, the butler's care
of the wine). Frequently, as has been pointed out, an act of
waste is at the same time an act of preservation. The prisons
are chief examples of this ambiguity at the literal, symbolic,
and paradoxical levels of the narrative. And what happens
after chapter 41 will reveal whether Joseph will act to preserve his family or let them be "devoured" by hunger,
whether Egypt will become a prison of waste or a place of
conservation. If Joseph does the natural thing, it will be
unnatural. By doing the unnatural, the natural will be
served. The paradox is perfect and profound.

As chapter 42 opens, the narrative shifts to Canaan, and
we find Jacob sending ten of his sons to Egypt: "Go down and
buy grain for us there, that we may live, and not die" (42:2).
Jacob keeps the youngest son Benjamin with him, "for he
feared that harm might befall him" (42:4). Both aspects of
Jacob's action indicate themes of preservation: he sends his
sons for corn so that they may live, but keeps the youngest
home as insurance against harm—not only harm to Benjamin
himself, but to the family. Jacob's acts of conservation are
not unlike Tamar's prostitution or Joseph's storing the grain.

The brothers travel to Egypt not knowing that Joseph is
governor. "Joseph's brothers came, and bowed themselves
before him with their faces to the ground" (42:6). This act
verifies the first dream; only the second remains unfulfilled.

Joseph then accuses the brothers of being spies (42:9-14),
puts them in jail for three days (42:17), releases all but
Simeon, and tells them to return home and bring their
youngest brother back to Egypt to prove that they are not
spies (42:18-20). They acknowledge what they had done to
Joseph and admit to one another that "there comes a reckon-
ing for his blood" (42:22). Their act of casting Joseph into the
pit was as unnatural and wasteful as Onan's act. This admis-
sion and the set of tricks that Joseph plays on the brothers

with the coins and the grain (42:25) allow them to demonstrate ability to obey and to show love and loyalty to both Jacob and their brothers—in short to reunite the family and preserve it. "Send the lad with me, and we will arise and go, that we may live and not die, both we and you and also our little ones" (43:8).

Looked at in this light what have appeared superficially as nothing but a series of arbitrary and confusing acts (Gen. 44) on the part of Joseph become significant elucidations of the underlying structures of the entire narrative. These tests of Joseph's brothers serve to do more than create drama and suspense, although they have that function; more basically, they offer further evidence of the importance of loyalty to a family, and by implication, obedience to the tradition that preserves a family and the law of its God.

Egypt *is* the pit for the brothers. Joseph has the same options they had earlier: he can kill them or do something less unnatural and more ambivalent. The three sets of dreams are again important here and give us a frame for Joseph's final decision. Although the consequences of his dream are unnatural, they are not violent and not necessarily wasteful. The consequences of the Pharaoh's dream are both violent and wasteful. The contrast of the two pairs is reconciled in the dreams of the prisoners—to preserve is to survive, to waste is to die. Joseph's brothers and his captors have always opted for the alternative that allowed Joseph to live. It seems likely that he will not do otherwise to his brothers. But it also seems essential that they be presented with the same kind of prison, the same ambivalences and the same paradoxes, so that they can finally ally themselves with the preservers rather than the wasters. The following chapters work out this pattern.

In chapter 44 the brothers demonstrate great affection for and loyalty to their father and one another (44:18-34). Indeed Judah offers himself as hostage in place of Benjamin.

Now therefore, when I come to your servant my father, and the lad is not with us, then, as his life is bound up in the lad's life, when he sees that the lad is not with us, he will die; and your servants will bring down the gray hairs of your servant our father with sorrow to Sheol. For your servant became surety for the lad to my father, saying, 'If I do not bring him back to you, then I shall bear the blame in the sight of my father all my life.' Now therefore, let your servant, I pray you, remain instead of the lad as a slave to my lord; and let the lad go back with his brothers. For how can I go back to my father if the lad is not with me? I fear to see the evil that would come upon my father. (44:30-34)

Judah's act is a radical and convincing one in the same way that Tamar's was: he is willing to put all personal concern behind in order to preserve not only the welfare of his father and brother, but the family itself—he will become a slave to a person he believes to be a foreigner. He has chosen the unnatural act which is paradoxically and at a deeper level the natural thing to do. He and the others will survive the pit as Joseph has earlier.

We have here both a climax and a classic case of Aristotelian reversal. Primarily we see it in the change in the brothers and their relationship to one another, secondarily in Joseph's new power relationship to his brothers. He is now in a position of dominance, as his dreams predicted; and he now has the choice, prefigured in the dreams of the butler and baker, of acting to make his brothers either servants or prisoners, by preserving or wasting, by finally offering them life from his "death," which his father had mourned long ago.

As chapter 45 begins, Joseph is overcome by his brother's speech and offer, and he makes himself known to his brothers in a very emotional scene in which Joseph himself indicates the controlling deep structure of the entire narrative.

And now do not be distressed, or angry with yourselves, because you sold me here; for God sent me before you to preserve life. For the famine has been in the land these two years; and there are yet five years in which there will be neither plowing nor harvest. And God sent me before you to preserve for you a remnant on earth, and to keep alive for you many survivors. (45:5-7)

In this speech Joseph forgives, demonstrates his belief, and clearly acknowledges the whole paradoxical purpose of his "death" as God's way of preserving the family. He also commits himself to the law of the family and begins to reassemble the family in the land of Egypt.

So it was not you who sent me here, but God; and he has made me a father to Pharaoh, and lord of all his house and ruler over all the land of Egypt. Make haste and go up to my father and say to him, "Thus says your son Joseph, God has made me lord of all Egypt; come down to me, do not tarry; you shall dwell in the land of Goshen, and you shall be near me, you and your children and your children's children, and your flocks, your herds, and all that you have; and there I will provide for you, for there are yet five years of famine to come; lest you and your household, and all that you have, come to poverty." (45:8-11)

This is the first time that God's direct control of Joseph's entire history is specifically acknowledged, although the narrator earlier indicates God's continuous intervention in human affairs when Joseph refuses Potiphar's wife and mentions that interpretation of dreams belongs to God. It is noteworthy that this acknowledgment comes during the climactic episodes of the narrative and suggests how the Joseph story relates to those that precede and follow it. In terms of the narrative it shows clearly that paradox is only the result of the human perspective and our limited understanding of the ways in which God operates.

The only significant event left to be worked out is Joseph's second dream and the movement of Jacob to Egypt—which, of course, are complementary acts. Jacob sets out for Egypt, stopping in Beersheba to offer sacrifices to God, and God tells Jacob: " 'Do not be afraid to go down to Egypt; for I will there make of you a great nation. I will go down with you to Egypt, and I will also bring you up again; and Joseph's hand shall close your eyes' " (46:3-4).

Jacob moves with all his sons and their progeny into Egypt with the blessings of his God and of Pharaoh, under the care of Joseph. "And Joseph provided his father, his brothers, and all his father's household with food, according to the number of their dependents" (47:12). The connection of the conservation of both human seed and food as themes of preservation in the narrative are here merged.

The story moves toward a conclusion with Jacob's confused

blessing of Joseph's two sons—the younger is declared to be greater than the older and the younger's descendents shall become a nation in themselves (48:17-20). This, in spite of Joseph's protestation, is an exact duplication of his own position in his father's household (and of his father and grandfather before him); and it gives further evidence that the younger son can dominate an older one when it is necessary to preserve the family. Likewise, incest (Judah/Onan/Tamar) is preferable to either waste or exogamy, and subservience preferable to freedom in order to preserve the family. Always in the Joseph story the structures of preservation supersede those of waste, even when preservation demands that one tradition be temporarily violated. The profound paradoxes of the story are a direct result of the tensions created by acts and events which are both natural and unnatural at the same time. Dreams become reality, subservience becomes dominance, prisons become places of preservation. The major operative patterns, symbols, and structures of the Joseph narrative are orchestrated into a symphony whose movements, themes, and motifs are tonal variations of the same structuring key.

The opening prepares us for the end, where the family is once again together and the members are in the same essential relationship to one another as before. This is not the "eternal return" of the pre-Hebrew myth, but instead a mythic pattern that is linear and eschatological. The situation at the end is also very different from that of the beginning; the similarity is more apparent than real. The Hebrew sense of man's relationship to God in history is very clear. The literary device of paradox stands at the center of the narrative pattern and the final thematic significance of the story.

Further, this analysis makes very clear the literary forms of repetition, pattern, and character that operate in the story and give it an elegance and eloquence quite apart from its religious, historical, or theological significance. And most important, it demonstrates that a close look at the narrative shows structures that allow the narrative pattern to speak its final significance in faultless symmetry.

VI The Literary Context of the Moses Birth Story (Exodus 1–2)*

JAMES S. ACKERMAN, Department of Religious Studies, Indiana University

The Exodus narrator is looking both to the past and to the future as he begins his story.[1] Exodus 1–2 introduces a larger epic cycle, centered in the figure of Moses, a cycle which recounts the creation of Israel as a nation and the formative years in the establishment of her covenant relationship with God. The event which forms the center of this cycle is the escape at the sea (described in Exodus 14–15), culminating the confrontations between Moses and Pharaoh. The narrator is highly conscious that in the birth of Moses a chain of events is being set in motion which will lead to the event —the creation, from a mixed rabble of enslaved peoples, of a new nation through which the divine purposes of freedom and justice will begin to be realized. Thus the Exodus is conceived as a new act of God's creation, at least equal in importance to the establishment of the cosmic order described in the early chapters of Genesis. We should not be surprised, therefore, when we find repeated allusions in Exodus 1–2 to the primeval stories in Genesis 1–11. The story includes a series of mundane events: the building of two store-cities in Egypt, the defiance of Pharaoh by two clever midwives, a child placed carefully in the reeds at the river's edge, a young man's standing up for his dispirited people, his flight from Egypt, his helping seven sisters to water their

*This essay is dedicated to James Muilenburg, formerly Professor of English, University of Nebraska, retired Professor of Old Testament, Union Theological Seminary (New York), whose vision and charisma drew me and countless others into biblical studies, and whose sensitivity to language and style provided the original impulse toward what I hope will be a new and fruitful direction in biblical scholarship.

flocks. But through the continual allusions to the primeval stories in Genesis 1–11 we become aware of the cosmic import of these apparently insignificant events which surround Moses' early years. Through Moses and Israel, the story suggests, God will reshape or re-create the world. Through the events which follow, a new reality will become known to man. The dominant mood of Exodus 1–2, however, is anticipatory: the structure and symbolism point beyond Moses' early years toward the escape at the sea, the giving of the law at Sinai, and Israel's wandering through the wilderness toward the promised land. All these themes are introduced in Exodus 1–2, indicating the direction in which the epic will move.

There is a historical base to the persons and events described in the book of Exodus, but the story presents them to us as they have been refracted through the prism of Israel's experience as a people. The historian would prefer to know the name of the king of Egypt who oppressed the Hebrews; the narrative gives us instead the names of two insignificant midwives who "delivered" them. (That pun does not work in Hebrew, but early listeners would surely have relished it!) The Bible is certainly teeming with data very important to the historian, but concentrating exclusively on them will not bring the reader closer to an understanding of the text. The teacher of literature should not use the Bible to elucidate the "history of Israel." The history and culture of the ancient Near East are subsidiary concerns, important only as they provide the background out of which the Exodus 1–2 portrait will emerge.

Exodus 1:1-7

This section serves as a transition from the stories of the twelve brothers in Genesis to the story of Israel which begins in Exodus. The transition is made very effectively through the twofold use of "sons of Israel"* (all asterisked biblical quotes have been made directly from the Hebrew text). In verse 1 the phrase refers to the twelve sons of Jacob or Israel who migrated into Egypt with their families; in verse 7 the phrase refers to the Israelite people who, we are told in the story which follows, have grown mighty and more numerous than the Egyptians. Note that the narrative flow of events, which ended in Genesis 50 with the death of Joseph, does not pick up again until Exodus 1:8. Exodus 1:1-7 provides us with a break in the action, so that we can make a large leap in time and prepare ourselves for the drama which will soon unfold.

These verses, however, represent far more than a device for pulling us through time while allowing us to catch our breath. Note the stately, deliberate, repetitive language, especially in 1:7. Since economy of language is a hallmark of Hebrew literary style, we must be aware that the apparent redundancy is flashing us signals. They reflect the theme running through the episodes that culminate in the birth of Moses—the mysterious power which permits the Hebrews to survive, and even to thrive, in the face of mounting oppression and persecution. Exodus 1:7 introduces this theme through a series of five Hebrew verbs which supplement one another and intensify the effect, explaining Pharaoh's fear and setting into motion the oppressive measures he undertakes. "And the Israelites *were fruitful*, and they *teemed*, and they *multiplied*, and they *became vast* in exceeding abundance, so that the land *was filled* with them."*

Lest the modern reader should judge this a classic case of verbal overkill, we would stress again that the story is extremely careful in its use of language. It has set the stage for Pharaoh's fearful acts of "wisdom" which follow. But even more importantly, it is also pointing back through the book of Genesis, deliberately selecting language which will underline the cosmic context of what is about to happen. The Creation story climaxes in Genesis 1:28 when God blesses the newly created man and woman through a series of imperative verbs: *"Be fruitful* and *multiply*, and *fill* the earth and *subdue* it; and *have dominion* over . . ."* Similarly, after the deluge, which blotted out the sin of man and returned the world close to its former estate, Noah, the new Adam, is given a comparable five-part divine blessing upon emerging from the ark: *"Do fruitful* and *multiply* and *fill* the earth, *terror* of you and *dread* of you shall be over . . ."* (Gen. 9:1-2).

The Exodus passage has preserved the fivefold verb structure in 1:7, and three of the verbs are the same in all three passages, so we can assume that it is inviting us to perceive the relationships among the three stories. It has omitted the final two elements occurring in both of the Genesis passages which emphasize man's conquest and powerful rule over the rest of creation. These characteristics are not compatible with the situation facing the Hebrews in Egypt. The story has taken the first three verbs from the Genesis passages and arranged them in a 1-3-5 sequence, selecting new verbs for the 2-4 positions to give further impact and emphasis to the statement. Note one further change: the divine blessings in the Genesis passages were a series of blessing-commands. In Exodus 1:7 the verbs are in the past tense. The narrator is clearly saying that the destiny of man, as announced at the Creation and after the Flood, is in the process of being fulfilled by the descendants of Israel.

The stress in the narrative, however, is merely on Israel's fecundity, not on its obedience. Israel is peculiarly passive in the early episodes of Exodus 1–2. The Israelites seem to be fruitful and multiply in these stories, not through any virtue or obedience on their part, but simply as a result of the mysterious purposes and hidden presence of God. The proliferation had already begun during the generation of Joseph, when the descendants of Israel were confined to the land of Goshen in the Nile delta region (Gen. 47:27). Now they are described as even outnumbering the Egyptians. A constant theme through the patriarchal stories in Genesis 12–50 is God's promise that the seed of Abraham will multiply exceedingly, becoming a great nation, and that the descendants of Israel will one day possess a land of their own.[2] The same words "make fruitful and multiply" are used repeatedly; as we hear the opening words of the Exodus story, we know that the fulfillment of these promises is beginning to take place. The narrator need make no mention of the God of

77

Israel, but we are being told that the deity is at work, renewing life and vitality among his people. Israel has multiplied; it must soon have dominion over its land. The perceptive listener has heard one shoe drop, and he will cock his ear to wait for the other.[3] One of the two major promises is in the process of fulfillment (a great nation from the seed of Abraham). We know that Israel dwells in an alien land, so we find ourselves anticipating the chain of events which will lead to Israel's securing her own land, the second promise made in God's covenant with the Patriarchs.

The modern reader may wonder why such an exciting story must begin with a prosaic listing of names. This beginning becomes particularly disconcerting when one looks back to Genesis 46:8-27, where virtually the same tradition is spelled out in even more specific terms: all seventy of the descendants of Israel who entered Egypt are listed. It was important to the cohesiveness of the early Israelite community for the major clans of all the tribes to be remembered and to celebrate their participation in the one great story. But why must the narrative repeat the essentials from the earlier list as Exodus begins? Note the reference in 1:5 to the seventy descendants "coming forth from the loins of Jacob"* who finally entered Egypt. Again, the text underlines the cosmic context of what is about to happen. Genesis 10 describes the seventy descendants of Noah who were scattered abroad and who established, according to ancient tradition, the seventy nations of the world. Israel is here being portrayed as the microcosm of the macrocosm—the fulfillers of the divinely ordained destiny of man laid out following the Creation and the Flood.[4] Consider the sequels to the Creation story and the Flood story. Adam and Eve were expelled from the Garden of Eden; Noah's offspring also scattered. The result of the dispersal of the seventy descendants of Noah was alienation and confusion, epitomized in the vain attempt to build the tower of Babel. The seventy descendants of Jacob/Israel are also wandering into the land of Egypt from the east. They will be pressed into bondage in the vain effort to build a second Babel. But the final result, from the biblical viewpoint, will be a series of mighty acts culminating in the Exodus from Egypt and the covenant at Sinai—a second dispersal, but this time aimed at re-creating the human community, offering man the hope of overcoming the broken relationships which had been part of his condition since primeval times.

Exodus 1:8-14

The character of the narrative shifts abruptly with verse 8, away from the sober, reflective tone of the preceding verses. The pattern of peace, harmony, faith, divine guidance, and protection which had run as a fairly consistent thread through Genesis 12–50 is being challenged by a villain the likes of whom had not appeared in the patriarchal narratives. Note the consummate skill of the narrator, establishing the changed situation of the Hebrews and the motivation leading to their bondage through two characterizations: an introductory description of the king and a revealing consultation between the king and his people.

The one characteristic we learn about the new king gives the story an appropriately foreboding introduction: he did not know Joseph. The verb "to know" has a wide variety of meanings in ancient Semitic languages. Although verse 8 could mean that the new king did not remember Joseph's service, recently discovered texts indicate that the verb, especially in political contexts, should be translated "to acknowledge the authority of." For example, when Moses appears before Pharaoh in Exodus 5:1 as a messenger from YHWH to demand that the Israelites be allowed to leave Egypt to serve their god, the king replies that he does not *know* YHWH (i.e. acknowledge his authority), and therefore he refuses to accede to his demands. Thus one pharaoh does not "know" Joseph, and his successor does not "know" YHWH. The meaning goes beyond this. The Egyptian court vaunts itself on its wisdom, but they do not *know* the real order of things. They show no awareness that their actions run counter to the new cosmic order breaking in upon them, crushing the oppressor and setting free the oppressed.

There are other kinds of humor—here, a pun—when the king is introduced as not knowing "Joseph" (literally, "the one who adds, increases"). The motivation given for the repressive policy towards the Hebrews includes "lest . . . if war should break out, they be added ("Josephed") to those who hate us."* Thus, the policy is not simply motivated by lack of recognition for Joseph's contribution to Egypt and the authority he had once held in the land; it is a deliberate attempt to prevent the Joseph phenomenon from recurring among the Hebrews in Egypt. What the king overlooks is that Joseph had brought prosperity for his Egyptian lord, the earlier king, creating "increase" in the land. But this new king is a subtractor, a decreaser. He could have brought continued blessing to his land, as before. But he sees the Hebrew increase only as a threat to his people. Ironically, by attempting to decimate the Hebrew population, he will unleash a flurry of divine activity which will bring decrease, but not in the way he had intended!

The proliferation theme recurs twice in this introduction of Pharaoh. Pharaoh perceives Israel's new situation, and in speaking to his people he uses adjectival forms of two of the verse 7 divine-blessing proliferation verbs. For Pharaoh, these are bad omens; from Israel's perspective, they are part of God's plan. The battle lines have been drawn here, and although God has not yet been mentioned, we know that the ensuing conflict will be cosmic. Pharaoh says, "Come now, let us outsmart them,"* but his "wisdom" leads him to actions which attempt to thwart the purposes of God announced to man in the two beginnings (Adam and Noah) and to the progenitors of Israel in their quest for fulfillment in the land of Canaan. The text is relying on its readers' knowledge that Egypt was renowned for her court wisdom throughout the ancient world, and that Pharaoh thus represents the epitome of human wisdom. But there is heavy irony here. Pharaoh, like Haman in the book of Esther, is being portrayed as the wicked fool who, intending to destroy Israel through total reliance on his "wisdom," sets into motion a chain of events which will lead to his own destruction.[5] Just as Haman craftily built the gallows on which he himself would eventually be hanged, so the King of Egypt's enslaving the Hebrews would lead to the death of Egypt's firstborn sons (Exod. 12:29-30) and the destruction of Egyptian troops at the sea (Exod. 14:21-31).

The Revised Standard Version renders Pharaoh's statement "the people of Israel are too many and too mighty for us," whereas the Hebrew text more literally means "the people of Israel are more numerous and stronger than we are."* This statement of numerical superiority may trouble readers who wonder how the descendants of one man could outnumber all the Egyptians after several centuries. Perhaps Pharaoh is only describing the land of Goshen in the delta. I would suggest that we take the statement literally. This gross exaggeration gives us the situation as Pharaoh sees it, reflecting his paranoid condition.[6] We know that Pharaoh's attempt to counteract Israel's further proliferation is doomed to failure because this is part of the divine promise. Can we not guess what will come of Pharaoh's other intention—to prevent Israel from "going up," leaving the land? The perceptive reader has been given a hint, straight from Pharaoh's mouth, of the outcome of the coming conflict.

These verses also deliberately use language and develop themes which point back to the Tower of Babel story. In both there is an emphasis on human ingenuity. Both are introduced by the interjection *haba* "come now," with the main verb in the Hebrew cohortative "let us," followed by *pen* "lest," describing the situation which the protagonists are seeking to avoid. Both stories refer to building activity and describe similar building materials. Both stories stress that man's proud wisdom and purposive activity are in vain, and can lead to his own destruction, when they run counter to the order of things as perceived by Israel. In each story man's purposive activity precipitates a divine counterreaction which results in redemptive dispersion, first in Abraham, then in Israel (note the prefiguring parallels drawn between Abraham and Israel in Gen. 12:10–13:1).

The climax of the Babel story was in God's descending

(yarad) in power to overthrow the tower and scatter its people. When will he descend in Egypt—to destroy Pharaoh or help Moses and Israel? Although we soon discover that Pharaoh's activity turns counterproductive, no mention is made of God's descent or active intervention. This is all the more striking in the light of God's promise to Jacob that he would descend *(yarad)* with him into Egypt (Gen. 46:4). God remains behind the scenes throughout these early Exodus episodes. But we, the readers, perceive his unseen activity in the frustration of all of Pharaoh's plans. We are led to expect a more powerful descent, as in Babel, but it has not yet occurred. The cycle is so structured that we can anticipate a climax involving God beyond the episodes of Moses' birth and early years. We can patiently relish the buildup in the assurance that more is yet to follow. And we are not disappointed: at the burning bush YHWH announces that he has "descended" and will use his power to set his people free (Exod. 3:8); again at Sinai YHWH descends in power to give his people the way by which they are to maintain their freedom (see Exod. 19:18-24).

Exodus 1:11 describes the action taken by Egyptian authorities in order to neutralize what was perceived as a national threat; the Hebrews are pressed into state slavery. Egypt was replete with projects demanding concerted effort which were policed by governmental authority; copper and turquoise mines in Sinai, gold mines near the coast of the Red Sea, river levees and sluices to control irrigation, and royal building projects. The Hebrews, according to these verses, were employed primarily in reconstructing two major cities in the Nile delta: Raamses and Pithom.[7] In the Tower of Babel story the proud and ambitious *haba* ("come now") of man is met by the mocking, yet shattering echo of God's *haba*. The same effect is achieved in Exodus 1:8-10. Pharaoh initiates the Hebrew bondage, lest *(pen)* his fears be realized. But, says the text, "as [the Egyptians] oppressed them, thus *(ken)* they multiplied and thus *(ken)* they burst forth."* The carefully conceived *pens* of man are met and overwhelmed by the well-established *kens* of God's order.[8]

Such word-play for ironic contrast is characteristic of biblical Hebrew. The language encourages its audience to relish the discomfiture of the oppressors who have all the resources of human power at their disposal. The Hebrew life style is idealized: they remain proud wanderers, aliens wherever they go, beyond the protection of the settler's law—subject to abuse and forceful subjection, but ultimately indomitable. The oppressor may try to control them through force; but this only intensifies their desire to remain Hebrews. State slavery, as it was practiced in the ancient world, was indeed a means of population control and reduction. The life expectancy of a slave working the mines or on some building project was not long. But the story reports that something mysterious and uncanny happened in Egypt. There was a direct correlation between the oppression to which the Hebrews were subjected and their thriving throughout the land.

The conclusion of these verses stresses a strong counter-theme which will be very important in the ensuing episodes. Through verse 12 the narrative had continued to develop the theme of proliferation. It had idealized the Hebrew lot, almost reveling in the persecution because it precipitated an even stronger expression of God's life-giving power. But verses 13-14 introduce the countertheme which brings the first two segments into tension with each other, creating of them an introductory frame which sets the stage for the other episodes in Exodus 1–2:

So the Egyptians made the Israelites *serve* with harshness; and they made their lives bitter with hard *service*, with mortar and with bricks, and with all the *service* in the fields. And all their *service* which they *served* for them (was done) with harshness.*

Note that just as the first paragraph had ended with five different verbs describing the new life and vitality of the Hebrew population in Egypt, the text here includes various forms of the Hebrew verb "to serve" five different times. This is not happenstance, nor does it represent unimaginative use of language. The monotonous, drumlike repetition of serve . . . service . . . service . . . service . . . served, re-

creates the soul-deadening feeling of slave labor.[9] The second
five-verb sequence invites the reader to ponder the contrast.
On the one hand we have five verbs depicting life and fruit-
fulness, wrought by the quiet power of the hidden God (1:7);
on the other hand, we have the fivefold stress on death-
bringing service, imposed at the command of the Pharaoh
who is anything but hidden (1:13-14). Through this artful
juxtaposition the narrative points to the conflict which will
follow. It raises a central question of this epic cycle: which
power will Israel serve—the life-giving power of God or the
death-bringing power of Pharaoh?

Exodus 1:15-22

The king has acted to forestall the threat of insurrection or
invasion by exploiting the Hebrew labor force. His action,
paradoxically, brings both life and death to the Hebrew
community; the more they are oppressed, the more they
spread through the land. Yet, the oppression is experienced
by the Hebrews as a form of death. These verses continue
and heighten both of the conflicting themes. The motivation
for the king's action was established by verse 12, where his
witnessing of the continued Israelite proliferation only intensified his paranoia. The form of the king's action was established in verses 13-14, where the slaughter of the newborn
Hebrew males is portrayed as a natural extension of the
deathlike bondage. From our perspective the king's action
seems unwise, in that he is destroying one of his chief
economic resources. This has led many scholars to question
the motivation for the king's decision to slay the newborn
Hebrew males. If he were trying to decimate the Hebrew
population, why just the newborn? And further, why only
the males? According to these scholars the original tradition
from which this segment of our story is derived is related to
the popular folk motif of the king who is warned that a male
child would soon be born who would eventually supplant him.
This is the motivation for the persecution which is given in

later Jewish tradition, also closely paralleling one part of the Jesus birth story (Matt. 2:1-18).

But, 1:15-22 is not simply a rough "scissors and paste" editing job, an apparent *non sequitur* to what had preceded. The narrative follows the crazy kind of logic which had characterized the Egyptian court in 1:9-10.[10] We have already heard the king say, "We're outnumbered by the Hebrews, so let's get rid of them by not allowing them to escape." From the Egyptian point of view, Pharaoh's next step makes sense. By cutting off the male Hebrew population he can calm his fears of invasion and insurrection, whereas sparing the Hebrew females will, through assimilation, allow the Egyptians to add greatly to their population.[11]

Earlier, the Hebrews had remained passive, requiring no human intervention to deliver them from extinction. But in determining to slay the newborn males, Pharaoh has escalated the persecution, necessitating new forms of action to counter the threat. Earlier, too, the scope had been nationwide, with the king taking action against the "Israelite people." Here the arena is much more localized, showing the king plotting with two midwives to slay the "Hebrew" male children. (One can argue that this reflects a conflation of sources preserving different perspectives of the tradition: one, the "people of Israel" seen as a nationwide threat; the other, the "Hebrews" confined to a small locale served by two midwives. But such an observation is irrelevant in appreciating the literary craft of the narrative.) Note how the narrative gradually focuses the story upon the figure of Moses, moving from the nationwide oppression (1:8-14) to the slaughter of the newborn males within a given region (1:15-22) to the plight of one single family, through whose wiles the murderous plot of Pharaoh is reversed (2:1-10).

The consonantal Hebrew text, which is the form in which the story was preserved until vowels were added in the 7th century A.D., contains a description of the midwives which can be rendered either "to the Hebrew midwives" or "to those midwiving the Hebrew women." Those who put the vowels into the text opted for the former interpretation, but many

scholars argue that the story makes better sense if the midwives are Egyptians. How could Pharaoh trust Hebrew
midwives to carry out such a commission against their own
people, they ask? As in the portrait of the Egyptian princess,
the story, in commending the God-fearing midwives, is pointing up the goodness which exists potentially in some Gentiles. They do not know the laws which will be given to Israel
at Sinai, but there are certain universal norms of human
conduct which many Gentiles will acknowledge and respect.
Thus, it is maintained, we see in the midwives and the
Egyptian princess a general human decency (called "fear of
God" in the midwives' case) which prevents them from murdering helpless children, even at the king's command.

Why not follow the Hebrew text "to the Hebrew midwives" as it now stands? As we shall see, there is all the
difference in the world between the clever Hebrew midwives
and the dumb Egyptian princess. First, the midwives have
Semitic names. They have been only loosely assimilated into
Egyptian society, and when the crunch comes they know who
they are and where their loyalties and values lie. Second,
Pharaoh does not suspect that the midwives will dare protect
their own kind. He also knows that slavery crushes the
spirit. He is counting on the demoralized Hebrew midwives
to do anything to save themselves, even when it is at the
expense of other Hebrews. Exodus 2:13-14 illustrates the
isolated, demoralized conditions produced by slavery. Such
conditions have existed among black Americans in recent
times. For another analogy, we know that many Jews held
subordinate positions—positions which demanded callous
brutality towards those about to die—in Hitler's death
camps.

The conflict has already been sketched in the two introductory paragraphs: God is bringing freedom and life to the
Hebrew community, and Pharaoh is intent on bringing slavery and death. Pharaoh, here relying on the combination of
fear and hopelessness produced by slavery, is sure that death
will prevail. And for a brief moment in the story it looks as
though he has calculated correctly. The Hebrew of verse 17

begins· "And the midwives feared. . . ."* We anticipate "Pharaoh" as the object of this verb. But no, it is "God." They bowed before a higher law than the edict of the king—an authority demanding that they abet the life-giving power at work in the Hebrew community. Later in the cycle the Israelites will murmur against Moses and want to return to the security of Egyptian bondage, but the first response of the people in the struggle between life and death, freedom and slavery—as embodied in the choice made by the midwives —indicates that God will ultimately be successful.

Note how Shiphrah and Puah defend themselves with straight faces against Pharaoh's charge of insubordination. Their lives are at stake, and yet their sly comparison between the vigorous Hebrew women and the pampered Egyptians comes through as totally credible to the "wise" king: "Oh yes, of course, that would be a problem, wouldn't it?" There is a great relish in this uneven conflict between the effete elite and the crude, but shrewd, vital, and resourceful, oppressed. The king fails to realize that not only is he being deceived, but he is also being mocked. The mode of deception clearly depicts the contrast between Egyptian and Israelite societies by pointing up the difference in the women. One thinks of the contrast between Potiphar's wife, who attempted to seduce Joseph because she was bored (Gen. 39), and Judah's daughter-in-law Tamar, who was forced to deceive and seduce her father-in-law in order to preserve her portion of the family inheritance (Gen. 38). Even more telling are the echoes of the final two stanzas of the "Song of Deborah" (Judg. 5:24-30), in which the deceitful activity of Jael, who boldly steps forward to strike down Sisera when Israel's existence is at stake, is contrasted with the great pathos of Sisera's mother and court ladies, who assuage their fears over his late return by anticipating the acquisitions—slaves and spoil—which will be brought back in his victory procession.

There are a surprising number of deception stories in the Bible.[12] My perspective on these stories was radically altered one day when our class was discussing Genesis 12:10-20, where Abraham avoids Egyptian persecution by passing off his wife as his sister. A black student from Harlem interjected immediately that that was precisely the situation of her people during the slavery period, where black men's lives were often endangered when the master lusted after their wives.[13] Such stories had had little meaning to me before then.[14] But when one considers the Hebrew status—both in Egypt and in Canaan—as an outsider, beyond the protection of the law, subject to the capricious whim of the ruling lord, it is easy to understand why deception would be a highly admired characteristic in Hebrew culture. Shrewd cunning was the only resource of the defenseless, here pitted against the overwhelming power and "wisdom" of Pharaoh.

Verses 20 and 22 juxtapose the action of God and Pharaoh, the conflicting forces of life and death, paralleling in many ways the climax of the preceding paragraphs. In verse 20 God stands by the midwives, protecting them from Pharaoh's wrath for noncompliance. Verse 21 (which some scholars label a later expansion of the text—or a feature which has been clumsily interwoven into the tradition) emphasizes that they were blessed with "households,"* which means "enduring progeny." Their clever boldness had secured continued offspring for the Hebrew community, so the midwives are rewarded in kind.

The fate of the midwives is symbolic of the condition of the community "the people multiplied and grew very strong" (1:20). This terminology, which has run like a continuing refrain through the narrative—concluding the first paragraph, beginning and ending the second, here ending the third—does not let us overlook the central theme which the narrative has been developing. The countertheme, stressing Pharaoh as death-bringer, also reaches its climax in verse 22. It was introduced in 1:9 as a response to 1:7 and continued in verses 15-16 as a response to 1:12. Here again in verse 22 it is a reaction to the continued proliferation of the Hebrews throughout the land in verse 20. Thus the themes intertwine and work together, producing a continuing escalation as the forces of life and death struggle to prevail.

Exodus 2:1-10

Scholars have pointed out that the foundling child motif appears in many hero birth stories throughout the ancient Near East.[15] But as we shall see, the story of Moses' birth has its own unique features. Furthermore, this episode, as it now stands, does not give the impression of being an independent entity which has been casually included in an arbitrary collection of traditions surrounding his birth and early years. It is itself a rare work of art, and the groundwork has been carefully laid in chapter 1 for its telling. The interwoven themes of life and death have just reached a high crescendo, and we look to this episode for the resolution of the conflict. But there is a strange, low-keyed quality to the "clash" of the two forces, neither explicitly mentioned. With great subtlety the narrative has muted the proliferation formula which had regularly sounded throughout chapter 1. Yet as we listen, we are led to the clear perception that, in the silence, the outcome of the first chapter's struggle is being determined. We know that through the birth of the one child, the forces of life have prevailed; through the rescue of Moses from the waters, the victory over death and bondage is now assured.

How to account for the older Miriam and Aaron, when the Hebrew text seems to indicate that Moses is the firstborn of this marriage is a question that has engaged scholars, but need not affect our literary analysis. Israelite literature has a cryptic quality which gets right to the heart of the matter, shearing away all details considered irrelevant to the outcome of the story. Consider the lessened impact if the episode had begun with the births of Miriam and Aaron. We presumably know the larger context of Moses' family, so why intrude the larger picture upon a close-up of one small, but extremely significant, chain of events?[16] In Exodus 4:22 Israel will be called God's "first-born son," and it is entirely appropriate that Moses, who will lead Israel toward nationhood, share in that status by being described as the "firstborn" of a Levite couple. Furthermore, we are thereby invited to ponder this death threat to Moses, Israel's "firstborn son," in the light of what will later happen to the firstborn of Egypt. There is a strong feeling in Israelite thought that history will return to haunt the oppressor. There are deeper truths than our quest after historicity would uncover. Through this art the narrative invites, even demands, the suspension of this instinct, so that we will move with the flow and perceive the truth being proclaimed.

We observe a sudden turnabout in verses 2-3, where a series of minor details clamors for our attention. They stress the special nature of this child, as if to say that none of the usual motivations for child exposure applies to him.[17] He is a healthy child, loved by his mother, legitimate in every respect, protected from death at great risk. By enumerating these details the narrative stresses that the child is being prepared for his destiny with the tenderest of motherly care. But it does not lapse into melodrama or sentimentality. With a twinkle it serves us up a delicious irony; by exposing the child the mother is, in fact, complying with the letter of the law—what more can one ask?

As the child is placed at the edge of the waters (that ambiguous symbol of life *and* death), his sister stations herself nearby to learn "what would be done to him." Note the confluence of two themes we had observed in chapter 1: the general passivity of the Hebrews, pointing up the behind-the-scenes activity of the hidden God, and the brazenly crafty response of Hebrews who cannot accept edicts aimed at destroying them. In 1:1-7 and 1:8-14 the Hebrews are portrayed as completely passive, continuing to thrive even when subjected to bondage. In 1:15-22 we see in the midwives' story that the Hebrews must act to defend themselves, though, we are told, this action would have been futile apart from God's protection. The situation recurs with renewed intensity in this episode. The careful strategy of mother and sister reenacts the pluck of the midwives. But we are shown here even more subtly than before that the ultimate outcome depends only to a certain point upon human initiative; even the most pious scheming cannot succeed apart from the quiet, even unspoken, intervention of God. The text uses the passive verb ("what would be done to him") at this point to stress the necessity of human passivity: the two active agents in our story to this point have been Pharaoh and the hidden God. We must wait to see which will prevail, though the sequence in chapter 1 gives us a good indication of what to anticipate.

The cosmic implications of this struggle were evident in chapter 1 through constant allusion to the proliferation formula of the Creation and Flood stories. Furthermore, in inviting us to connect the seventy offspring of Noah (nations of the world) with the seventy descendants of Jacob/Israel, the narrative depicted Israel as the microcosm of the universal macrocosm. Again at this point we are asked to look back as we behold the *ark* floating in the reeds by the river's edge. The only other occurrence in the Bible of the Hebrew word *teba*, translated as ark or basket, is in the Noah story. In that instance, divine judgment was about to fall upon a corrupt mankind, and the ark became the vehicle through which man's hopes and God's purposes for the future were to be realized. Here, the death threat originates from a fearful Pharaoh, not God; and the intended victims are the enslaved Hebrews in Egypt, not all mankind. But for the Israelite community the fate of the child in the ark was just as important, if not more so, to the future destiny of mankind as was the fate of Noah.[18] Through Noah man was saved from extinction, partially purged of the corruption which had engulfed the world. Through Moses, as we shall see, Israel was to be delivered from the spiritual death of bondage and oppression. And the experience of Israel under Moses was but a microcosm of that which, it was thought, would one day come to all the nations of the world.[19]

The story has been so structured—we have already been reminded of Noah's survival in the ark; we have already witnessed the repeated frustration of Pharaoh's attempts to destroy—that we are now expecting some intervention from God, or at least from someone friendly to the Hebrew cause. And we have been cleverly misled: who should come along but Pharaoh's own daughter! How does she appear on the scene? She "came down"—the verb which is traditionally used for a divine manifestation (see discussion above on God's descent in the Babel story). Handmaidens accompany her descent to the river's edge, and she is about to enter the water, attended by her servant girl, when she spots the ark stuck away in the reeds.[20]

The suspense builds as we come to the moment of decision. But even before we get there the text, through subtle arrangement of verbs, has hinted at the outcome. At the beginning Moses' mother "*saw* that he was a goodly child . . . [and] *took* for him a basket." Now "the daughter of Pharaoh . . . *saw* the basket . . . (and sent her maid) and she *took* it."* Is the narrative giving us a clue that the princess will respond, as had the mother, with love and compassion, or are we being set up for a cruel irony? (Note, incidentally, the artful way the verb "took" threads its way five times throughout this episode.)

Verse 6 begins with a crudeness which surprises: "And she opened and she saw him—the child—and behold, a babe—crying."* Some of the ancient translations have attempted to smooth out the roughness of the text, but I would argue that the Hebrew text, as is, reflects artistry we have come to respect. The direct object pronoun has been omitted from the first verb, connoting the same kind of haste and anticipation with which children open gift packages. The next verb, on the other hand, has a repeated direct object once as a pronoun, and then, specifically, "the child," replicating the process of standard recognition. The reader is to make no mistake. The repetition of the word from verse 3 emphasizes that this is the same child who had been loved and cared for by his mother. Now we are asked to shift perspective, to see this child from the princess' viewpoint: "and behold, a babe—crying."*[21] The princess does not know, as the reader does, what has gone before. But the child's crying, characterizing its helplessness, wins her pity, and she quickly surmises from the circumstances that the child is a Hebrew.

Scholars often stress that the narrator is portraying the

princess' mercy and kindness as a foil to highlight her father's cruelty. Such an instance of benevolence among some Gentiles enriches the story, preventing it from being easily reduced to a narrow ethnocentric struggle between the good guys (us) and the bad guys (them). An Egyptian princess spares him; a Midianite priest will welcome him into the clan; his own Hebrew people will turn upon him, challenging his claim to authority. Indeed the princess does the right thing in this story. She sends for a Hebrew wet nurse, perhaps realizing that the danger of discovery would be minimized, and also that an Egyptian wet nurse would be inclined not to give the child good treatment.[22] Her offer to pay wages to the unknown Hebrew wet nurse for her work, in the context of the master-slave relationship between Egyptian and Hebrew, is seen as a further sign of the princess' compassion and humanity.

This may be the correct interpretation, but the theme in chapter 1 of the cunning oppressed, supported by the benevolent power of the hidden God, establishes an ethos which inclines us in a different direction. Note that finding a Hebrew wet nurse was not the princess' idea. Moses' sister materializes from nowhere, trying to be "helpful" with her innocent suggestion. The princess' one-word response "Go" connotes a feeling of supreme authority, a brusque manner in dealing with underlings, and perhaps some relief in having the problem so quickly resolved.[23] The princess believes she is in complete control of things, but actually she is being controlled by the bright wit of a young girl. The princess may attribute her feeling of pity to an innate spontaneous response of her generous nature. But we may be witnessing the work of the same power which will harden a later pharaoh's heart.

The combination of haughty condescension continues in verse 9, where the princess says, "Take this child and nurse him and I, even I, will give you your wages."* Why the "even I," if not to point up the boorish quality of such "refined" benevolence? The princess expects gratitude and a chorus of "hallelujahs" in the slave quarters, but we who hear the story know there will only be ear-to-ear grins and great delight over this final "put on" of ole' massa.

The ethos we feel here is the humorous irony often found in slave literature. Imagine the enjoyment, the sheer relish, of early audiences to this turn of events. The child is delivered from Pharaoh's clutches by being given over into his daughter's hands! Now our "wise" and unsuspecting villain will through his daughter pay wages to a Hebrew woman to nurse her own child, thus defying his edict, and that very child will one day arise to lead his people to freedom and leave Egypt in ruins. As Moses was drawn out of the reeds by the water at the "benevolent" command of the princess, he will one day draw his people through the water (the "Reed Sea," the same word in Hebrew as in 2:3) at the absolute command of God.

The story faithfully reflects the practices traditionally followed for adopting a foundling child:[24] after the child has been found, a wet nurse is contracted to raise him for three years. After that period, when the child is weaned, he is legally adopted and given his name. And even here the humor continues. The princess names him "Moses," but, unfortunately, she does not handle the Hebrew language very well. "Moses" is part of an Egyptian name, meaning "son of," such as we find in Thutmosis, Ahmosis, Ramses (Ramosis), etc. But the story is of course concerned with the meaning of this name in the Hebrew language, and it has intriguing possibilities. The princess is quite correct that *m-sh-h* means "to draw out" in Hebrew. So far, so good; she shares in the great "wisdom" of the Egyptian court. But she missed the lesson concerning the formation of Hebrew participles. She thinks that "Moses" means "the one drawn out of the water," but the passive participle would be "Mashuy." [25]

Because she does not have total command of the language, she mistakenly names him with the active participle ("the drawer out")! An insignificant detail? Hardly. Names had great importance in ancient Near Eastern thought because they were thought to describe the inner essence of the person. The princess thought that Moses' basic characteristic would be passive   the one who has been found, drawn out, brought up, and that his very name would be a reminder of the gratitude which he should feel for her benevolence. But she mistakenly names him "the one who draws out," and that is precisely what he will do. The princess thought the name referred to Moses' past as a passive babe; in fact, because of her clumsiness with the Hebrew language, the princess is unwittingly confirming the destiny which, we will soon discover, the God of Israel has determined for him.[26] He will indeed draw Israel out of bondage, through the waters.

We now have sufficient perspective to look back at what appeared to be excess verbiage, twice repeated, which occurred in 1:15-22. It was not necessary for the Pharaoh, in commanding the slaughter of the Hebrew male children, to add that the daughters should be allowed to live. Why does the story include this "unnecessary" statement? Three different daughters play a role in delivering Moses from death, and the word "daughter" occurs six times in this part of the story. Certainly our attention is being drawn to the ironic connection between Pharaoh's intent to spare the daughters and the fact that a succession of daughters, the last being his own, contributes to his undoing.

Surely a woman will play an important role in any birth story, but why is there such an extreme stress on the activity of women in this story? Not only are the three women mentioned: Moses' mother, his sister, and the Egyptian princess. The clever Hebrew midwives had played an important part in setting the stage for the discovery of the ark in the reeds. Early in this story Pharaoh was introduced to us as setting himself against the purposes of God through his absolute "wisdom" and power.

The reply to this challenge is that the wit and compassion of women—symbolic of that which is least and weakest in ancient culture (as were the Hebrews themselves)—are sufficient to undermine the intentions of the proud oppressor. Why? Because the power of the God of Israel, though muted and behind the scenes, stands with the oppressed and manifests itself through that which is least and weakest.

Exodus 2:11-15d

Suddenly Moses is grown up. We are led smoothly into his adult life by a repetition of the same verb in verses 10 and 11. The use of "grew" at the end of the birth story means that the child has grown and is now ready for weaning (cf. Gen. 21:8). The second instance of the verb indicates that Moses has reached maturity. The narrative need not fill in all the gaps; it is not a biography of Moses. Interest in Moses is restricted to those events which relate to the destiny of the new nation Israel. The remarkable circumstances leading up to Moses' birth were important because they foreshadowed the eventual demise of Pharaoh's power at the hands of the God who brought life to his oppressed people. Now that Moses has been designated as the hero—child born of and preserved by a special providence, we are free to move immediately into a quick collage of episodes from his young adult life which point up his qualifications for the position of leadership to which he will soon be called.

This passage contains two episodes building up to the quiet climax in 2:15-22. It will reintroduce earlier themes, but there are also new emphases which alter the mood of the story. In the introductory verses the Hebrews had remained passive, totally sustained by the life-giving power of their God (1:1-7; 1:8-14). In the next two paragraphs the Hebrews were driven into action by the growing intensity of the persecution (1:15-22; 2:1-10). But the action has been sly and shrewd. There were no overt acts of hostility against the persecutor—only crafty ploys aimed at survival. And we know that these acts have been successful because God is working behind the scenes in behalf of his people. The hero child, hidden in the reeds, symbolized both the passive, secretive people and the mystery of the hidden God thus far portrayed. The mysterious, hidden nature of hero and Deity is a theme which will move throughout the epic. At times the Israelites profoundly feel the absence of God and turn against his designated leader.[27] Even at Mt. Sinai, the place of the covenant, the people are not permitted to come near the holy mountain, lest they die.[28] Moses is not allowed to approach the burning bush and is granted only a brief glimpse of God's back on the mountain, because no man can see God and live.[29] The hiddenness and mystery of God will remain a part of Israel's experience. Moses will also remain a hidden figure throughout this epic, shrouded in mystery and paradox. As he was hidden from his persecutors at birth, he will remain hidden from his people, waiting on the mountain for the words of the covenant; and when he returns, it will be with his face veiled to protect Israel from the gleaming rays of God's glory.[30] Finally, in death Moses will be hidden from all the world, so that "no man knows the place of his burial to this day." [31]

In 2:11-12 we are about to discover the other side of Moses, the forceful, aggressive leader acting in the midst of his people, presenting God's demands to a recalcitrant Pharaoh, urging his people through the waters as they flee before the Egyptian chariots, standing on the hilltop with his hands held high as Israel goes into battle against the Amalekites, proclaiming the ten "words" at Mt. Sinai, and smashing the tablets in wrath when he discovers his people playing the harlot with the Golden Calf.[32] Just as the first two stages of our story pointed up the hidden God and concluded with the hidden, passive child, this stage will develop the other side of Moses, as with ever-increasing openness he takes the initiative in responding to the needs of the afflicted. The activity of Moses, we will soon discover, is but a precursor to the manner in which God will take the initiative to act with openness and power in behalf of his people.

The tension in the preceding segments was produced by a conflict of powers external to Moses. As the child's fate hung in the balance, the reader might wonder whether the life-giving power of God or the death-bringing power of Pharaoh would prevail. As this passage opens, a new tension is produced by a struggle of competing claims within Moses. Though the text tells us immediately that the Hebrews are "his brothers,"* we know that he has been nurtured in two cultures and has two natures—Hebrew and Egyptian. Which of these loyalties, so diametrically opposed, will prevail when the challenge comes? Whether Moses even knows what we have been twice reminded—that the Hebrews are his brothers—is not really germane. The important point is that Moses has not yet become a Hebrew. Hebrew blood and his mother's nursing do not suffice. Only through feeling compassion for the oppressed and acting in their behalf can he identify himself as a Hebrew. Note the interesting reversal of the "rags to riches" motif.[33] In most foundling stories the hero is removed from the royal court and raised among the common people, finally returning as a young adult to claim and establish his rightful heritage of wealth and power. In this story, however, Moses did not become the hero, the legitimate agent of God, until he burned all the bridges between himself and the wealth and power of the Egyptian court.

This paragraph contains two episodes, both introduced by "and he went out," and we have learned that the Bible does not use repetitive language carelessly. We are being asked to make associations, to see parallels. Moses' "going out" from the royal court is preliminary to the larger "going out" of Israel which will follow.[34] In Exodus 3:10-12 the same verb is used three times when Moses, in the critical event at the burning bush, is commanded to bring Israel out of Egypt.[35] Before he can lead others out of Egypt, however, it is necessary for him to go out from the royal court, and finally, to flee the land of Egypt. The precondition of these departures is a spiritual "going out" in which, through acting in behalf of his brothers, he breaks ties with his Egyptian heritage.

In the first episode (2:11-12), Moses sees . . . sees . . . and then sees. Moses' first two acts of seeing are the observation of conditions which we know existed in the Hebrew community before his birth. He not only sees "their burdens" (cf. 1:11), but through the addition of one letter in the Hebrew—a preposition ("he looked upon")—we are informed that Moses is not simply an observer; he is responding with strong feeling to the hopeless misery of the slaves.[36] His eyes are being opened. In Moses' second act of seeing he observes an Egyptian overseer beating a Hebrew to death. Again we see the past recurring in the present. Pharaoh the death-bringer is still at work. The fate previously intended for the newborn males is now being visited upon adult males. Moses instinctively knows what he must do. Passive defiance and tricks will not serve. Unlike the sly midwives and his mother, he resorts to open violence. But the theme of shrewd caution continues: he knows he must act, but he first carefully looks in all directions. And, for the third time, he sees "no one"; it is his opportunity to act. He saves the Hebrew by smiting the Egyptian to death—the same verb which described what the Egyptian was doing to the Hebrew. It cannot be accidental that this is also the same word which will later describe what God does to Egypt through the plagues (called "the ten smitings" in Hebrew).

Another aspect of slavery is dramatized in Moses' next encounter: two Hebrews are violently struggling with one another. Moses immediately intervenes to defend the cause of the person being wronged. His question to the wrongdoer ("Why do you smite to death your neighbor?")* is not asked out of idle curiosity. The question is formulated in the words of an indictment which could initiate a judicial process, and the implication is that Moses has both the authority and power to back up his intervention. This assumption is immediately challenged by the wrongdoer. In 1:11 the Egyptians had set "princes" to supervise the labor for the building projects. The wrongdoer asks Moses if he is such a prince, having the authority to pronounce and enforce judgment over them. The unspoken implication is that Moses is getting a little too uppity, forgetting who he really is. How dare he lord it over his fellow Hebrews? The irony is that, by intervening to restore community among his people, Moses is affirming himself as a Hebrew.

The confrontation with the quarreling Hebrews not only foreshadows the murmurings and rebellions against Moses' authority during Israel's sojourn in the wilderness; it also gives us insight into the deadened spiritual condition of the slave community. We see the same close relationship between physical death and spiritual death which had been traced in the prolegomena to Moses' birth. Hebrew men are being beaten to death by Egyptians. But the sense of community among the Hebrews has been so crushed by bondage that Hebrews are turning in hopeless violence on one another. The sneering attack on Moses' right to intervene carries the implication that only Egyptian authority should be respected. The Hebrew wrongdoer prefers the authority which crushes and brings death to the power that would re-create community. The wrongdoer's first question is an eloquent reflection of the self-hatred which flourishes among oppressed peoples whose spirit is crushed. They have been so thoroughly brainwashed regarding their "rightful position in life" that they turn viciously on any one among them who would rise up to give them hope.

The wrongdoer's second question opens up yet another characteristic within the slave community. Moses is cast in the role of the troublemaker who, in killing the Egyptian, will make things even worse for his people. Hostages will be taken, reprisals carried out. The crushed spirit finally stops hoping for things to get better, but it never stops fearing that things will get worse. Not only is Moses wrong for stirring up false expectations, but he may well bring down wrath which will further worsen conditions for the people he is trying to help. These fears will be realized following Moses' first encounter with Pharaoh. The Egyptians, assuming the Hebrews are growing both lazy and uppity, add to their work load by forcing them to gather the straw for bricks. The Hebrew leaders are beaten when the brick quota is not reached, and their response is to turn on Moses and Aaron: " 'The LORD look upon you and judge, because you have made us offensive in the sight of Pharaoh and his servants, and have put a sword in their hand to kill us' " (Exod. 5:21).

Moses is not yet the full-blown hero. He cannot answer the question regarding his authority to intervene, because he has not yet been called by God. The midwives had feared God and acted to defy the king. But Moses fears the king and flees for his life. His dual heritage had given him only the potential to buck the system. Through his early years with his mother he had gained an awareness of his origins, and his growing up in the princess' household had spared him the crushing physical and spiritual effects of bondage.[37] Nevertheless, the Egyptian stranglehold is so strong on the Hebrews that even Moses must succumb and flee. The death spirit is contagious throughout the land. And we see that Moses, as strongly as he identifies his unfettered spirit with his people, is unable to face the contagion on his own. He flees across the Sinai to the land of Midian, east of the Gulf of Aqaba.

Some scholars theorize that 2:15 was at one time a direct continuation of the Moses birth story which ended with 2:10. In its present context "this thing" which Pharaoh hears of is Moses' acting in behalf of the Hebrew people. For doing what? Slaying an Egyptian overseer? Surely a prince of Egypt would not be punished for slaying a low-grade official in the Egyptian hierarchy. If one removes verses 11-14, the "thing" Pharaoh hears of is that a Hebrew child had escaped his death edict and been raised by his own daughter. Most of these same scholars had argued that the original motivation for Pharaoh's edict was because of a dream that he would one day be overthrown and replaced by a Hebrew. The child had been raised in secret, and his existence was only discovered after he had reached adulthood.

I have already argued against this interpretation in an earlier part of this essay. These traditions might well have been used for various purposes as they were preserved in oral form. But the story makes sense as it now exists, and this negates the necessity to theorize concerning possible earlier forms of the tradition. The discussion in this segment has centered on the broken spirit of the oppressed and the way it is manifested in the narrative. But let us recall a theme which was strongly developed in chapter 1: the paranoid fear which poisoned the spirit of the oppressor. With the civil rights days in America during the early sixties behind us, we might be surprised to remember that the rights of black people could at that time be violated almost at will. But a very special kind of wrath consistently descended

upon any white person who "deserted" his people to affirm
the cause of black people. Such desertion, which implicitly
challenged the values of the white oppressors, was regarded
as gross betrayal of group solidarity and was often severely
dealt with. The Exodus story has already emphasized the
ever-increasing fear among the Egyptians before the growing Hebrew multitudes. In acting to defend the Hebrews,
Moses was challenging the basic foundations—social, political, and religious—on which Egyptian society had been established. It should come as no surprise that Pharaoh would
seek to crush him.

Exodus 2:15e-22 [38]

Introduction. Like other literary works, many biblical
narratives begin by describing a fairly stable situation (The
whole earth had one language/Moses was keeping his
father-in-law's flocks) into which is introduced a new element
or a secondary action establishing a new condition and setting the scene for the main action which will follow (Men
moved in from the east and settled in the valley of
Shinar/Moses led his flock and came to the mountain of God).
The opening verses provided us with the two stable elements
necessary for the action to begin: Moses has moved into the
land of Midian and is resting by the well; the priest of Midian
has seven daughters. Readers might anticipate the outcome,
allowing the two pieces of information to interact in their
minds. A man, a group of women, and a well—aha! We
remember other well stories, where the Patriarchs of Israel
found their brides. Will Moses do likewise? Another motif
from the preceding birth story might also echo in the reader's
mind. Moses is fleeing before Pharaoh; he has been saved
once by other daughters. What role will these daughters play
in rescuing him from pursuit?

Parenthetically, the narrative has given us the same type
of artistic flourish which we learned to appreciate in 2:10 and
2:11. The same verb is used to close one unit and open the
next, again used with two differing meanings: Moses *dwelt* in
the land of Midian; Moses *sat* by the well.

Action, Conflict and Dialogue. This section is packed with verbs. A high intensity is achieved, and the conflict arises and is resolved all in one verse—almost like a thirty-second shoot-out in a Western film. The action is framed by the threefold use of the verb "to come." The daughters come to water the flocks; the shepherds come to drive them away; the girls come to their father with the news of what happened. By comparison, the narrative is far more detailed in describing how the daughters watered their flock. There are two possible explanations: to convey the bustling, energetic, activity of the young women—establishing their attractiveness for the listeners. Or, more likely, to convey the backbreaking effort involved in watering the flock—establishing even greater outrage among the listeners when the rowdy shepherds come along and drive them away from their hard-gained water.

Moses reacts as would any good member of the audience, driving the bullies away. And the Israelite experience that there is a power which works for justice among men, even when the odds are one against many, is reinforced. The Hebrew text says that Moses arose and delivered the young women. These two verbs are technical terms to describe action which rescues the powerless from oppression. In the Bible the verbs often depict the activity of God, but they can also describe the deeds of a man empowered to act by a divine commission.[39] Despite this allusion, it is quite noticeable that there is no mention of God's spirit here, and we must assume that the omission is intentional. As already noted, Moses is not yet the full-blown hero, divinely commissioned, empowered to act by the spirit of God. Note that the young women are not Hebrews; they are weak and helpless, and they are in a situation where they are unable to defend themselves. Moses' actions are not primarily ethnocentric in their orientation. His response to the girls' plight is an instinctive reaction against oppression, and this is the major characteristic of the hero which our narrative has been emphasizing throughout. When called at the burning bush to lead Israel from bondage, Moses will stress his many limitations. But through the sequence of acts demonstrating his fierce passion to protect the helpless, the story has shown us that Moses is uniquely qualified to fill the hero's role in Israel.

The dialogue between the puzzled father and the excited girls is a gem. As in the conflict sequence, the scene is very brief; but the closeup effect of the thirty-second exchange achieves a strong impact. The father is surprised that the flocks have been so quickly watered. Why? Moses did not force-feed them! This can possibly mean that the conflict between the girls and the shepherds had been a recurring one, and the daughters had consistently been forced to wait for whatever water was left after the shepherds' flocks had drunk their fill.

The daughters are astounded that the Egyptian stranger, having no family ties with them, has intervened to reverse this long-standing pattern. Their incredulity is captured in one phrase: "and he *even* drew water for us."* That detail had not been mentioned before. Either in their excitement and gratitude they are attributing more to their deliverer than he had actually done (remember, *they* had drawn the water before the shepherds came), conveying their larger-than-life perception of his deeds; or it had indeed been necessary to draw new water because the shepherds' flocks had moved in when the girls' flock was driven away. Moses himself, having driven the shepherds away, had stooped to perform this menial task (a traditional woman's role? Cf. Gen. 24:15-21; 29:9-11). Their wonder, then, is triggered just as much by Moses' tender, humble compassion as by the strength through which he routed their tormenters (cf. Num. 12:3). In sending his daughters out to fetch Moses, the father is extending the full hospitality of the clan to this stranger who had already acted as if he were part of the family. We are invited to compare the response of this wandering shepherd family to Moses with that of his Hebrew "brothers."[40]

Resolution. Here we sense the staccatoed time sequences of action and dialogue dissolving into a broader temporal perspective. We see why the action and dialogue sections were narrated so quickly that there was no time for suspense to materialize. The main focus of the episode is how Moses came to join the clan of Reuel through marriage. In typically cryptic fashion the story does not describe the father's offer to Moses, Moses' reactions, how long it took him to decide. Instead the narrative jumps right to the point: Moses accepts the offer and marries one of the daughters he had earlier rescued.

Through the introduction to this episode we might have anticipated that the narrative would result in a love story. Not so. It is true that, as with Isaac and Jacob, marriage did result from the encounter at the well. But there has been no attempt to develop the love theme. We must assume that this downplaying was deliberate, that we are to wonder instead at Moses' motivation for intervention—his natural sympathy for people being brutalized by the powerful. We might also have assumed that the daughters would help rescue Moses from Pharaoh, as other "daughters" had rescued him at birth. But the tables are reversed; Moses does not need their help to escape from Pharaoh. From the perspective of the epic cycle, Moses' one great need is not the absence of Pharaoh, but the presence of God. Though we do not yet know it, this Midianite clan will provide Moses with the "help" he needs—the occasion to approach the mountain of God.

Just as the birth episode had concluded with the princess naming the child, this episode, which, as we shall see, structurally parallels the birth story, ends with the naming of Moses' firstborn, giving us assurance that his line will continue. The birth and naming of the child are not a parenthetical aside, a mere historical annotation. As in Moses' birth episode, the naming of the child has a many-faceted significance. "Gershom" comes from the Hebrew root *g-r-sh* "to drive out," which verb was used in 2:17 to describe what the shepherds did to the seven daughters. Perhaps Moses was stirred into action because he saw an analogy between his situation and the predicament of the young women—both had been driven away by circumstances beyond their control.

"Gershom," born in the remote land of Midian, symbolized to Moses his "driven out" condition.

The text, however, relates the child's name to the Hebrew root *g-r* "alien sojourner." Abraham had been told that his people would be alien sojourners in a land not their own (Gen. 15:13). The irony is that Moses, expelled from his "home," for the first time experiences the condition which had been his people's lot for many generations. Driven from the land he has considered home but which was not, yet feeling that his ties with the clan of Reuel do not fulfill his final destiny, Moses is now ready to begin a new quest for the home promised to the Fathers in generations long gone by. We might assume that, since our story has reached its happy ending—Moses escaped from Pharaoh's reach, warmly welcomed into a seminomadic clan, free to wander with family and flocks—there will be nothing more to tell. But we must be attentive to even the smallest clues: the name "Gershom" indicates that Moses has not yet reached his final home. His stay in the land of Midian is not the end of the story; he is still restless, strongly feeling his alien sojourner status, of which his son will be a constant reminder.[41]

Exodus 2:23-25

This is the concluding section of the seven-part story. Both the opening and closing episodes serve as links to what precedes, tying together themes and events which will become operative in what follows. Exodus 1:1-7 showed the seventy descendants of Jacob-Israel as the microcosm of the seventy-nation macrocosm that descended from Noah. Through them the nature and purpose of man to fill and rule the earth, announced at the Creation and following the Flood, would be fulfilled (as promised to the Patriarchs of Israel throughout the book of Genesis). As we shall see, Exodus 2:23-25 acts as a similar conclusion to what has just preceded it.

Both passages, however, also serve as introductions to what follows, marking a new stage of divine activity. In 1:1-7 the commands and promises made in the past begin to move toward realization through God's behind-the-scenes activity. The descendants of Israel become a great nation in Egypt, and the proliferation formula of 1:7 introduces the major theme around which the conflict of the story will center. This introductory characteristic applies even more strongly to Exodus 2:23-25, which contains standard terminology introducing many Bible stories describing a divine summons to a hero to rise up and deliver Israel from the hand of the enemy (cf. Judg. 3:15, 4:3, 6:6, etc.). Our discussion will center only on those aspects of 2:23-25 which *conclude* the story of the birth and young manhood of Moses before his call.

The opening passage, in describing the fruitful proliferation of the descendants of Israel, mentions the death of Joseph, God's agent through whom the life of the people had been preserved (cf. Gen. 50:20). The closing passage gives us another death—the death of Pharaoh, the death-bringer. Paradoxically, the people of Israel experience the deathlike quality of bondage even more strongly as a result. Historically, the death of a great king always fanned the embers of hope among subject peoples throughout the empire, hope that the successor would be ineffective and that the time of liberation was therefore near at hand. The wrongdoer's response (2:14) to Moses reflected a group among the Hebrews which had played it safe by refusing to hope, because when the hopes do not materialize the resulting despair becomes unbearable.

Through this reminder of the situation of Israel in Egypt, the impression that the story of Moses cannot have ended is reinforced. Twice again we hear the word "service,"* variations of which had been drummed into the story five times in 1:13-14, when it introduced the death theme. Thus, we are made aware that although Moses has escaped the death threat, the conflict between life and death has not yet been resolved for his people. In fact, the first four descriptions of Israel in verse 23 show her at her lowest ebb. Though Pharaoh is dead, there is no one to hope in. Moses is far removed from the scene, and the God who had been with the forefathers has apparently faded from the people's memory. It is quite remarkable that there is no direct object for the outcry of Israel. They scream into the void, underlining their utter despair. But God heard . . . remembered . . . saw . . . knew. The cry goes into the void, but God is there also. We know that the story is ready for a dramatic new turn.

We have moved in the course of this story from (1) a passive people blessed by their quiet God to (2) a crafty people acting on the sly, successful because of divine protection to (3) an openly active human being who still falls short of fulfilling God's purposes. But in this final passage (4) God perceives (heard . . . saw) and responds (remembered . . . knew), and as Greenberg points out, the iterative effect of these four verbs is that of a bell "tolling the good tidings: the time of God's action has at last arrived."[42]

The text does not restrict itself to the terminology used in the preceding paragraphs, but it leaves enough connections for us to draw an ascending order of relationships. God *saw* the sons of Israel, just as Moses had *seen* their burdens and had *seen* an Egyptian beating a Hebrew to death, and the daughter of Pharaoh had *seen* the ark placed carefully in the reeds. As Moses had responded with compassion to the plight of his people, the princess had pitied the helpless babe crying in his lonely isolation. God hears the Israelites' cry for help and, the text concludes, "he knew" (i.e., "pondered what to do"; cf. Gen. 18:20-21).[43] Should not God even more appropriately take pity on his firstborn son, the children of Israel?

Although any graphic representation of the structure of the Moses birth story within its literary context will be misleading because the themes and language are intertwined with great sophistication, it might still be helpful to lay out, in some crude fashion, a graphic representation of how the literary units fit together into a whole.

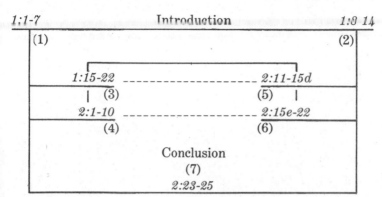

| 1:1-7 | Introduction | 1:8 14 |

(1) (2)

1:15-22 — — — — — — — — — — 2:11-15d

| (3) | (5) |

2:1-10 — — — — — — — — — — 2:15e-22

(4) (6)

Conclusion
(7)
2:23-25

Introduction

1:1-7

(1) The scope of this passage is nationwide. The descendants of Israel are portrayed as the microcosm of the macrocosm—the agents through whom man's destiny, laid out at the Creation and following the Flood, is to be fulfilled. Israel, however, is entirely passive. Joseph the life preserver had died, but life flourishes among the Hebrews in Egypt. It is the behind-the-scenes activity of God which brings life and progeny to the people, as had been promised long ago in the covenant with the Fathers. The time of fulfillment is now at hand.

1:18-14

(2) The scope of this episode is nationwide. Though Pharaoh continues the life theme by alluding to the verse 7 proliferation formula, he emerges as the chief opponent of God, determined to counteract the Hebrew vitality through bondage. Strong allusions from the Tower of Babel story overlay this episode, stressing the proud, purposeful "wisdom" which destroys human community. The Hebrews remain entirely passive; the activity of the hidden God—bringing increased life in the context of increased bondage—foils the efforts at population control. The theme of fear is introduced, once implicitly and once explicitly, as the

109

Egyptian response to Hebrew life. And the fivefold repeated root "service" in verses 13-14 contrasts with the five verbs for proliferation in verse 7, establishing the struggle between Pharaoh, the death-bringer, and God, the preserver of life.

Sections 1 and 2, then, introduce the conflicting protagonists: God and life versus Pharaoh and death.

<table>
<tr><td>1:15-22</td><td>2:11-15</td></tr>
</table>

1:15-22

(3) The scope narrows to a community in Egypt (the Hebrews). The king's secret request to the midwives heightens the death theme. Because the struggle has escalated, the Hebrews are stirred into limited action. The midwives (a word occurring seven times in this episode) ignore the king's request because they also fear God. When the king would judge them, asking them why they preserve life when he had commanded death, they are saved by a combination of their brazen quick wits and the all-embracing protection of God. The proliferation formula is again alluded to, triggering a yet more fran-

2:11-15

(5) The setting is the Hebrew community in Egypt. This passage is divided into two episodes, each introduced by "and he went out."

The bondage theme is reintroduced, and we see that the death intended for newborn Hebrew males is also being inflicted upon adult Hebrew males. Moses is now an adult, and the conflict between life and death which had been waged around him at birth is now internal, in the struggle of loyalties to his two backgrounds. As a babe he had lain helpless and passive, his fate determined by human cunning and compassion undergirded by divine providence. Here he sees and has

tic (and public) response from Pharaoh: throw the newborn Hebrews into the river. Only the daughters are to be saved.

compassion, just as three daughters had seen and looked out for him. He remains cautious, but his smiting the Egyptian signals a new level of Hebrew activism in response to death and bondage. It also foreshadows the future open activity of God in laying the ten "smitings" (plagues) on Egypt.

Further aspects of the death of bondage are portrayed in the next episode, where we see brother smiting brother. Moses' intervention to establish justice in the matter, re-creating the broken community, foreshadows the laws of Sinai given with the same intent. Moses' judgment question, attempting to preserve the community, parallels the king's judgment question in 1:15-22 attempting to stamp out the community. The response of the Hebrew wrongdoer, standing in sharp contrast to the response of the midwives and reintroducing the fear theme, establishes two opposing types within the Hebrew community and foreshadows the murmurings against Moses in the wilderness. The Hebrew wrongdoer scorns and fears Moses, who would bring life; Moses fears Pharaoh, who would bring death. He is not yet the perfect hero filled with God's spirit. Pharaoh's attempt to slay Moses, driving him into the wilderness, parallels his earlier command to throw the newborn Hebrew males into the river.

Sections 3 and 5 continue the conflict between Egypt's bringing death (on newborn and adult Hebrew males) and Israel's (God's) preserving life (midwives and Moses). A contrast is also intended between the plucky Hebrew midwives, who rightly react against Pharaoh, and the soul-deadened Hebrew wrongdoer, who wrongly reacts against Moses.

2:1-10	2:15-22
(4) The scope is further narrowed to one Hebrew family. Both the life and death themes are muted, only implicit. The outcome of the struggle rides with the fate of the child who, floating in the ark, is depicted as a new Noah preserving life for mankind. Again the partnership between Hebrew shrewdness and divine providence is evidenced. The crying child is rescued by the activity of three "daughters" who	(6) Although the scene changes to a different land, the action centers around water, preserving the structural parallel with 2:1-10. The scope also narrows to the plight of one family. As before, the setting is the misuse of power at the expense of the helpless, who are driven away from the source of life. As Hebrew boys had been rescued by the midwives (mentioned seven times) and Moses by three daughters, Moses

"saw," "know," and "pitied" (a mocking of Pharaoh's sparing the daughters); but the story clearly implies that, ultimately, what "was to be done" to the child lay in God's hands. The hiddenness of the child parallels the hiddenness of God's activity throughout chapters 1-2. Moses is depicted as the firstborn, and the active participle name he receives from the princess is a turning point in the narrative, marking his move from a passively resisting community to an increasingly active leader. The name is also a portent or his ultimate destiny: he will "draw out" his people from the reed waters, just as he had been drawn out.

spontaneously rescues the seven daughters, although they are not his "brothers." This foreshadows Israel's understanding of her ultimate destiny, mediating her new experience of God to all afflicted peoples of the world (Gen. 12:3; Exod. 19:4-6). The naming of Gershom, the firstborn, gives us an indication of Moses' present condition and of his future destiny.

Sections 4 and 6 are linked through the water motif, the Nile from which Moses is saved and the well in the wilderness where he rescues seven daughters.

Conclusion

2:23-25

(7) The scene returns to the land of Egypt, gradually panning back from the outcry of Israel to the cosmic response. The setting of the Moses birth and youth story concludes, aptly, with the death of the death-bringer. Paradoxically, this causes the Hebrews to experience the death of bondage even more intensely. They cry for help—to no

one—and God hears, sees, and takes note of their plight, just as earlier figures in the story had perceived the plight of others and had pity. Moses had done what he could and been threatened with death, but the stirring of the Deity heralds a new stage of resistance to bondage and a new *modus operandi* by which God will make himself known. Our ending is only a beginning.

Anyone who saw "The Pawnbroker" knows that a major cause of the film's effectiveness was the visual flashback scenes in which the pawnbroker perceived and interpreted the present through analogous experiences from the past. The Bible story creates added dimensions of meaning through the same allusive device, which, because it is verbal, has more of an "overlay" effect than "flashback." As has been noted, the first of the seven sections established the cosmic setting in Creation and the Flood for the mundane events which follow, preparing us to find other allusions to the primeval stories. In 1:8-14 there are clear references to the arrogance of the Tower of Babel story, and 2:1-10 presses back to the preserving ark of the Noah story. If we move further back in the sequence of primeval narratives, the preceding story is that of Cain and Abel; 2:11-15 talks of Moses as his brothers' keeper, defending one who is being beaten to death, then intervening to prevent one brother from smiting another. Preceding Cain and Abel is the Garden of Eden. Do we have an allusion to that in 2:15-22 when it talks about the daughters being driven away (a theme emphasized by the naming of "Gershom") from the water, the source of life (cf. Gen. 3:24)? Is the narrative, moving back with its allusions through the primeval story sequence, portraying a God who, through Moses and the people of Israel, is in the process of reversing the alienation and broken community which had been man's condition since earliest times?

We can only briefly touch on the implications of these allusions. Pharaoh's Babel-like building activity is doomed to fail because bondage crushes the human spirit. Moses in the ark is, like Noah, the preserver of life for mankind because he will point the way to freedom. His intervention to prevent one Hebrew brother from smiting another is an attempt to overcome the hostility between brothers which had existed since Cain killed Abel. Paradoxically, the seven daughters are driven away by the shepherds because God, confirming the new situation of pride and hostility embodied in man's disobedience, had driven Adam and Eve out of Eden, away from the tree of life. Is Moses' returning the driven-out daughters to the well a symbolic act for the new life which will be made possible through Israel's covenant relationship with God?

The opening chapters of Exodus, through their reverberating language and thematic motifs, contain echoes of the entire book of Genesis. Similarly, the following chapters of Exodus pick up the reverberations of the language and themes of these first two chapters, now enhanced with new content and meaning. A dominant theme which we have noted throughout this story, broken only by the final three verses, is the behind-the-scenes activity of God. This contrasts sharply with the description of divine intervention beginning in Exodus 3 and building to a climax in Chapters 15 and 19. In Exodus 3:7, which further develops the new form of divine activity begun in 2:23-25, God states: "I have seen the affliction of my people . . . and have heard their cry . . . . I know their sufferings, and I have come down to deliver them . . . and to bring them up." The key word in this series is *yarad* "come down," which, as in the Tower of Babel story and elsewhere, heralds the mighty acts of God. Though mentioned explicitly only in connection with the midwives, the presence and activity of God are clearly perceived in the events surrounding Moses' birth. But what accounts for the silent, hidden characteristic of the Deity in this part of the narrative? I would propose that part of the answer lies in Genesis 46:3-4, where God says to Jacob, "Do not be afraid to go down to Egypt; for I will there make of you a great nation. I will go down with you to Egypt, and I will also bring you up." The key word in this series is again *yarad* "go down."

Here the word is not heralding a mighty act of God; it is akin, I would suggest, to the archetypal theme of the descent into the underworld.

In her formative years it was not unusual for ancient Israel, as she stated the meaning of certain events in her sacred history, to express her stories in language and concepts similar to those of the surrounding cultures. Note, for example, the strong stress on the parting of the waters—an ancient motif of creation—in the story of Israel's escape from the Egyptians at the sea (Exod. 15:4-10; cf. Gen. 1:6-7, Isa. 51:9-11, Ps. 74:12-17, etc.). Israel saw cosmic significance in God's activity at the sea, which had brought her into being as a people. The other major pattern in ancient Near Eastern culture was the story of the god who died in the long summer drought and was stripped of his/her royal clothing as he/she descended into death's habitation. The final outcome, however, was the triumph over death, and the deity would ascend from the realm of the dead, bringing rain and fertility again to the parched earth. In Canaanite culture this god was Baal.

Jacob/Israel's descent into Egypt is patterned on and foreshadowed by the series of descents in the Joseph story. Joseph is seized, stripped of his robe, and cast into a pit (Gen. 37:19-24). He is then sold to a group of Ishmaelites, who bring him down (literally "cause him to descend" *yarad*) into Egypt. Jacob is shaken by the brothers' story of the "death" of Joseph, mourning: "I shall descend *(yarad)* to Sheol to my son." He means that the news of the death of his favorite son has brought him near to death, and soon he will (through death) descend into Sheol, the underworld, and be joined with his son. Those readers who already know the outcome of the story can relish the *double entendre* in Jacob's words: he will descend to be with his son, Joseph, but his going down *(yarad)* will be into Egypt rather than to Sheol.

Joseph is sold as a slave down into Egypt, but because of the divine blessing he rises very quickly to a position of authority in his master's household. The incident with Potiphar's wife, however, in which Joseph is again stripped of a garment, leads to his being cast into prison. The prison is twice referred to as "the pit"* (Gen. 40:15, 41:14). Such a designation for prison rarely occurs in the rest of the Bible,[44] so one might suppose that the narrative wants us to be aware of the sequence of Joseph's "descents": thrown into the pit, sold into Egypt, and cast into the prison-pit. Sheol (the underworld) is often called "the pit" in Hebrew Scriptures, and death is referred to as "descending *(yarad)* to the pit."[45]

We might conclude that the narrative uses heavily connotative language in order to heighten the drama and import of Joseph's descent into Egypt and his rise to power in the royal court. His brothers call him "Baal (lord, master) of the dreams" and cast him into the pit after stripping him of his royal garment.[46] He descends into Egypt and is then cast into the dungeon pit. But the power and presence of God are with him, overcoming all the powers of adversity which had threatened to overwhelm him and raising him to fullness of life in a position only envisioned in dreams! The psalmist, using mythic language to describe overcoming some personal adversity, writes: "O LORD, thou hast brought up my soul from Sheol, restored me to life from among those gone down to the Pit" (Ps. 30:3). Such a statement precisely describes Joseph's situation at the conclusion of the story when he is reunited with his family and stands in full favor with the Egyptian court. Moreover, such a statement could just as precisely be made by the Israelites upon their deliverance from Egypt!

The Joseph story serves as a prototype for Israel's understanding of her experience in the Exodus. Chapters 1–2 describe the descent of Israel into the realm of "death," whereas the rest of the Moses cycle describes God's intervention to bring his people up out of bondage. As with the pit, Egyptian slavery, and prison in the Joseph story, there are three symbols of death and evil in Chapters 1–2: Egypt, where Israel has been pressed into bondage; the Nile waters, into which Moses is cast; and the wilderness into which Moses flees. They fall into the 2-4-6 positions in the seven narrative units of Exodus 1–2.

The remarkable element in both the Joseph and Hebrew bondage stories, a quality which must have surprised and delighted early audiences, is that *the symbols of death and evil are transformed into means of deliverance.* Joseph's life is saved when, instead of being murdered, he is thrown into the pit by his brothers (Gen. 37:21-23); Egypt becomes the means by which the descendants of Jacob are saved from starvation when drought hits the land of Canaan; Joseph's contact with the butler in the "dungeon-pit" becomes the means by which he rises to favor in Pharaoh's court. Similarly, in Exodus 1-2, Egypt, the pit of Sheol,[47] becomes the womb which gives birth to Israel; the "death" of bondage precipitates a crisis in which the Hebrews are fruitful and multiply and which leads to the creation of a nation. The waters, a traditional symbol of evil and death,[48] especially in the context of Pharaoh's command, become the means by which the future deliverer of Israel is borne up. And finally, the wilderness, a feared and threatening region thought to be inhabited by powers of death,[49] becomes the area which permits Moses to escape Egyptian persecution and find the clan whose wanderings will lead him to the mountain of God.

We have traced the following sequence for the hidden activity of God in Chapters 1-2 of the Exodus narrative: Egypt, waters, wilderness. The rest of the Exodus narrative will preserve this same sequence in recounting the mighty acts of God which are about to unfold following the call of Moses at the burning bush. (1) God's plagues fall upon the land of *Egypt*, weakening the resolve of the oppressors and finally allowing the Hebrews to flee (chaps. 5-13); (2) when the Hebrews are trapped by a contingent of Egyptian troops in chariots, the *waters* become God's means by which the pursued are delivered and the pursuers are destroyed (chaps. 14-15); and finally, (3) as the Hebrews begin their perilous journey toward the promised land, God reveals himself in the *wilderness* at Sinai (19:1) through laws intended to create the greater cohesiveness and unity Israel will need to survive the ordeals which lie ahead (chaps. 19-24; 32-34).

It is the varying uses of *yarad*, "to go down," in Genesis

40:4 and Exodus 3:8 which structure the differing perceptions of God in these juxtaposed Egypt-waters-wilderness
sequences. The reason for the hiddenness of God in Exodus
1–2 is that God has descended with his people into the pit of
Egypt. He is not being portrayed as a transcendent God, far
removed from his suffering people. If anything, he is even
more immanent than in the "mighty acts" which follow. He
remains quiet and hidden because he is totally identified with
his people in their powerlessness and suffering. The prosper-
ing of the oppressed emphasizes the mystery that, despite
their descent, God and his people will not succumb to the
powers of death and evil. The turning point in the struggle
between God and Pharaoh has come already in chapters 1–2
while God is still hidden; the mighty acts which follow are the
dramatic execution of the victory which is already won.

VII Moses: Tragedy and Sublimity

HILLEL BARZEL, *Department of Comparative Literature, Bar Ilan University, Tel Aviv, Israel*

In approaching the Bible as literature, we may look upon its stories as a totality, rather than as a composite of different literary sources. Here the religious approach, which sees the Bible in its uniformity, is similar to that of the literary-artistic approach, which also analyzes monolithic, integral works, though from a literary rather than a religious point of view. A collection of stories relating to a single biblical hero can therefore be analyzed as a uniform creation, in terms of its artistic qualities and the impression of the hero left on the reader's mind by the portrait built up by the stories taken together. Our literary approach to the Bible may employ critical terms in analyzing the means of expression as well as other artistic aspects of the text.

Another way of exploring the Bible as literature is to see the role of the Scriptures in literature itself or in the other arts. Whenever we find the Bible or any part of it used as a subject, motif, or source-model in the creative arts, we have a subjective, literary impression related to the Scripture. The artist can be likened to the reader or literary critic who avoids the often puzzling issue of sources, but takes in the effect left by a biblical story or figure as an integral whole, making no attempt to take it apart on any grounds of scientific or historical inquiry.

Moses, too, can be considered from a literary point of view, disregarding questions of sources. The portrayal of Moses in the Bible can be considered as part of a work of literature issuing uniformly from a single narrator. Undoubtedly, however, Moses must also be seen in the light of the special qualities of the text in which he appears in order to avoid any

overly subjective impressions and conclusions having little to
do with Scripture as written and to ensure that any literary
judgments are securely founded in the text.

We shall examine the figure of Moses in the Bible in the
light of two themes—tragedy and sublimity. Our first task
will be to establish the relevance of these terms to the Old
Testament as a whole. We shall then specifically employ
them in considering the figure of Moses. The discussion will
finally be rounded out with examples drawn from poetry and
sculpture. Let us consider the tragic aspect first.

I

Tragedy as a literary genre is, of course, a consummation
of the Hellenic spirit. Neither in form nor in content did the
ancient Hebrew produce any literature resembling Greek
tragedy. Greek tragedy was based on mythological tales in
which gods appear like men. A constant theme in works such
as *Prometheus Bound* and *Oedipus Rex* is the materialization
of the sphere of the gods and its effects among mortals. The
Bible, on the other hand, though it contains instances of the
dialogic relationship between man and his creator, typically
places the Godhead at a level of intensity and abstraction far
beyond human comprehension. The representation before an
audience of a divinity or semidivinity is quite inconceivable in
a society which takes the commandment, "You shall not
make for yourself a graven image, or any likeness of anything
that is in heaven above" (Exod. 20:4) in its most absolute
sense.

To this factor must be added the nature of the environment
in which artistic creativity takes place. It is true that in
Greek society tragedy was born out of ritual elements, but
from its very inception it possessed Dionysian qualities which
called for liberation from the divine imperative and from the
bounds of moral demands cherished by religion. Nietzsche in
"The Birth of Tragedy Out of the Spirit of Music" explains
how these Dionysian qualities at the root of Greek tragedy

are no vulgar liberation whose chief effect is to give free rein to man's lower instincts, but an appeal to the spirit of unconquerable stirrings, of the truly tremendous and exalted. On the other hand, the pertinence of the carnivalesque and bacchanalian element in the Greek birth of tragedy cannot be denied. In its subsequent development, too, tragedy became a part of the Greek tradition of amusements and entertainments, not unlike the Olympic Games. Tragedy as a social agent was thus destined to provide an answer to life's profane demands as well.

The same cannot be said of the immutably sacred Bible. The Psalms were written to accompany the Levite temple ritual. The words of the Law were transmitted by priests to edify the people. Poetic and prophetic works were inspired first and foremost by the demands of ritual, religion, and popular edification and have always been so used. The development of a literary genre even secondarily based on entertainment was unthinkable in a society which knew only tabernacle and temple, and fostered no rival cultural-spiritual institution divorced from holiness and the sacred ritual. Amphitheatres in Palestine of the Second Temple period were an expression of Hellenization, built in towns with an appreciable non-Hebrew population.

In his essay "Job and the Possibilities of Biblical Tragedy," Baruch Kurzweil insists that the spirit of the Hebrew Bible is opposed to the spirit of Greek tragedy because it cannot present the clash of two equal figures of value, a situation conceived by Hegel as essential to the birth of tragedy. Kurzweil bases his argument on Hegel's theory that our tragic emotions are aroused when we observe a conflict between two value-bearing people.[1] The play the German philosopher had in mind when he formed his theory of tragedy was *Antigone*, but we could also say in analyzing a Shakespearian tragedy that, for example, Desdemona's death at the hands of Othello arouses tragic emotions in us because both of them—strangler and victim—are equally decent, honest people. This is what distinguishes their case from that of the Boston Strangler, whose deeds arouse shock, but no tragic sentiment. In the latter case, a character devoid of values does injury to creatures unlike himself. The result is a feeling of horror, but not a sense of tragedy. Greek tragedy grew up in a world of relative values. Gods could sin, for they, too, were possessed of earthly desires. Conflict in Greek tragedy, even when it involves gods or their offspring, is an arena for the clash of value bearers who stand on common spiritual ground. Not so in the Bible, where man is relative while God is absolute. In the conceptual framework of the Old Testament, it is unthinkable whenever the Godhead is involved in the dramatic conflict, to talk of equal value bearers clashing. Thus, according to Hegel's theory of tragedy, the Bible can depict no tragic conflict; and those heroes who have contact with the Godhead are thereby removed from any possibility that their stories can be viewed as tragedy.

Kurzweil adduces additional arguments based on Franz Rosenzweig's poetics as expressed in his *Der Stern der Entlösung*.[2] In Rosenzweig's opinion, the end of the Greek hero's tragic journey is reached with his own naked, isolated, and hopeless self. All bridges between him and those forces which have guided him in his struggle—those forces he rebelled against—are cut off. This condition is possible, in Kurzweil's opinion, only in a world not anchored in a doctrine of salvation. The Old Testament, in which an ever-present loving kindness enables a sinful hero to turn time and again to his God and find succor in him, cannot, therefore, present the totally hopeless situation we might define as tragic. Thus, thinks Kurzweil, the medieval Christian world also could find inspiration only for ritual or religiously based mystery plays, not for tragedies. So long as Western society was thoroughly and monolithically Hebrew or Christian —emphasizing, that is, the concept of salvation and the ever-present possibility of return to a merciful, redeeming Godhead—tragedy had no place in it.

If we accept Kurzweil's position, then, we are clearly precluded from considering biblical figures such as Job or even Moses from a tragic point of view, especially if we carry out our examination from the perspective of the biblical narrator and enter into the inner spiritual logic of the books in which these characters appear. If Moses seems to be in conflict with his God, it is not a tragic conflict; he accepts God's command. This acceptance leaves no doubt as to which of the two has primacy in the Bible's system of values. On the other hand, Moses can always beg for mercy and forgiveness; if there is no forgiveness, there is at least the redeeming quality of the dialogue itself. No discussion of a figure such as Moses could possibly attempt to adopt such basic tragic concepts which, like those of Hegel and Kurzweil, are drawn from an Hellenic spiritual environment utterly alien to that of the Hebrew Bible.

II

Nevertheless, if we are to examine the Bible as literature, we should also take into account responses not necessarily based upon the intention of the scriptural narrator. Though not a formal tragedy in the Greek sense, a story may evoke a tragic response. The modern reader could very well respond to certain biblical stories with sentiments of tragedy, not because of a subjective approach to the text, but because, in spite of the framework of the scriptural narrator's values, room is left for the situation he describes to speak in the language of plain facts and to affect our responses directly. Even as the narrator is condemning Saul (for example, Samuel says that he has done evil in the eyes of the Lord), he does not alter the facts of Saul's life and does not neglect to portray Saul's moments of greatness. In these descriptions of Saul, room enough is left for that kind of emotive response which we may undoubtedly call tragic. The emotions aroused by tragedy are described in Aristotle's well-known definition as pity and terror, compassion and awe. These terms cannot be analyzed in detachment from the context of the Greek tragedies in which they appear. In the context of the responses which Aristotle expected tragedy to elicit from the spectator, compassion and awe are bound up with catharsis

and depend upon that characterization of the hero and that
type of plot described in Aristotle's *Poetics*.

Compassion and awe exist primarily as strong emotions
arising from extreme traumatic situations. And though the
Old Testament draws balanced pictures of light and shade,
moments of joy and episodes of failure, yet descriptions of
the traumatic far exceed those of peace and tranquillity. The
words of the prophets are structured in a pattern of reproof
and consolation, but the consolations are few and the re-
proofs are many. In Isaiah and Jeremiah, we read through
many chapters of wrath and tribulation before reaching the
utopian millennium for Israel and all peoples. In the Bible's
narration of the lives of those heroes whom it depicts from
beginning to end, it is the moments of failure and sorrow
which stand out. Compassion and awe could well accompany
our responses to the lives of Saul, Jonathan, Jeremiah or Job,
and justify our calling them tragic heroes.

In discussing the portraits of biblical heroes, the Aristotelian theory of responses can be joined with the concepts
of social estrangement and reintegration which Northrop
Frye rightly emphasizes in his discussion of the tragic—or
even the comic—hero. The former is presented to us in his
estranged aspect, at a far remove from any social integra-
tion, while the latter is portrayed in his close links with
society and his environment.[3] An analysis of the characterization of tragic heroes reveals that all their customary linking circuits—to themselves, their family, their people, and
their tasks—are shattered. The inevitable consequence of
cutting all these links is death. Compassion and awe are
aroused in us when we see this process of total estrangement
at its peak. (The hero need not necessarily be an average
person, especially good or bad: even Greek plays Aristotle
could have called to mind, such as *Prometheus Bound* or
Oedipus Rex, did not, as far as can be seen today, deal with
average characters, but rather with outstanding personalities.)

In Saul we have an excellent instance of the fate of a hero
whose circuits of reference are all gradually disrupted. Saul

loses his respect for himself: the "evil spirit" which troubles him is evidence of that. He also loses the respect of others. The first king over Israel has been rejected and will lose his crown, as the prophet Samuel frequently reminds him. Even Saul's children Michal and Jonathan prefer the king's rival, David, over their father. The depth of Saul's utter estrangement and loneliness is reached in his last encounter with the dead prophet: "And Samuel said, 'Why then do you ask me, since the LORD has turned from you and become your enemy?'" (I Sam. 28:16). The narrative of Saul's death as told in I Samuel dramatizes the moment in a way that could almost vie in tragic intensity with the finale of a great tragical classic:

The battle pressed hard upon Saul, and the archers found him; and he was badly wounded by the archers. Then Saul said to his armor-bearer, "Draw your sword, and thrust me through with it, lest these uncircumcised come and thrust me through, and make sport of me." But his armor-bearer would not; for he feared greatly. Therefore Saul took his own sword, and fell upon it. And when his armor-bearer saw that Saul was dead, he also fell upon his sword, and died with him. Thus Saul died, and his three sons, and his armor-bearer, and all his men, on the same day together (I Sam. 31:3-6).

The biblical narrator closes the story of Saul's life with the scene of David and his men mourning over the death of their king, intoning David's lament over the "beloved and lovely" Saul and Jonathan (2 Samuel 1:23).[4]

III

The reader's reaction to the story of Moses may also include a feeling of tragedy. Moses appears in the Bible in a remarkable variety of roles: prophet and general, lawgiver and judge, reprover and poet. But for us to see him as a tragic figure, two broad facts of his life and achievements, very much bound up together in Scripture, are the most pertinent. The first is the metaphysical: Moses' coming into the presence of the Almighty. The second is national: Moses as a messenger to his people. In each of these fields he registers exceptional achievements. The concept of "face to face" comes to symbolize the Almighty's relationship with Moses. Moses is accorded what is given to no ordinary mortal: he achieves maximum proximity to God.[5] "Thus the LORD used to speak to Moses face to face" (Exod. 33:11), "and there has not arisen a prophet since in Israel like Moses, whom the LORD knew face to face" (Deut. 34:10). Moses is accorded divine revelations from the start of his mission, and knows the true, ineffable name of his sender. Moses displays supernatural powers in fasting for forty days and nights on Sinai. He brings miracles with his staff, he works "all the signs and the wonders" (Deut. 34:11). He brings the children of Israel and all mankind the Ten Commandments engraved on tablets. As a national leader, Moses succeeds in his initial task, which is to carry through the Exodus from Egypt; he divides the Red Sea, and Pharaoh's army drowns with all its chariots. The great forty-year trek in the wilderness is successful under his resolute leadership. This leadership brings military victory in hard-fought wars with the forces of Amalek, Midian, Sihon, and Og. Challenges to his leadership made by the sons of Korah, Dathan and Abiram, and others are unequivocally put down.

And yet this whole body of achievements is shattered against thresholds which Moses cannot cross. These moments when Moses is fettered make him into a tragic hero. "Moses said, 'I pray thee, show me thy glory.' And he said, 'I will make all my goodness pass before you, and will proclaim before you my name "THE LORD"; and I will be gracious to whom I will be gracious, and will show mercy on whom I will show mercy. But,' he said, 'you cannot see my face; for man shall not see me and live.'" (Exod. 33:18-20). Immediately after the Bible has related how God spoke to Moses "as a man speaks to his friend" we find the declaration limiting Moses' status. Moses is not satisfied with vague, metaphorical promises that God's presence will go with him among the people, but desires the attainment of absolute knowledge of God. The expression "thy glory" in this context is a substitute for "thy face," as we can gather from God's answer and from the conclusion of this dialogue: "'Then I will take away my hand, and you shall see my back; but my face shall not be seen.'" The prohibition is absolute: "for man shall not see me, and live." This statement contains two important pronouncements. One is universal: no mortal can see God's face and live. The other is particular and applies to Moses: he is a mortal like any other. Thus, so long as we are dealing with Moses, the missionary to his people, he has the right to dwell in the presence of the Lord and that dwelling is expressed in terms of maximum proximity. But when he speaks as an individual and wishes to know God fully, he is refused. Here he learns that his own nature is essentially human, not divine. He is treated no differently from any other mortal, and his great metaphysical stature avails him naught. This moment arouses a feeling of compassion and awe in the reader.

A similar threshold is placed before Moses in the national sphere. All Moses' efforts are directed towards bringing his people into the promised land. Canaan is the be-all and end-all of his actions and desires. Yet, at the decisive moment, just as in the metaphysical sphere, he comes up against an impassable threshold. God commands Moses to go up on Mount Abarim, Mount Nebo, to behold the land of Canaan and die. "'For you shall see the land before you; but you shall not go there.'" (Deut. 32:52). This decree is justified by Moses' sin of sacrilege and disrespect for God, similar to Aaron's. Moses' death does not come about through old age or failing physical or mental ability; the text emphasizes that he died with his powers unabated (Deut. 34:7).[6] The nonattainment of the chief national goal in Moses' life as an individual is a consequence of his transgression and a witness of failure. Moses does not readily resign himself to his foreordained fate, as we may gather from his reporting, "'And the LORD said to me, "Let it suffice you; speak no more to me of this matter."'" (Deut. 3:26). Nevertheless, Moses has had his boundary drawn before him: "'For you shall not go over this Jordan'" (v. 27), and there is no sign of any willingness to relent. Like his being halted upon a metaphysical threshold, so also his being halted just below the peak of his ambitions as a leader could well arouse tragic emotion in the heart of the reader who identifies with the hero and his fate.

IV

Franz Kafka's monothematic works are permeated with the tragedy of man's standing helplessly upon a threshold. It is, therefore, not surprising that he grasped the significance of the threshold in Moses' life. He writes:

"The essence of the Wandering in the Wilderness. A man who leads his people along this way with a shred (more is unthinkable) of consciousness of what is happening. He is on the track of Canaan all his life; it is incredible that he should see the land only when on the verge of death. This dying vision of it can only be intended to illustrate how incomplete a moment is human life, incomplete because a life like this could last forever and still be nothing but a moment. Moses fails to enter Canaan not because his life is too short but because it is a human life. This ending of the Pentateuch bears a resemblance to the final scene of the *Education sentimentale.*" [7]

Here Kafka enlarges upon one of the thresholds in Moses' life, namely, his being barred from entering Canaan.

In his famous fable about the man before the gates of the Law, [8] Kafka uses the metaphysical notion, "for man shall not see me, and live." The narrator presents a kind of antithetical figure to Moses: a simple man among men, [9] who desires to attain the absolute, to enter the Law. It is worth pointing out that this fable is told to Joseph K. by a priest in a church, and though it talks about "law," the reference is clearly to *the* Law, i.e., the limitless, the infinite, the absolute—in other words, to God. Kafka's fable portrays a man who has striven all his life to cross over the threshold, succeeding only partially. As he lies on the verge of death, his fading eyesight beholds the radiance shining through from beyond the gates, but more than that he shall not see. Moses, too, is granted a modicum when he asks to be shown the face of God: he sees his back and perceives his magnitude, but cannot fully comprehend the mystery of the Godhead. Therein lies the major point of resemblance between the First-among-Prophets and everyman. Though the words of Kafka's fable are told by a priest in a church, i.e., in a Roman Catholic environment, the aim of the narrator is to expound a universal truth which he regards as fitting to all religions and all seekers after God. The priest's fable appears in "Prolegomena to the Law," and is indeed a sort of preamble disclosing the essence of the holy books of all nations and all languages. Kafka grasps the nub of worldwide religious belief in the spirit of the biblical story of Moses' rebuttal. The fable shows man in his essential limitedness, which in Kafka's view predetermines his death in a state of tragic estrangement that shatters all illusions. The story of Moses with its metaphysical moral consolidates and strengthens the notion of locked gates. And if that is the case with Moses, who had spoken with God face to face, how much more is it true of the man outside the gates of the Law who talks only with the paltriest entrance guard? The same duality found in the biblical story is also present in Kafka's fable. On the one hand, Moses speaks with God as a man speaks to his friend. The Bible, too, asserts the general existence of a gate through which the righteous—all righteous people—may enter. The keeper of the gate can say to the dying man that the gate is meant for him and him alone. To put it another way, every religion promises man a chance and attests to the existence of a road leading straight to the Godhead. On the other hand, the gatekeeper knows that the chance of any given individual's getting in is infinitesimal. For no man shall see God and live. The story of Moses reveals the true nature of the metaphysical limitation latent in him. The limitation which casts a tragic shadow on his portrait is at the heart of Kafka's fable.

David Frishman, among the greatest of Hebrew writers, writes in his poem "Moses":

> At the peak of the solitary mountain, cut into the stone,
>   Is a fresh bed.
> And on that bed lies a tired man one hundred
> And twenty years old.

And his eye is not dimmed, his vigour yet unabated
But his heart so empty and fallen;
The beat of Death's wings sounds out already
As he devours his prey.

And the dying man sighs "O my God,
I have lived in vain!
All my days have I acted and ached for my people—
And have achieved nothing.

I loved this people from the land of Egypt
And have brought it out;
And yet I have not led this people
Into the Land of Israel!

I have brought my people out of the realm of bondage,
For I was sick of bondage;
And yet I have not brought this my people
Into the realm of freedom.

For great is the desert, terrible is the desert,
Between land and Land;
And great and terrible, awful is the gulf
Between bondage and freedom.

And great is the ill, terrible is the ill,
If a man can arise
And descend to his people, to the house of bondage,
And rise up to redeem them,
And yet conquer no other land for them. . . .
Would that naught were begun,
Would that he had not taken them out of bondage if freedom
Is not his to give![10]

Moses' failure finds expression in this poem in terms of liberation and freedom. The leader's being barred from bringing
his people into Canaan testifies also to his inability to find
freedom for the refugees from Egypt. The tragic moment is
not perceived as disappointment at the nonattainment of a
personal goal, but as a failure in leadership. The moment of
death is illuminated by the light of the tragic estrangement in
which the hero abandons the last of his aspirations. The
tragic hero's rupturing of social links, in Frye's terms, is also
bound up with his inability to fulfill his role. Oedipus, by his
sin, brings a plague upon the citizens of his town. Tainted by

this sin, he may no longer fulfill the tasks of a leader of Thebes. On his deathbed, in Frishman's portrayal, Moses ponders his own failure to give his people freedom. His whole life's work is called into question. The severance the leader feels is a severance not only from his life as it draws to a close, but also from the very mission of his whole existence.

V

In employing the concept of tragedy, we were constrained to distinguish between tragedy as a literary genre with certain structural rules peculiar to it, and tragic emotion evoked by a literary work. While tragedy as a literary genre is certainly not a part of the Bible, the ability to arouse tragic feelings is perhaps one of its distinctive qualities. In discussing the sublime, then, we mean such texts as arouse in the reader a feeling of the sublime. Clearly, arousal of such feelings is accomplished by certain properties in the text. In this case, unlike that of tragedy, there is not the slightest doubt of the relevance of discussing sublimity in the Old Testament. By the sublime we understand the perception of a totally boundless, supremely forceful experience which awakens in us a certain kind of feeling. Given the basic character of the Hebrew Bible, whose chief theme is the belief in one God, unbounded ruler of heaven and earth, whose omnipotence is beyond all grasp of the human imagination; experience of the sublime becomes one of the fundamental attributes of its style and characterization, especially in those parts which are neither legal-ritual nor documentary-historical. Thus, Coleridge rightly recognized that the sublime is not a legacy of classical Greek literature, but a concept which originated with the Hebrews.[11] Wordsworth regarded anthropomorphic polytheism as a force that had shackled the thinking of even the greatest of ancient Greek and Roman poets. The Hebrews, thanks to their resistance to polytheistic beliefs, had no such shackle. Hence, Wordsworth speaks of the impassioned imagination of the prophetic writing in the Bible and contrasts it with

Greek and Roman literature which remained confined within well-defined forms.[12]

In discussing tragedy, we found cause to disagree with the exclusive attribution of the tragic world view to the Greeks; likewise with the sublime, there seems to be no reason to deny its presence in Greek literature, or for that matter, in the literature of more patently polytheistic peoples. Bradley rightly points out that even an experience of limited scope can create in us a feeling of the sublime since it is not outward size that counts, but inward vital or moral intensity, which can equally well exist as an attribute of a thing or creature of reduced dimensions.[13] In fact, Bradley comes close to Kant's distinctions, though, of course, the latter stressed the interconnection between the sublime and the infinite. Kant saw no place of greater sublimity in the Old Testament than in the commandment, "You shall not make for yourself a graven image, or any likeness."[14] He taught that the sublime must ever be great, while smallness could be permitted to be only beautiful.[15] But he also understood that size and forcefulness are not really dependent on the infinite. The Dionysian qualities stressed by Nietzsche in his analysis of tragedy are in many ways close to the sublime. Nevertheless, it is clear, in dealing with the Old Testament, that the intensity of the concept of a boundless Godhead lends special qualities to the book regarding its ability to arouse the reader to emotions of sublimity.

The feeling of the sublime is not confined to chapters devoted to descriptions of the exalted Godhead, but is capable of spilling over into moments of encounter in which the Godhead radiates its force upon whoever stands before it. The description of the revelation visited upon Elijah, when God appears not in an earthquake, but with a still small voice, is surely colored by the sublimity of both sender and receiver. Ezekiel, on beholding the chariot, draws the sublimity of the divine onto himself and his visionary prophecies. The same can be said of Daniel's apocalyptic visions and of the scene of Isaiah's dedication.

The sublime can be subjoined to the terrible, the threatening, or else to an uplifted feeling centered between the "awesome sublime" and the "noble sublime." In both these aspects Kant links the sublime to a feeling of gratification, but stresses that element of awe which always accompanies emotions of sublimity. Bradley's detailed discussion of the problem of the uneasy feeling aroused in us by sublimity,[16] however, indicates that the sublime need not necessarily be accompanied by feelings of uneasiness or awe that might bring it close to tragic emotion. On the contrary, sublimity is likely to be accompanied by amazement and an uplifting of the spirit which have nothing whatever in common with that awe included by Aristotle among the feelings aroused by tragedy. Sublimity in the Bible may be accompanied by feelings of compassion and awe, but may just as easily exist in its own right, unconnected with tragic emotion. It is most likely, however, to be accompanied by feelings of elevation and gratification. Perusal of the passage where Elijah is seen disappearing heavenward on a fiery chariot, for example, might well arouse sentiments of amazement and joy at the infinite greatness which conquers even death.

VI

Counterbalancing those episodes where Moses appears in his limitations are many passages in which Moses is portrayed as a being raised above conventional smallness. Here, too, there are the same fields where Moses' elevation is particularly apparent: in the one, the emphasis is on his national achievements, and in the other, his metaphysical attributes. Moses' great moment as a leader occurs after crossing the Red Sea. With the parting of the waters and the drowning of Pharaoh and his army, the children of Israel have made good their escape from the house of bondage. At this point there prevails a state of complete harmony between Moses and his people. "Thus the LORD saved Israel that day from the hand of the Egyptians; and Israel saw the Egyptians dead upon the seashore. And Israel saw the great work which the LORD did against the Egyptians, and the people feared the LORD; and they believed in the LORD and in his servant Moses" (Exod. 14:30-31). The great hand of the divinity has manifested itself through the staff-holding hand that parted the waters. In the Red Sea miracle, the reader is presented with a leader endowed with irresistible powers. The feeling of sublimity in the story of the crossing of the Red Sea is carried over from the prose narrative into the Song of the Sea (Exod. 15:1-18). The song is intoned by Moses; naturally, its images of grandeur and glory apply to God alone. When Miriam the prophetess goes out with timbrels and dances, she, too, sings of the exaltedness of God and makes no reference to her brother: "And Miriam sang to them: 'Sing to the LORD, for he has triumphed gloriously; the horse and his rider he has thrown into the sea'" (v. 21). Nevertheless, the scene reflects Moses' image at its peak. This is one of the few episodes in Moses' life where no mention is made of conflicts or disputes, be they with the children of Israel, with priests, with spies—least of all, with God. The exultation of victory is complete and is coupled with magnificent natural vistas. The imagery is bathed in sublimity. The "depths" and "mighty waters" are limitless. The figure of Moses cannot be dissociated from these images. In this scene of the Red Sea we are shown Moses exalted, unbound by his human fetters.

He experiences a similar moment in the metaphysical sphere:

When Moses came down from Mount Sinai, with the two tables of the testimony in his hand as he came down from the mountain, Moses did not know that the skin of his face shone because he had been talking with God. And when Aaron and all the people of Israel saw Moses, behold, the skin of his face shone, and they were afraid to come near him. But Moses called to them; and Aaron and all the leaders of the congregation returned to him, and Moses talked with them. And afterward all the people of Israel came near, and he gave them in commandment all that the LORD had spoken with him in Mount Sinai. And when Moses had finished speaking with them, he put a veil on his face; but whenever Moses went in before the LORD to speak with him, he took the veil off, until he came out; and when he came out, and told the people of Israel what he was commanded, the people of Israel saw the face of Moses, that the skin of Moses' face shone; and Moses would put the veil upon his face again, until he went in to speak with him. (Exod. 34:29-35)

The sheen of Moses' face bears witness to a supernal, divine radiance accorded him. The radiance appears after he has spent forty days and forty nights in the presence of the Lord on Mt. Sinai (v. 28). Both his prolonged fast and his inscribing the tablets at God's dictation show his special status. He is not like other mortals. Moses is unshackled from his human limitations. While his fasting and his dwelling in the presence of God were of definite duration—forty days and forty nights—the radiance in the skin of his face is transformed into an abiding phenomenon. Sublimity and supernal radiance are here intertwined. Moses is at the summit of his spiritual achievements. This is Moses' second ascent into the abode of the Lord. The results of the first had been disappointing: Moses' prolonged absence had brought on the golden calf. The sheen on Moses' face thus comes after the sin of the past has been atoned for. The tablets are now unbroken. Moses' spiritual primacy is established for all time to come.

VII

Uppermost in the mind of Michelangelo, who is sometimes regarded as the greatest artist of the sublime, were those passages of the Bible describing Moses at the height of his ascendancy. Indeed, it is the sublimity he felt to be immanent in Moses which he portrayed in his well-known statue of the prophet. The upper part of the statue includes Moses' horns, which the Renaissance master, basing himself on the Vulgate's mistaken choice in translating the Hebrew root *q-r-n* in its sense of "horn" instead of "light" or "radiance" (the Latin text reads *cornuta facies sua*), understood as the horns of a beast. The horns symbolize both physical and spiritual vigor and turn upward in apparent invocation of a higher instance. Moses' gaze, too, is turned afar, and apparently aimed into the unlimited distance, thereby freed from the limitations of the direct glance whose distance is determined by that of the object beheld. The beard, unusually long, reinforces that quality of boundless immensity which the whole statue endeavors to express. So also with Moses' arms. The free arm is sinewy and muscular; the other, which holds the sacred tablets, is less so: they embody the synthesis of physical and mental strength in one man. Art critics have often remarked on the disproportion between the upper and lower halves of the body. The legs are larger than normal. Their solidity conveys the image of Moses as the day-to-day leader of his people during the forty years of wandering in the desert. Some see "divine wrath" reflected in the face. In any case, the Florentine master obviously discerned in Moses no tragic aspect, but only a heroic vein whose sublimity is "noble" rather than "awesome." The statue fuses together physical strength and spiritual leadership. Critics point to the resemblance between Michelangelo's Moses and statues of Roman emperors, but the Renaissance sculptor's approach could not have expressed itself in such a forceful intensification of the prophet's image had the approach not been anchored in certain impressions drawn from the biblical text. The sculptor's impressions are drawn from those verses which describe Moses' transcendence, and not from those which stress his relativity and limitedness.

The same can be said of the following poem by H. N. Bialik, national poet of Jewry in the last generation. The poem, written on the 7th of Adar, the traditional anniversary of Moses' death, extols the transcendence of the spiritual giant over the physical giants, who have been allegorized as forces that have tried to rob Judaism of its unique and sustaining heritage.

ON THE PEAK OF A MOUNTAIN

> On the peak of a towering mountain
> There stands since the youth-day of time,
> Remote, with his arms spread to Heaven,
> A man, gray in silence, alone;
> In his left hand a staff wielding power,

Whilst his right grasps the tablets of stone;
On his face an effulgence of glory,
Heights of clouds—his girdle sublime.

At his feet are two giants prostrated,
Anakim in stature and main;
They contended against him with strength,
They attacked him in battled arrayed;
With an axe and a spear they presumed
To clamber on high and essayed
To wrest from his arms the Commandments
Engraven in stone—but in vain.

His eyes are aglow with a light
That is soft like the eyelids of mora,
Looking down on the giants below
With the gaze of the righteous and meek;
The knees of the giants are sinking
Beneath them, and bending and weak.—
Be still, in his presence exalted!
None like him has ever been born.[17]

The poem is based entirely upon images of the sublime. Instead of Mount Sinai, Bialik writes of "Har-El"—the Mountain of the Lord.[18] The feeling of locality, as well as of time, is immeasurably intensified. The radiance on Moses' face is interpreted as "an effulgence of glory" and is bound up with the ineffable immanence of the heavens in their heights. The sublime is communicated explicitly. In describing the battle with the giants (*Anakim;* cf. Deut. 9:2), the poet recalls the biblical battle with Amalek during which Moses held his hands aloft (Exod. 17:8-16). But here, the original scene is transformed exclusively into a picture of heroism and glory while the to-and-fro of the battle as described by Scripture goes unmentioned. Moses is portrayed only in the greatness of his stature.

A similar concept of Moses existed in the mind of the German-Jewish poet, Heinrich Heine:

What enormous stature! I find it impossible to imagine that King Og of Bashan was any bigger than he. How small Mount Sinai seems when Moses goes up upon it! For it is but the footstool on which rest the feet of the man whose hand reaches heaven where he speaks

with God (God forgive me my sin). It sometimes seems to me as if
this Mosaic God were but the reflection of the irradiance of Moses
whom He so resembles in sorrow and in love.[19]

Like Bialik and Michelangelo, Heine uses the sublime as a
standard by which to portray a character he admires, while
he goes even further than they in his elevation of Moses'
"enormous stature" to a level that rivals the greatness of God
almighty himself.

All three artists based their impressions on the text of the
Bible. To these impressions they naturally added the halo
which Moses had acquired over the generations—his identification with the Jewish heritage in the eyes of Bialik and
Heine and the Christian heritage in the eyes of
Michelangelo—as well as the artists' own idiosyncrasies. But
it is clear that in the absence of an unmediated response to
the Bible's written text, they could not have formed their
respective conceptions as they did. We have seen that when
our standard of analysis is the impression gleaned from the
Bible by the artist, one creative mind might draw tragedy,
the other, sublimity devoid of awe.

VIII

The possibility of a biblical character-portrayal—in the
present case that of Moses—that leaves the door open to
even-handed and even contradictory impressions stems from
the poetic doctrine on which the Old Testament biblical narrative is based. It is true that biblical narrative is written
from a clear ideological standpoint and passes unequivocal
judgments on its heroes. Some of them are judged as doing
that which is right in the eyes of the Lord, some as doing evil.
There can be no doubt, for example, that Moses is presented
in a favorable light, as are Abraham, Isaac, and Jacob, as
well as Elijah and Elisha. On the other hand, the biblical
narrator adopts a measure of objectivity in reporting facts.
King Solomon, builder of the first temple, is nevertheless
clearly stated to have erected altars to foreign gods. The

castigations of the rebel Jeroboam, son of Nabat, are quoted as spoken. King David hears his sentence of death explicitly pronounced by Nathan the prophet after his sinful dealings with Bathsheba and Uriah the Hittite. This episode is related with plain literalness, with no attempt to defend the king's image. The sojourn in the Garden of Eden and the expulsion from it in consequence of sin are set in a general archetypal mold—human behavior predestined to sin and error. These data constitute a fixed pattern for the biblical narrator.[20] Old Testament narrative is distinguished by its wonderful brevity and distillation, but is founded on a many-faceted view of human complexity. Its brevity is no sign that it ignores factors of depth, two-sidedness or many-layeredness, but shows on the contrary that it recognizes them: hence, paradoxically, the Bible's readiness to relate facts which speak for themselves, and its contentedness with short and sharp judgments.

The episodes comprising the story of Moses are fundamentally no different from chapters telling of other characters in the Pentateuch or the prophetic and historical books of the Old Testament. The two cruel scenes of failure in Moses' life, on Mt. Nebo and at the cleft in the rock, are as explicitly narrated as the descriptions of his contributions to his people's march to freedom and of the light shining from his face. One's impression of Moses as a tragic figure or as a person of sublimity and achievement depends either upon the reader or upon the artist who works raw material from the Bible into his imagination or his creations. The Bible story presents a pattern of human complexity which embraces, in Moses' case, both tragedy and sublimity, and both at their highest pitch.

VIII The Book of Judges
KENNETH R. R. GROS LOUIS

Most people in the twentieth century know more about the book of Judges than they think they do. Although the book as a whole is rarely anthologized in collections of literature from the Bible, several of its stories and characters have become commonplace because they have so often been adapted in Western art. The Samson story is surely one of the more popular among artists, if not one of the best-known stories in the Western world. But the Jephthah and Gideon stories have also been widely alluded to in literature and depicted in other art forms; and Deborah, while less visible in recent centuries, can rightfully take her place among the great women of the Old Testament. The richness of Judges as a source of artistic inspiration makes the book, from our perspective, one of the most important in the Bible. At the same time, the literary potential has been detached from the narrative as a whole. Artists and readers have turned admiringly to the individual stories, culled from them, reworked them, without paying much attention to the ways in which the stories might fit together, without, in other words, considering all of Judges as a literary work with its own themes and structure.

We might begin by looking at this book in relation to another collection of tales, the *Odyssey*. We assume that the Homeric poet had a number of stories about Odysseus to draw on, but that he selected, and judiciously, it seems, those stories which went together to transform what might have been an elaborate travel tale into an epic which explored the dimensions and facets of a larger-than-life heroic character. Many of the characters from the *Odyssey* have, like those in Judges, found their way into later literature with lives outside the context of Homer's epic. Modern criticism, however, has principally concerned itself with the overall structure and themes of the poem, with its unity and coherence. No such literary criticism exists for the book of Judges.

Judges is, of course, part of a larger story, of a larger design, whether we see that design as literary or theological; and because of this, any analogy between Judges and the *Odyssey* is not perfect. Yet, in considering the creation of the Homeric epic, we are reminded of a crucial process in the creation of Judges. We know that the book describes an unstable period in Hebrew history, following the triumphs of Joshua, and preceding the coming of the prophet Samuel. The period is, however, a long one; and we have only a few narratives, independent of one another, apparently unrelated, local fragments as they are often called. We are given in written form a series of episodes, possibly based ultimately on oral accounts of tribal heroes. The questions we should attempt to answer are: Why these heroes? Why these particular stories? Why in this particular order? The questions are always implicit in any study of the *Odyssey*, and we should assume that the book of Judges, like the Homeric poem, represents decisions about what to include and what to exclude. To put the problem in another way: What do the stories of these judges have in common? What are the links which connect and unify them?

We should note first the overriding pattern which gives surface unity to Judges, the pattern which occurs again and again, and which suggests a theory of history. The first chapter describes a situation, a very bad situation, in which a number of Canaanite strongholds have not been taken by the Israelites. The enemy is all around and among the Israelites, an enemy difficult to defeat because it has "chariots of iron." Making what seems to us a not unreasonable decision, the Israelites work out an amicable agreement with their enemies, accepting a few of their gods, allowing them to remain as tributaries without destroying their altars. Onto this situation of incomplete conquest and political chaos, the book of Judges imposes a pattern. An angel of the Lord says to the Israelites:

"I brought you up from Egypt, and brought you into the land which I swore to give to your fathers. I said, "I will never break my covenant with you, and you shall make no covenant with the inhabitants of this land; you shall break down their altars." But you have not obeyed my command. What is this you have done? So now I say, I will not drive them out before you; but they shall become adversaries to you, and their gods shall be a snare to you. (2:1*b*-3)

Following the death of Joshua, "the people of Israel did what was evil in the sight of the Lord and served the Baals":

And they forsook the LORD, the God of their fathers, who had brought them out of the land of Egypt; they went after other gods, from among the gods of the peoples who were round about them, and bowed down to them; and they provoked the LORD to anger. They forsook the LORD, and served the Baals and the Ashtaroth. So the anger of the LORD was kindled against Israel, and he gave them over to plunderers, who plundered them; and he sold them into the power of their enemies round about, so that they could no longer withstand their enemies. . . . Then the LORD raised up judges, who saved them out of the power of those who plundered them. And yet they did not listen to their judges; for they played the harlot after other gods and bowed down to them; they soon turned aside from the way in which their fathers had walked, who had obeyed the commandments of the LORD, and they did not do so. . . . Whenever the judge died, they turned back and behaved worse than their fathers, going after other gods, serving them and bowing down to them; they did not drop any of their practices or their stubborn ways. So the anger of the LORD was kindled against Israel; and he said, "Because this people have transgressed my covenant which I commanded their fathers, and have not obeyed my voice, I will not henceforth drive out before them any of the nations that Joshua left when he died. . . ." (2:12-14, 16-17, 19-21)

The pattern described here is imitated throughout the accounts of the greater judges. Israel does evil, God is angry, he raises enemies to punish the Israelites, they repent, a judge is chosen to save them, there is a brief period of peace, and the cycle begins again, as Israel does evil. The beginning of each major narrative is basically the same: "And the people of Israel did what was evil in the sight of the LORD." The pattern is a familiar one: apostasy, a period of servitude, supplication for aid, a response to the call, temporary salvation or peace. There is a certain futility about the alternation of glory and misery in Judges. When a judge dies, things return to the way they were before, or they get worse. The judges' two main functions—to protect Israel against its enemies, and to protect it against internal corruption—prove successful only for brief periods. There is not, however, anything aimless or meaningless about this futility, a sense we often get from the world of the Homeric poems, since here God comes repeatedly to Israel's aid, and his actions indicate a profound concern and affection for Israel. That affection is perhaps another unifying element of Judges. From God's perspective, after all, the Israelites are a pretty ungrateful and hopeless lot, returning as they do again and again to the ways which they should begin to realize lead only to disaster. The language of chapter 2 is important in identifying the kind of relationship which exists between Israel and God, and in pinpointing the particular sin of the Israelites. Consider the verbs used to describe the actions of the Israelites: they *forsook* the Lord God, *went after* other gods, *served* other gods, *bowed* down to them, *transgressed* their covenant. Their sin is obviously infidelity, but infidelity of a very special kind. As the language indicates, the Israelites continually prostitute themselves. They turn away from a loyal lover, break a covenant, make leagues with others, forsake their lover, bow to others, serve others, corrupt themselves, in a phrase, as the narrative says, they "play the harlot." What might this tell us about the Israelites? There are many reasons why an individual (or a nation) might play the harlot: immaturity, lack of faith in the initial object of love, lack of confidence, opportunism, lack of morals or of values. And all these words and phrases, I would suggest, characterize the Israelites in the book of Judges; indeed, some of them characterize the judges themselves.

In chapter 1, with its long list of towns taken and not taken, there are only two brief narratives, but they are important in setting the tone of the whole book. In 1:12, Caleb promises his daughter Achsah to the man who success-

fully takes the town of Kiriathsepher. Othniel accepts and
satisfies the condition. As he is about to go off with his
bride-to-be, she urges him to ask her father for a field. She
then makes the request to Caleb herself—"Give me a
present"—and he complies. We should be struck by the practical shrewdness of Achsah, as well as by her boldness in
asking for the field. She seizes the opportunity to get something which neither her father nor her husband had considered. Such opportunism and shrewdness characterize, as
we will see, most of the judges. The second narrative is in
1:23-25. "The house of Joseph sent to spy out Bethel. . . .
And the spies saw a man coming out of the city, and they said
to him, 'Pray, show us the way into the city, and we will deal
kindly with you.' And he showed them the way into the city;
and they smote the city with the edge of the sword, but they
let the man and all his family go." The decision, like Achsah's,
is shrewd and opportunistic, but it is also a decision which
involves betrayal and treachery. The line between being
shrewd and being a traitor is perhaps hard to draw, and may
depend on the perspective of the draftsman. These brief
narratives prepare us well for the stories of the greater
judges.

To this point, we have considered a kind of overview of
Judges. The dominant, unifying pattern is clearly the cycle
we have described, a theory of history, not only of human
history, but of individual histories as well. Someone does
wrong, he is punished for his error, either by his own guilt or
by an outside agent, a parent or authority figure of some
kind. He repents and asks for help which can come either
from within himself or from an outside source; the help
comes; balance or equilibrium is restored; the individual is at
peace with himself and his society, large or small, community
or family, until he does wrong again and the cycle begins
anew. In Judges this cyclical theory of history, both personal
and collective is not, however, futile or meaningless. God's
abiding love for Israel and his determination that Israel shall
love him impose an even larger pattern on the cycles. The
prodigal always goes home. The beloved is taken in again by

the lover. The cycles here are part of a larger theory of history directed by an infallible God rather than by fallible man. God, not the Israelites, is always the victor. To exhibit this pattern, this theory of history, the book of Judges presumably had many stories to choose from. Yet, to return to our opening question: Why these particular stories of these particular judges, of Ehud, Deborah, Gideon, Jephthah, and Samson? Presumably, there are other links here, other themes being developed in addition to a theory of history and God's great love of Israel. The stories, told with characteristic biblical honesty, are always dominated by an abiding faith that beneath the chaos there is a certainty, an order, if only Israel will be loyal enough to find it. Yet perhaps before it can accept that certainty and achieve that loyalty, Israel must understand and accept something about human experience, about man and the limits of his capacities to interpret the events around him.

What elements would stay in our memory if we could read the book as if for the first time? What is memorable about each narrative, each presumably purposely selected as were the episodes in the *Odyssey*? In the story of Ehud (3:12-30), we probably remember that Ehud is left-handed, that the king is a very fat man, that Ehud has a sword which sinks so deep into the king's belly that the hilt goes in too, and the king's fat closes over the entire weapon. We might recall other larger elements from the narrative; but I suggest these would be the main details—peculiar details, it seems to me—for us to remember. What does it matter that Ehud is left-handed or that the king is very fat or that his belly can swallow up a sword? The story begins with the familiar pattern we have already discussed—the people of Israel do evil, God angrily puts them under the yoke of Eglon, they pray for a deliverer, and the Lord raises up Ehud to judge and save them. Nothing else seems to the narrator worth mentioning about Ehud except that he is left-handed, a fact emphasized when he girds his sword on his *right* thigh. We recognize, however, a further distinguishing characteristic of Ehud—that he was chosen by God to judge Israel. The choice

seems almost randomly made. We are not told what at
tracted God to Ehud, as we will not be told what led him to
Deborah, a prophetess "who used to sit under [a] palm"; or
Gideon, the youngest son of a poor farmer in a small clan; or
Jephthah, the outcast son of a prostitute; or Samson, the
county-fair strong man. The people of Israel send tribute by
Ehud, but Ehud ironically prepares his own present—the
present of death. Eglon, we are told, is a very fat man, a
detail which characterizes his sumptuous style of living and
which also underlines the plight of the Israelites, who presumably have been forced back into the wilderness (Ehud
later rallies Israel's forces "in the hill country") because the
Moabites are in possession of the "city of palms," their king
relaxing "in his cool roof chamber," attended by servants.
The one small detail opens up for us the vast differences
between the lives of the Moabites and the conquered
Israelites—inside versus outside, cool versus hot, fatness
versus leanness, palms versus the hills. After the tribute-
bearers have been dispatched, Ehud tells Eglon that he has
something secret for him. The king, fatally curious, perhaps
hoping to relieve his boring life or wanting to fatten himself
in as many ways as possible, sends all his servants away.
Ehud, enjoying his metaphorical left-handedness, repeats his
curiosity-arousing statement, lures Eglon to his side, and
kills him. Ehud has seized the opportunity and shrewdly
played on the king's curiosity (we recall the first narrative of
chapter 1), but however praiseworthy his deed, he is also
performing an act of treachery (we may recall the second
narrative of chapter 1). His assassination of Eglon is similar,
but not comparable, to the opening up of Bethel for total
destruction. Whether either act is heroic or villainous depends on the perspective of the interpreter. The narrative
has several ironies, several expectations which are not
met—Eglon does not expect the secret message to be death,
his servants do not expect to find their king dead, the Israelites do not expect to be called to battle and victory on this
day by left-handed Ehud. The events could not have been
predicted.

The second of the longer narratives in Judges begins with the familiar pattern—the people of Israel do evil, God is angry, he sends Jabin and Sisera to punish them, they cry for help, and God selects a deliverer. As with Ehud, we are given no explanation of why it is Deborah who is chosen. All we hear about her is that she is a "prophetess" who lives "in the hill country" (4:4, 5). Why Deborah? The answer to the question, from God's perspective, is probably, Why not Deborah? The choice is unexpected, unpredictable, even somewhat mysterious. And yet, God has chosen a woman (we learn soon he has chosen two women) to be the strength of Israel, to help them defeat the enemy with its chariots of iron. Deborah summons Barak and tells him that the God of Israel has commanded him to gather his forces in preparation for a battle with Jabin's army, a battle which the Israelites, she assures him, will win. Barak is not so sure—"If you will go with me, I will go; but if you will not go with me, I will not go" (v. 8b). Why should he doubt the Lord's command? Again shortly before the battle, Deborah has to urge Barak on. "Up! For this is the day in which the LORD has given Sisera into your hand. Does not the LORD go out before you?" (v. 14b). There are two possible explanations for Barak's doubt. It suggests, first of all, how weak the faith of the Israelites is, how little confidence they have in the power of God. The second explanation, a more human one perhaps, is that Barak doubts Deborah's prophecy because she is a woman. He is not sure that he should believe this female prophet who lives in the country under a palm tree; is he being led into a trap? His concern suggests too the shrewdness of the people, a shrewdness forced on them by the powerful enemies who surround and live among them. Barak does go, of course, and destroys Jabin's army (the victory belongs to the Lord, we are reminded, not to Barak). Sisera flees and comes to what he believes is a safe place, and what we, at this moment, believe is a safe place. Deborah had said earlier that Sisera would be sold into the hand of a woman, but she turns out not to be the woman we had expected. "Sisera fled away on foot to the tent of Jael, the wife of Heber the Kenite; for there

was peace between Jabin . . . and . . . Heber" (v. 17). Jael
greets him warmly—"Turn aside to me; have no fear"—and
invites him into the tent, where she covers him with a rug
and gives him a drink of milk, although he asks only for
water. Relaxed and tired, Sisera asks Jael to keep watch and
to turn away any visitors. "But Jael the wife of Heber took a
tent peg, and took a hammer in her hand, and went softly to
him and drove the peg into his temple, till it went down into
the ground, as he was lying fast asleep from weariness. So he
died" (v. 21). This is a stunning and unexpected conclusion.
As with Ehud's assassination of Eglon, Jael's is an act of
deception, even of treachery (there is peace between Jabin
and her husband). Expectations have again been
reversed—Deborah emerges as an unexpected judge to give
guidance to Israel; Barak is not confident of victory; the
Canaanites, with their clear military superiority established
by iron chariots, are confident; Sisera believes he is secure in
Jael's tent.

Chapter 5 then presents us with a second account of the
Deborah-Jael story, although we now see the events from a
different perspective. Chapter 4 followed normal narrative
patterns, and we learned more as we read—we knew Deborah would succeed, but not how; we knew Sisera would be
defeated, but not when. The poem of chapter 5, however, has
a different perspective. It is after the battle, after everything is over, when it is time to try to impose some pattern on
the events, to explain them, to draw some lessons from
history. The first lines of the poem, which the text tells us is
sung by Deborah and Barak, identify the two main elements
of the victory: the power of God, and the willingness of the
people to offer themselves (although we find out in the poem
that there are some Israelites who are not willing to fight).

Hear, O Kings; [Deborah's point of view seems to be reflected]
    give ear, O princes;
  to the Lord I will sing,
  I will make melody to the Lord, the God of Israel. (v. 3)

The emphasis on "I" draws attention to the fact that the

judge and deliverer of Israel is a woman, a weak person, presumably, but one who turns out to be the people's strength. Deborah and Barak describe the power of God, who makes the earth tremble and the mountains quake (vv. 4, 5), but then, as if in contrast to that great power, they describe the state of the Israelites before God interceded for them. Their highways were unoccupied, travelers kept to the back roads, the villages were uninhabited. Having fallen away from their God, the Israelites were reduced to the lowest level of civilization. And yet, God is Israel's friend, a God of awesome might; and he intercedes as he has so often before, and will again. Deborah is chosen, "a mother in Israel," a phrase which further underlines her femininity, and which perhaps also points to the prior immaturity and childish lack of faith of the Israelites and their need for a mother. Their failings come in for particular criticism when Deborah and Barak, after recalling those who willingly sacrificed themselves, question those (vv. 16, 17) who did not fight at all. With the battle over, the emphasis must be on the loyal Israelites and God's victory so that the disloyalty of the tribes who remained home can be put into larger relief. The fact that some did not fight indicates to us again the lack of unity in Israel, the lack of mutual trust, which suggests why they play the harlot repeatedly, why they do not believe in God's power and love or in Israel's mission.

It is that mission that Deborah and Barak seem most interested in emphasizing in their song.

> The kings came, they fought;
>   then fought the kings of Canaan,
> at Taanach, by the waters of
>   Megiddo;
>   *they got no spoils of silver.*
>   (v. 19, italics mine)

The Canaanite kings see the war as being fought for material gain, and so, as we hear later, do their women. But Israel sees the war as being fought for a *cause* which needs to be propagandized because there are some tribes who still do not believe in the cause or that it is also God's.

From heaven fought the stars,
  from their courses they fought against Sisera.
                                        (v. 20)

A distinction is made between the Israelites' sense of mission and their enemies—Eglon sitting in his cool roof chamber in the city of palms, Sisera's mother imagining the spoils of victory being divided. Meroz (v. 23) is cursed, therefore, for permitting Sisera to escape; Jael is praised for killing him. Jael, the second woman in the narrative, is "most blessed of women." As Deborah and Barak rehearse her deed, we know, of course, the outcome—it has become a moment in past time—and the poem, rightly it seems, turns balladlike in creating for us the very instant of the murder.

> She struck Sisera a blow,
>   she crushed his head,
>   she shattered and pierced his
>   temple.
> He sank, he fell,
>   he lay still at her feet,
> at her feet he sank, he fell;
>   where he sank, there he fell dead.
>   (vv. 26b-27)

The poetry itself depicts for us the act of Sisera falling—we can imagine him, through the repetitions and rhythms of these verses, going down. The third female character is introduced, the mother of Sisera, worrying about her son's return, peering out the window. The juxtaposition is striking, and, from our modern perspective, we may be tempted to sympathize with Sisera's mother. From the perspective of the book of Judges, such sympathy would be wrong—she is the enemy. The narrative sets up distinctions which help turn us away from her, too. She is confident of victory—"Why is his chariot so long in coming?" (Those chariots of iron which so torment the Israelites also bring comfort to their owners.) She then answers her own question by picturing Sisera's men dividing the spoil,

> A maiden or two for every man;
> spoil of dyed stuffs for Sisera,
> (v. 30*b*)

and by imagining herself wearing a fine embroidered neck-
piece taken from the defeated Israelites. So Sisera's mother
sits and waits, while Deborah arouses an army, and Jael kills
the enemy, she sits thinking of women for her son's men and
luxurious apparel, while Deborah, also a mother, seeks for
her children "no spoils." Our temporary sympathy for
Sisera's mother is sentimental; we have perhaps fallen prey
to the loose loyalties which afflicted the Israelites. Deborah
and Barak remind us:

So perish all thine enemies, O LORD!
But thy friends be like the sun as he rises in his might.
(v. 31)

The story of Gideon follows the pattern we are now accustomed to—the people of Israel do evil, God is angry, he gives
them over to Midian, they cry for help, and he sends them a
deliverer. The opening verses again suggest the pitiful de-
cline in the life-style of the Israelites because of their evil
ways. They live in dens and caves, like animals; their produce
is destroyed by the enemy; they have no sheep, no oxen, no
asses. The enemy is powerful, this time because of its countless camels. An angel of the Lord repeats the terms of the
union between Israel and God, and points out that the Israelites have not lived up to their part of the agreement.
Nevertheless, God hears their cries for help and sends an
angel to Gideon, a poor farmer, who is beating his wheat in
the wine press to hide it from the Midianites. He announces
to Gideon: "The LORD is with you, you mighty man of valor"
(6:12*b*). To such an announcement, and from an angel, we
would expect an awed response. But Gideon, like Barak, is
not convinced. "If the LORD is with us, why then has all this
befallen us? And where are all his wonderful deeds which our
fathers recounted to us, saying, 'Did not the LORD bring us
up from Egypt?' But now the LORD has cast us off, and given
us into the hand of Midian" (v. 13). Gideon essentially shrugs

off the angel and suggests that if the Lord is with him, given present circumstances, he might be better off alone. Even one of the judges, it seems, shares the suspicion and uncertainty of Barak and of those tribes who did not fight with Deborah. The Lord himself now speaks,—"Go in this might of yours and deliver Israel from the hand of Midian; do not I send you?" Gideon replies with basically the same question we have raised about Ehud and Deborah—why me? He is, he argues, the youngest in his family, and his family belongs to the weakest clan in the area. The choice seems not only random, but almost a deliberate attempt to pick out the one who is weakest in order to point up the power of God. The Lord tries to persuade Gideon to accept the charge by assuring him of his support. But Gideon, shrewd and canny (and lacking in faith?), asks for a sign to prove that he is not being deceived. Only when fire springs from a bare rock is Gideon persuaded; he even builds an altar on the spot. We cannot blame Gideon too much, of course, given the plight of the Israelites. At the same time, we recognize that his lack of faith illustrates what has brought the Israelites to their present state. God has a divine plan for Israel; but while it is developing, the Israelites must exist in human history, too. Gideon carries out God's command to destroy the altar of Baal, for example, "but because he was too afraid of his family and the men of the town to do it by day, he did it by night" (v. 27). Gideon's fears prove justified in the morning when his fellow townspeople demand his death because he has destroyed Baal's altar. The state of the Israelites' morale is low indeed. Only his father's clever suggestion that Baal, if a god, can take care of himself, saves him.

Throughout the narrative, Gideon is suspicious, cautious, shrewd, so much so that his attitudes, after a while, seem to affect God's actions. Gideon's trumpet and messengers succeed in raising the spirits of various tribes, who willingly agree to follow him. But Gideon then puts God through additional tests by asking him first to keep the ground dry while covering a fleece of wool with dew and then asking him (though always cautiously, "Let not thy anger burn against me, let me speak but this once; pray, let me make trial only this once . . . [!]") to keep the fleece dry while covering the ground with dew (vv. 37-39). God passes both tests, and Gideon and his followers prepare for battle. At this point, God, presumably all too aware of Gideon's shaky faith, decides that "the people with [him] are too many," and sets up his own tests which reduce the army from thirty-two thousand to three hundred (7:2-8). His reason, consistent with Gideon's responses to him and his angel, is to prevent Israel from priding itself on the coming victory, from saying, "My own hand has delivered me." God wants to make it perfectly clear that the victory belongs to him. The tests he sets up reveal again the lack of faith among the Israelites (twenty-two thousand leave because they are "fearful and trembling"), and the randomness of his selection process (ninety-seven hundred are eliminated because they kneel at the river to drink instead of cupping the water in their hands). The Lord by this time knows Gideon very well—he tells him that the Midianites can be defeated, but adds that if Gideon is afraid, he should go into the enemy camp with his servant Purah to receive confirmation of the fact. Gideon and Purah go into the enemy camp. Only after he hears the account of a dream which is favorable to him does Gideon arouse his men for battle (vv. 9-14). The attack itself further illustrates Gideon's shrewdness. Essentially, it is a false attack by night, during which the three hundred Israelites trick the enemy into thinking they are surrounded by thousands (vv. 19-22). Deception is involved, as it was in the stories of Ehud and Jael, as it was in the narrative of chapter 1 of the man who opened his city to enemy spies. There is no direct confrontation; Gideon confuses the Midianites and drives them in groups into the hands of his comrades.

The final unraveling of the Gideon narrative provides us with further insights into the dominant theme of Judges. Some tribes refuse to help Gideon and are severely punished for their casual loyalties; Gideon illustrates flashes of wisdom in calming the angry men of Ephraim (8:1-3) and in refusing to be king of Israel (vv. 22-23); he exhibits a fatal flaw, however, in asking for the golden earrings of the enemy (the spoils) and in making an ephod, or priestly vestment, with the gold (vv. 24-27). We recognize the lack of unity in Israel, the lack of faith in God's plan of history; even the judges, exemplifying the shrewdness and cautious suspicion of the people, do not always make the right choices. Gideon's decision to request the spoils of victory is clearly an error, as Deborah and Barak have already told us (they fought for a cause); and while Israel has rest for a time under him, the ephod has been made, and Israel, we are told, will "play the harlot after it."

Abimelech, the son of Gideon's concubine, is obviously not one of Israel's judges. But his story, centrally placed in these accounts of the greater judges, is important to our understanding of the whole. Up to this point, Ehud, Deborah, and Gideon have successfully delivered Israel from external enemies. Later, Jephthah and Samson will also defeat outside enemies. Abimelech, however, is an internal enemy, perhaps representing the internal corruption in Israel itself. He is vain, ambitious, a military adventurer. He persuades the men of Shechem that they would be better off under one king (himself) than under his seventy half-brothers, the sons of Gideon (9:2). Shortly before Abimelech's appearance in the narrative, Gideon has wisely refused the kingship, pointing out that "the Lord will rule." The juxtaposition underlines for us the folly of Abimelech and the folly of the Israelites. The error is further emphasized by Jotham, the one son of Gideon who survives Abimelech's massacre, in his fable of the trees' search for a king. The most appropriate trees, the olive, fig, and vine, all refuse because they accept their inherent values; the bramble, however, agrees to be king. Jotham points out that if Abimelech has been selected in "good faith and honor" (not as the only available choice or because of his dangerous nature), then he should be king; if not, those who chose him should be cursed (vv. 7-20). Israel should not choose a king just to have a king, a strong person on whom they can rely instead of God.

The Israelites, not surprisingly, fall out among themselves. The deception which Ehud, Jael, and Gideon practiced against the enemy for praiseworthy ends is practiced by the Israelites against one another. We hear of treacherous schemes, ambushes in the mountains, movements of forces by night, armies lying in wait in the fields. But as in the other narratives, there are ironies, expectations which are not met—Zebul mistakes Abimelech's men for the shadow of the mountains; the people of Shechem feel safe in the "stronghold of the house of Elberith," which Abimelech burns to the ground; Abimelech tries to repeat his strategy to defeat the people of Thebez shut up in a strong tower, but a woman drops a millstone on his head and crushes his skull. The internal enemy is destroyed, but not without a final outburst of vanity. "He called hastily to the young man his armor-bearer, and said to him, 'Draw your sword and kill me, lest men say of me, A woman killed him'" (v. 54). Is Abimelech thinking of what men say of Sisera?

Following the defeat of their internal enemy, symbolizing the overcoming of their own corruptions, the Israelites have peace for many years. After a time, however, they return to their old ways, play the harlot, and are punished by God. Leaderless, somewhat repentant, they look around for someone to deliver them from the Ammonites. They turn to Jephthah, "a mighty warrior." But Jephthah asks them a question similar to the one God has been asking throughout Judges: "Did you not hate me, and drive me out of my father's house? Why have you come to me now when you are in trouble?" (11:7). He is, however, easily persuaded when they ask him to be their leader. Like Ehud, Deborah, and Gideon, Jephthah is a peculiar and unexpected choice to be Israel's deliverer. We know as much about him as we do about Gideon, much more than we do about Ehud and Deborah, and that knowledge makes the choice all the more surprising. He comes from the dregs of Israelite society, stained by his birth, denied entrance into his family, forced to become a mountain bandit. He is, like the other judges, opportunistic and shrewd (if not treacherous), cautious, not unwise. He attempts peace negotiations with the Ammonities, providing them with Israel's historical claim to the land and pointing out that he has not personally sinned against them. That having failed, he opportunistically makes a deal with God: "If thou wilt give the Ammonites into my hand, then whoever comes forth from the doors of my house to meet me, when I return victorious from the Ammonites, shall be the LORD's, and I will offer him up for a burnt offering" (v. 30). Jephthah expects victory once he has made his vow with God, and he gets it. He does not expect, however, that he will be greeted on his triumphant return by his daughter: "She was his only child; beside her he had neither son nor daughter" (v. 34). He is, of course, horrified; his opportunism has led him to both victory and defeat. And is this God's trick? His deception? Or is this conclusion to reclaim Jephthah's dignity? For he does fulfill his vow, painfully and slowly—only after his daughter has bewailed her virginity for two months in the mountains, two months during which Jephthah might have changed his mind. The sacrifice of his daughter may end Jephthah's story, but it does not end this particular narrative. Like the stories of Ehud, Deborah, Gideon, and Abimelech, the narrative concludes on an unexpected note, a kind of trick, in which those who cannot pronounce *Shibboleth* correctly are identified as enemies and slain. There is a remarkable coherence to these narratives; incidents and elements of each echo in all of the others.

The Samson story marks the climax of Judges in several ways. Most obviously, Samson is the last of the greater judges, the last deliverer whose feats are described in some detail. The story begins with the usual pattern which opens each of the other major narratives in this book. Israel's evil ways have this time led them into the hands of the Philistines; but no deliverer immediately appears to save them. Part of the pattern is broken by the author—Ehud, Deborah, Gideon, and Jephthah were full grown when they were selected to be saviors of Israel. We know the circumstances of Jephthah's birth, but otherwise, we know of no earlier events in the lives of these judges which might have suggested their significant selection by the Lord. In this last major narrative, however, God intervenes more directly. The angel of the Lord appears to a barren woman to announce that she will conceive and bear a son who will "deliver Israel from the hand of the Philistines" (13:5b). The choice seems less random than it did in the earlier accounts. God's champion has in a sense been preselected, molded in the womb to be the deliverer.

Given this background, and the seriousness with which Samson's parents treat the announcement, Samson turns out not to be quite what we might have expected. The other judges (except Deborah) have their flaws, but there was no reason to expect them to be perfect. This judge, on the other hand, has a miraculous birth, and the success of his mission is predicted even before he is conceived. We expect someone very special. What we get is a country strong man, a kind of simpleminded, muscle-bound boy, who loves to play games and make up riddles, who wants his own way and forces his decisions on others whether they like it or not, one of whose main interests is women—Philistine women at that. The more we learn of Samson, in the context of the circumstances of his conception and birth, his selection as Israel's judge strikes us as the most random and arbitrary of all.

His parents try to dissuade him from marrying a Philistine (a woman he has only seen once), but he stubbornly insists: "Get her for me; for she pleases me well" (14:3b). His desire may be prompted by the Lord, as the narrative tells us, but he reveals himself as no diplomat in the discussion. After slaying a lion and eating the honey produced by bees swarming over its carcass, he challenges the Philistines with a riddle, "Out of the eater came something to eat. Out of the strong came something sweet," and bets them that they cannot provide the answer within seven days (14:12-14). There is nothing inherently wrong with the game—it is good fun and illustrates Samson's zest for life and for challenges. But it is an immature bet, an adolescent game; it also reveals Samson's weakness when he gives in to his wife's pleas for the answer. We will certainly recall this incident when Samson is being hounded by Delilah, and we must wonder why Samson does not recall it as well. His response to his wife's treachery (by now an expected mode of conduct in Judges) can only be described as excessive. He kills thirty men (v. 19). His extravagant responses become typical behavior. He burns the Philistines' crops because his Philistine father-in-law gave his wife to his companion (15:1-5; he inquired about her only "after a while"); he slaughters the Philistines because they burn down his wife's father's house (vv. 6b-8; a burning occasioned, he seems to forget, by his destruction of their crops). The early audiences presumably delighted in Samson's exploits against their enemies. But from a literary perspective, Samson is petulant, conceited, immature. Pervading our reading of his actions, however, is our knowledge of his miraculous conception and birth. *We* know he is being driven, if not controlled, by the Lord, whom Samson calls on for help in the most casual and informal of ways. The difficulty is that Samson is never sure what is expected of him, or at least he is incapable of maintaining his dignity for very long.

In chapter 16, Samson goes to Gaza and spends the night with a harlot, escaping a Gazite plot with enormous bravado. "After this," we are told, he loves Delilah (v. 4). She will, of course, be his last woman. Delilah willingly agrees to the Philistine suggestion that she "entice" Samson to discover the source of his great strength. Her reward, her spoils of victory, from each of the lords for her treachery will be eleven hundred pieces of silver. Samson, as he did with his wife, plays hard-to-get for several days, telling Delilah his strength is powerless against the bindings of seven fresh bowstrings or new ropes, or lost if seven locks of his head are woven and tightened with a pin. The tension mounts for us because we know Samson has played this game to no final success once before. He finally reveals his secret, battered as he apparently is by Delilah's constant pleadings. "His soul was vexed to death" (v. 16b). He is seized, his eyes are gouged out, and he is taken to the mill at Gaza to work with slaves. Expectations have been reversed throughout the narrative—Samson's mother knew she was barren and expected no children; we know of Samson's conception and expect a different kind of judge; Samson's parents did not expect him to marry one of the enemy; Samson expected to win his bet with his lion riddle; his wife's family did not expect him to return for the woman who had betrayed him; Samson does not expect Delilah to deceive him. And now, the Philistines gather to offer a great sacrifice to their god, to celebrate their triumph over Samson. They call for him, "that he may make sport," and he brings their temple down around their heads (v. 30). He achieves, like Jephthah, his great moment of dignity at terrible personal cost.

How shall we answer our opening question: What do these judges have in common? In one sense the answer—and it is a very significant answer—is that they have nothing at all in common. All we know of Ehud is that he is left-handed, Deborah is a prophetess who lives under a palm tree, Gideon a poor farmer, Jephthah the son of a prostitute, Samson a strong man whose strength resides in his hair. They do different deeds. They have, some of them, different kinds of blemishes. They plan their strategies differently. Ehud conceals his weapon and performs an act of individual assassination; Deborah prophesies that Sisera will be sold into the hand of a woman; Gideon plans a night mock attack; Jephthah makes a deal with God to ensure victory; Samson depends on the force of his arm. About each, however, there is something memorable. What they have in common, if we can call it that, is their rich diversity. The book of Judges delights in surprises, in diversity of character and situation, in reversals of expectations. The hand of the Lord falls where it will, often in unexpected places—on a southpaw, on two women, on the youngest son of a poor farmer in a weak clan, on the son of a prostitute, on the son of a barren woman. As in the creation stories, there is delight here in the diversity of being, in the fullness of being, in the range of those chosen by God to save the people he loves. These are old-fashioned, country people—Deborah under her palm, Gideon on his farm, Jephthah and his daughter and the simplicity of the relationship, Samson the county fair bell ringer. There is wonder here at the variety of man, at the value of every kind of man. Implicit in Judges is a conviction of the worth of every kind of human gift and human characteristic, a vast democracy of spirit, once this weak and worthless cast is transformed by God's spirit. Even a characteristic such as human treachery is not all bad under certain circumstances.

But there is even more to Judges than this sense of the variety of man, of the potential value of each man. The book presents stories which contain, in addition to ironies, many seeming contradictions. Ehud is left-handed but the strong right arm of God works through him; Deborah and Jael are women, supposedly weak, but through God they are made strong; Gideon is a simple, suspicious farmer, but he becomes a hero and is asked to be king; Jephthah is an outcast, from the dregs of society, but he reveals enormous nobility of purpose and spirit; Samson is constantly being outwitted, but he just shrugs it aside; he is robust and happy-go-lucky, but he is also God's champion.

Samson in a sense epitomizes the judges. He is, like Israel, a special child of God. He also is, like Israel, immature, opportunistic, rash. His weakness for women culminates in the loss of strength through the wiles of Delilah—like Israel, he has played the harlot once too often. He is enticed, as Israel is enticed; the source of his strength is taken from him, as God, the strength of Israel, removes himself to punish the Israelites; he is overcome, bound, and subdued, as Israel is sold into the power of her enemies and driven into the hills and mountains. Samson's blindness seems to symbolize and crystallize the blindness of Israel when it gives in to temptation and weakness and does evil in the sight of the Lord. Samson suffers literally the darkness which the Israelites suffer figuratively when they turn away from God and are forced to live in caves and dens, when their highways are unoccupied, their villages empty. But as the strength and favor of God are renewed repeatedly to the Israelites, so Samson's God-given strength returns in a natural manner; indeed, so natural is the return—"The hair of his head began to grow

161

again after it had been shaved" (v. 22)—that it suggests, like the coming of dawn after night, how natural it is for God to give Israel new strength against its enemies.

What ultimately unifies Judges is its delight in contradiction. It edifies because it describes for us in a series of swift, vivid narratives the paradoxical nature of human experience. Things are not always what they seem, as the characters of the judges exemplify. That is why the story of Abimelech is so central to the book. He is not a judge, but he *could* be. He is, after all, like Jephthah, an outcast, the son of a prostitute. The narrative of Abimelech establishes the whole background of the age, the tone and setting in which the judges operate. He is a military adventurer, a professional killer, able and entirely unscrupulous, very dangerous. He illustrates what Israel could become if it were not for the judges.

Man has a dual nature. He can go the way of Abimelech or the way of Jephthah. Man's experiences are also paradoxical. Eglon sends all away because he expects to receive a secret message, and the message is death; his servants do not enter for fear of angering him, and all the while he lies with Ehud's dagger buried in his fat belly; Sisera is delighted to find safety in Jael's tent, and she drives a nail into his temple; Gideon declines the kingship, takes the jewels instead, and they turn out to be a snare to him and to his people; Abimelech successfully burns down one tower, but when he tries the same thing a second time, he is killed; Samson toys and riddles with his women, but then confides in them, at first only at the loss of a bet, and ultimately, at the loss of his eyes and life. The narrative does indeed select stories carefully—to illustrate a theory of history, to underline God's abiding love for his people; to suggest the many ironies, contradictions, surprises, which the human world involves; to remind the reader that human experience can be, from a human perspective, ultimately paradoxical; to imply strongly that the resolution of the paradoxes lies in God; to urge the Israelites, then, to return to their God, to stop playing the harlot.

IX The Book of Ruth*

D. F. RAUBER (deceased), Department of
English, San Diego State College

[Professor Rauber, in his two opening paragraphs, comments on "the dearth of literary criticism in biblical studies,"
and argues that the "literary scholar should be an equal
partner" among other specialists on the Bible.]

Many readers may be surprised at the charge that literary
considerations are largely absent from treatments of Old
Testament subjects, for they have recollections that the art
of the biblical writers is always being discussed. In most
cases, however, the payment of literary tribute to the artists
is almost ritualistic: a slight bow is made in the direction of
the Muse, a few generalities are shuffled off, and then attention turns to what really matters. When the treatment of
literary values is not on an extremely elementary level, it is
almost exclusively confined to questions of literary origins
—the history of a genre and cross-cultural parallels.

For example, look at this introduction to Ruth by L. P.
Smith in *The Interpreter's Bible:*

The old rhetorics were fond of citing the book of Ruth as a perfect
example of simple narrative. Modern specifications for short-story
writing are here admirably met. "Plot is simply thinking in terms of
scene and suspense." Scenes consist "in significant detail of action,
character and setting." The author "holds suspense by dramatic
detail," and the final suspense is resolved "just before the curtain"
(II, p. 829).

The internal quotations are from Blanchard's *The Art of
Composition*, apparently a standard sort of freshman

---

*From *Journal of Biblical Literature*, vol. LXXXIX, Part I, March, 1970,
pp. 27-37. Reprinted by permission of the Society of Biblical Literature.
Original title, "Literary Values in the Bible: The Book of Ruth."

rhetoric. And it is precisely this, that treatments are so often on a freshman level, that reveals the extraordinary degree of literary naïveté pervading the field. Any literary scholar who used this sort of material in connection with the most unimportant of modern short-story writers would be laughed out of court, and rightly so. What are we to think, then, when such commonplaces are applied, not to a minor writer, but to one who is, in theory at least, regarded as a master?

Not all accounts of Ruth are this simple-minded. Commentators usually do place the work in a literary genre and do mention certain generalized characteristics of that genre. Driver, for instance, notes that "the narrative is told with much picturesque and graceful detail, and affords an idyllic glimpse of home life in ancient Israel." M. E. Chase, starting from Goethe's remark that Ruth is "the most beautiful of all idylls," expands upon these lines, observing that the gleaning scene "has a pleasing, pastoral quality which reminds one of other ancient settings of Arcadian simplicity, drawn by Theocritus or by Vergil." Yet such treatment is hardly searching.[1] It may be objected that the works I am citing are specifically introductions and therefore by definition generalized accounts. This is true, but it is also true (in my experience at least) that literary analysis of Ruth hardly goes beyond this sort of thing, and that is my main contention.

The objection to this kind of literary evaluation is not that it is condensed and offhanded, but that it is so simplistic that it gives a radically wrong impression of the work. There is a common thread running through the criticism, the tone of which is contained in phrases such as "picturesque and graceful." In brief, Ruth is seen as being very definitely in a minor mode. Miss Chase later makes this explicit when she speaks of this "short, even slight story" and concludes that "as a work of literary art, the story of Ruth cannot be justly called profound in its emotional appeal" (p. 196). J. T. Cleland sounds the same note in *The Interpreter's Bible* (II, p. 832): "The book is a slight, though exquisite, piece of work. . . . From the literary point of view, it is a gem, a gracious and beautiful short story." My contention is that these judgments are quite misleading and untrue to the work. And the reason is simply that these commentators do not study the story very seriously as an art product. If we accept Ruth, provisionally at least, as high art and look at it directly, without condescension, we find very quickly that it is far more than a palely fragrant flower in the garden of the pastoral.

More and more I become convinced that the great key to the reading of Hebraic literature is sensitivity to pattern, and nowhere is response to patterning more important than in Ruth. The whole of chapter 1 is concerned with establishing a dominant pattern for the work, which is first given indirectly in various manifestations and then, near the end of the chapter, given overtly. This controlling pattern can be stated abstractly as emptiness-fullness. The first example is in verse 1: "there was a *famine in the land.*"[2] That is, with respect to physical nature, the land itself, emptiness is dearth and famine, and the implied opposite, of course, is plenty. In verse 3 occurs a second manifestation, again in negative form: "And Elimelech Naomi's husband died; *and she was left,* and her two sons." Here is the same theme on the social level: fullness is the complete and harmonious family, and emptiness is the loneliness of the widow. In the verse cited, Naomi's deprivation is only partial, and purposely so, for the artist wants the complete desolation two verses on to strike with greater force: "And Mahlon and Chilion died also both of them; and *the woman was left of her two sons and her husband.*" Stricken, Naomi yearns to fulfill completely the pattern she intuitively recognizes by dismissing her daughters-in-law, so that in its exterior appearances her life will reflect her interior state of total emptiness. In this attempt at dismissal appears the third manifestation of the pattern:

And Naomi said, Turn again, my daughters: why will ye go with me? are there yet any more sons in my womb, that they may be your husbands? Turn again, my daughers, *go your way; for I am too old to have an husband.* If I should say, I have hope, if I should have an husband also to-night, and should also bear sons; Would ye tarry for them till they were grown? (vv. 11-13).

Here the theme is seen on a deeper and more personal level, emptiness presented as the barrenness of an old woman as over against the fullness of bearing.

Not only is this a carefully developed series, but it is also highly ordered. It starts on the widest of levels (man and the earth), then narrows down to the social level (man in the family), then narrows down once again to the most personal level (Naomi, the individual woman, in her anguish). There is added power in our sensing that the beginning and end of the series bend around to meet. Our minds sweep from the intense point of personal grief back to the opening as we recognize the parallel between the barrenness of the old woman and the barrenness of the exhausted earth. We see the similarity, and then the difference. The cycle of nature is endlessly repeated, but Naomi is old and for her, or so to her it seems, there will never come a time in which the Lord will visit her again as he will visit "his people in giving them bread." Note also that through the strong contrast between the youth of the nubile daughters and the barren old age of Naomi, the author has expanded his whole construction. We are dealing now with both of the great nature cycles—spring and winter as well as dearth and plenty, cycles which are both similar to one another and distinct.

The verses being discussed also introduce a fourth manifestation of the pattern in Naomi's denial of hope. This represents a preliminary summing up in that the essence of the separate manifestations—famine, isolation, barrenness, old age—is given as hopelessness, the final emptiness. Then at the end, in verses 20 and 21, the whole set of symbols is drawn together, summed up, and intensified by direct statement: "Call me not Naomi (Pleasant), call me Mara (Bitter): for the Almighty hath dealt very bitterly with me. *I went out full, and the* LORD *hath brought me home again empty.*"

Thus does the artist develop his pattern. The whole chapter is basically an introduction, a setting of the stage, a posing of the problems. The movement has been a skillfully managed downward spiral, a sinking to the very depths. I do not suggest that Ruth is another Job. On the contrary, while

Ruth is a profound work, it is not bitter or austere, and the artist has gone to considerable pains to arrest any such notion by planting and partially developing a countermovement. The most obvious example is the famous verse 16: "For whither thou goest, I will go; and where thou lodgest, I will lodge." That is, we know that Naomi is not alone and will not be. But even more impressive from the viewpoint of technique is the masterful way in which the author ends the chapter in verse 22: "and they came to Bethlehem in the beginning of barley harvest." It is almost impossible in the clumsy medium of analytic prose to do justice to the artistry of the apparently simple phrase "in the beginning of barley harvest." It is, for one thing, a very fine transitional device with the meaning, "So much then for prologue and setting; now on to the main action." It is also in itself a beginning, the announcement of a healing movement and a preview of the solution, for harvest is pre-eminently the symbol of plenty. But over and above all of these effects is our response to the superb control of the artist, who by this exhibition of perfect poise convinces us beyond any doubt that all is well, that this is indeed a divine comedy.

The second movement begins with "and they came . . . in the *beginning* of barley harvest" and ends with the complementary "So she kept fast by the maidens of Boaz to glean unto the *end* of barley harvest and of wheat harvest" (v. 23). As this formal opening and close suggest, this movement centers around the image of the harvest. On one level it is a celebration of the fertility of the earth; on another, the working out of the restoration theme. With respect to the latter, the heart of the development is in the meeting of Ruth and Boaz, which is placed by the artist almost exactly dead center in the chapter: "Then she fell on her face, and bowed herself to the ground, and said unto him, Why have I found grace in thine eyes, that thou shouldest take knowledge of me, *seeing I am a stranger*" (v. 10). Here is another major device of the artist. "Seeing I am a stranger" is a hugely evocative and charged condensation. A nerve is touched in the consciousness, and our imaginations at once expand to draw into this outwardly simple story large portions of the total experience of the people Israel. Surely *the stranger* is one of the most important images of the Old Testament, one especially prominent in the central experience of the exodus and the intense reflection upon that experience solidified in the Torah. . . . [It might] be insulting to belabor this point, but a few examples are in order to establish the breadth and tone of the concept. There are the touching and powerful words of Moses himself at the birth of his son, words which sum up so much of his life and character: "I have been a stranger in a strange land" (Exod. 2:22). There is the legal application in the law: "Thou shalt neither vex a stranger, nor oppress him: for ye were strangers in the land of Egypt" (Exod. 22:21), with its explicit connection between the Egyptian experience and the social obligation. There are also the great positive statements of Leviticus which widen the applicability of the obligation: "The land shall not be sold for ever; for the land is mine; for ye are strangers and sojourners with me" (Lev. 25:23). And this whole set of interrelations is contained within a larger pattern. In both Leviticus and Deuteronomy a great parallel is established between Torah and the land. For example:

If ye walk in my statutes, and keep my commandments, and do them; Then I will give you rain in due season, and the land shall yield her increase, and the trees of the field shall yield their fruit. And your threshing shall reach unto the vintage, and the vintage shall reach unto the sowing time: and ye shall eat your bread to the full, and dwell in your land safely (Lev. 26:3-5).

This is not only a promise of reward but also an insight, expressed with lyric passion, that the following of the law by men corresponds to and is linked with the following of the natural patterns by the trees and the vines.

My argument is that the artist intends this vast complex of correspondences, insights, and apprehensions to echo strongly in Ruth and to bear on the action. His technique is to explode within the specific situations of his story potent memories of major themes in the grand Hebraic tradition.

That the stranger theme is meant to reverberate in the story is seen by Boaz's response to Ruth. He shows first that he understands what it means to be a stranger: "and how thou hast left thy father and thy mother, and the land of thy nativity, and art come unto a people which thou knewest not heretofore" (v. 11). But this is also a deliberate echoing of something even deeper in the Hebraic past than the exodus; it brings Abraham and the patriarchs to mind and especially such glowing texts as: "Now the LORD had said unto Abram, Get thee out of thy country, and from thy kindred, and from thy father's house, unto a land that I will shew thee" (Gen. 12:1). This is a reminder of the very deep roots of the stranger concept in the Hebraic experience and excellent evidence that the author is drawing upon those depths.

To return to the text, Boaz goes on to say, "The LORD recompense thy work, and *a full reward be given thee* of the LORD God of Israel, under whose wings thou art come to trust" (v. 12). In its dramatic setting this is a splendid and illuminating verse. We should never forget that we are dealing with a living situation and not with the laying out of abstract patterns however noble. From the dramatic point of view what is all-important here is our apprehension of the exact mental and emotional state of Boaz. Now one of the insights in the Exodus and Leviticus passages quoted above can be stated as the proportion, "As the LORD is toward men, so should a man be toward his unfortunate neighbor." But at this point Boaz attempts to evade his responsibility by placing the whole burden upon the LORD. It is true that the LORD will recompense Ruth fully on one level, yet it is Boaz who will recompense her fully on the human level. Boaz has, I suspect, dim intuitions that this is his destiny, but he does not see clearly. In what follows, however, we see him already responding to this pattern of fulfillment on the simplest of levels, that in which Ruth's "work" is her gleaning in the fields. The recompense here is in Boaz's instructions to his young men and even more directly in "and he reached her parched corn, *and she did eat, and was sufficed,* and left" (v. 14). With delight we see that this is only a foreshadowing of the "full reward" to come, for we know what Boaz really knows but does not yet realize that he knows. At the same time, we smile at Boaz in the comic mode, because we also delight in the fact that our insight is superior to his. In this sophisticated construction are revealed essential qualities of our author—a psychological penetration both gentle and strong, a largeness of mind which expresses itself by understatement, wit, and subtlety. The combination is very much like that represented in English literature by Chaucer, or better yet, George Herbert.

Our comic delight is heightened when we note that Ruth, in her enormous and touching innocence, has understood very little. But Naomi sees and understands perfectly, and with the advent of this understanding comes an upward surge of her spirit, a lifting from the depths. She breaks out, "Blessed be he of the LORD, who hath not left off his kindness to the living and to the dead" (v. 20), and we know that Naomi, who was herself among the dead, now lives again.

All that remains to be done is to draw what Boaz partially knows into the full light of consciousness. This is accomplished by Naomi, through the instrumentality of Ruth, in the third movement of the drama, which is one of completion. The patterning of the movement is again marked. For example, the psychological completion of the process of understanding in Boaz is reflected on the physical level by the completion of harvesting represented by the threshing and the harvest festival. Also, the theme of completion is clearly announced at the start in the powerful word *rest*: "Then Naomi her mother in law said unto her, My daughter, shall I not seek *rest for thee*, that it may be well with thee?" (3:1). In this highly formalized art we would expect a return to this theme at the end, and not in vain: "Then said she, *Sit still*, my daughter, until thou know how the matter will fall: for *the man will not be in rest, until he have finished the thing this day*" (v. 18). The gist of this is that everything important has been accomplished; only details remain to be taken care of.

The charm of the midnight scene on the threshing floor is celebrated, and I will not comment further upon it. Not so

famous, but even more impressive to me, is the fine way in
which full realization is, as it were, forced upon Boaz. The
critical verse is 9, and again I must comment that here, as in
the previous example, the artist uses to great effect the
principle of perfect symmetry, exact centering. The key
verse is: "And he said, Who art thou? And she answered, I
am Ruth thine handmaid: spread therefore thy skirt over
thine handmaid; for thou art a near kinsman." The parallelism between this and the central scene in the previous
chapter is unmistakable. This too is a meeting—"Who art
thou?"—but on a deeper level. I do not think that the emphasis in Ruth's response should be placed upon *kinsman*, at
least in the literal sense. For this would be no revelation;
Boaz knows this. Rather the magic, and it is magic, is performed by "spread therefore thy skirt over thine handmaid."
In Boaz's mind this triggers a memory, recalls to him his
previous words, "And a full reward be given thee of the LORD
God of Israel, *under whose wings thou art come to trust*."
Once this correspondence has been made, the full meaning
and implications of his previous words flood in upon him. He
apprehends the proportion I spoke of before and its applicability to him. In a moment the process of understanding is
completed. Everything culminates and merges in this image
of ingathering: the wings of the LORD sweeping in to himself
the people, the arms of Boaz gathering in to himself the
maiden Ruth, the arms of the young men drawing into the
barns the grain. It is a moment of imaginative splendor and
depth.

After such a revelation there must be a relaxation of tension. And since there are the details and practical matters to
be cleared up, the author turns his attention to these, partly
in the rest of this chapter and partly in the scene at the gate
which opens chapter 4. After this scene, which is best described as an interlude, the artist proceeds to construct a
concluding movement of the greatest power and literary
interest. The mode here is entirely one of triumph and celebration. The center of the development is verse 13: "So Boaz
took Ruth, and she was his wife: and when he went in unto

her, the LORD gave her conception, and she bare a son." In this verse, written deliberately in an austerely noble style, the author returns directly to the emptiness-fullness theme developed so carefully in the introduction. He balances the total emptiness there with a complete fullness and fulfillment here. The fertility of Ruth and the fruit of her womb are triumphant rejoinders to the barrenness which darkened the first chapter. Here also is the human manifestation of the theme of harvesting which has pervaded the work from chapter 2 on. Here also is re-establishment of the full family and social harmony.

But while the verse itself is simple and unadorned, the author has taken steps to ensure that its importance will not be missed. He does this by bracketing it between two passages of evocative splendor, by making it part of a complex construction. Preceding is a noble recollection of past glory: "The LORD make the woman that is come into thine house *like Rachel and like Leah, which two did build the house of Israel*" (v. 11). Our minds fill with the whole of the patriarchal past, and this reinforces the fullness theme, for it brings to mind the strong patriarchal emphases on fertility and "the seed." In addition, by positing so direct a parallel between Ruth and the mighty figure of Rachel, the artist has broken out of his small domestic world into the mainstream of the historical and imaginative splendor of Israel. This expansion into the past is carefully matched on the other side of the key verse by an equal burst of glory in the future: "and they called his name Obed: he is the father of Jesse, the father of David" (v. 17). The whole construction is a double cone in which a large past is made to focus in on the simple birth; then, from the focal point of that birth expands an equally large future. The sureness of the artist's touch is especially seen by the introduction of a certain asymmetry: the figure from the past, Rachel, is related directly to Ruth; the figure from the future, David, to her child. Then, to round off the whole figure, in the genealogies of verses 18-22 the whole course of history is presented in another way, this time in a continuous, unbroken flow from Pharez to David.

But this is only part of the celebratory triumph. The author does not forget that he is telling a human story as well as a national and symbolic one. He returns also in the end to his human starting point, Naomi. Verse 16 is the locus here: "And Naomi took the child, and laid it in her bosom, and became nurse unto it." Nothing more perfectly reveals the rich humanity of this artist than this turning, amidst all the thunders of glory, to the woman Naomi. She too must be made full. The poignancy of the poet may be seen by placing side by side "I went out full and the LORD hath brought me home again empty" and "Naomi took the child, and laid it in her bosom." We sense also the author's feeling that the theme of glory ought to be contained somewhat, and he does this, in a very Hebraic fashion, by showing all the glory rooted in the simple Naomi and her maternal and domestic yearnings.

Further—and this is additional evidence of the great craftsmanship of this artist—looking back we see that we have been prepared, that the author has planted foreshadowings or symbolic representations of this final scene in the intervening chapters. The reminder in chapter 2 is slight and glancing; it occurs when Ruth returns to Naomi from the fields with the fruit of her labor: "and *she brought forth, and gave to her* that she had reserved after she was sufficed" (v. 18). The same symbolic preview of birth and presentation is given more directly in chapter 3. Boaz has filled the apron of Ruth with grain, and Ruth presents herself before Naomi, the apron held out bulging with grain, saying, "These six measures of barley gave he me; for he said to me, *Go not empty unto thy mother in law*" (v. 17). Thus the beginning and end of the thematic development are firmly linked; thus all the themes and figures come together and are fused in splendor and tenderness.

This, then, is my reading of Ruth. I would like to emphasize that it is not intended to be exhaustive. There are numerous other patterns and progressions. For example, I have given only one example of the bracketing device. This could be expanded to show that the work can be viewed as a complex set of interlocking bracketings, which operate to give the work an extreme unity. Another interesting literary point is that the author has succeeded in combining in this work a very high degree of patterning with an almost perfect narrative flow. Indeed, he rather obviously plays off his systems of patterns against the continuous flow of the story. But the analysis is complete enough for the present purposes.

It is, of course, up to the reader to decide how convincing the reading is, but assuming that it and the principles of analysis underlying it are accepted, certain consequences follow. In the first place, the reading supports my initial contention that the conventional literary judgments are extremely limited. The work is not a charming trifle; rather, we are impressed by its great resonances. It is indeed a gem, but gem in the sense of a gathered and concentrated power, a bright clarity beneath a somewhat deceptive setting of lyric grace and simplicity. The charm and the grace are present, but they are not all that is there by a long mile.

But once it is admitted that Ruth is an artistic creation of very high order, it follows that we must become more cautious about making easy judgments about its significance and purpose. For example, Miss Smith in *The Interpreter's Bible* (II, p. 831) says, "This points to the obvious conclusion that the book was composed as a plea for the inclusion of foreigners in the 'assembly of Israel.'" Fohrer denies this and claims that "like the Job legend, the purpose of the narrative from the very outset was edification."[3] I am not especially concerned about the content of these assertions, for I think they have a partial truth, just as it is true—in a way—that *The Tragedy of King Lear* is about filial ingratitude and has—in a way—a purpose of edification. But under these assertions is a hubristic assumption that for a work of high literary art we can say with confidence, "The purpose of X is ...." and fill in the blank with twenty-five words or less. It is, I maintain, one of the main functions of the literary critic to oppose this view. The task of the literary critic is to explore the complex world of the artist and to suggest ways in which we can respond as fully as possible to its multiplicity, its suggestiveness, its richness. But all this is denied us, if lurking in the back of our minds is the secret conviction that art is really little more than the decorative embellishment of the prosaic, that the purpose of a great artist can be reduced to copybook maxims.

Literary studies are also valuable because they present for contemplation structures which differ greatly from the scholarly presentations and are therefore challenging. The most striking example of this in my interpretation is the rôle of the scene at the gate in chapter 4. In the literary interpretation the scene is relatively unimportant, is indeed a deliberate descent into the ordinary with the rhetorical purpose of setting off and separating two scenes of great importance. Yet it is precisely this scene which has attracted the most discussion and analysis in the scholarship, with what I believe to be a violent distortion in the artistic shape of the work. That the author of Ruth had a certain interest in the legal situation is obvious, but that it was not his main interest should be equally apparent. Yet in most scholarly treatments discussion of the legal problems tends to occupy center stage and to push into the wings what most deeply concerned the artist. It is certainly the function of literary analysis to draw attention to this kind of imbalance.

I do not push forward either my own views or the literary view as the truth and the whole truth, but merely as valuable and valid; valid, furthermore, even though it conflicts with the scholarship. I know, for instance, that textual scholars hold that the genealogies of chapter 4 are a later addition and that many of them believe the Davidic materials in general to be additions. This may be true, but it does not destroy my reading. My technique has been to *assume* that Ruth is a unity and to investigate it under this assumption. The result has been the discovery of a set of patterns very hard to explain by any sort of cut-and-patch work or any theory of semiautomatic folk art. But whatever the final truth about the actual composition of Ruth is, and it is undoubtedly complex, analysis in terms of the work itself and the artistry of the work seems necessary as a brake on the tendency of the scholars toward fragmentation. It seems to me that the ordinary scholarly position involves a model of literature in which attention is directed away from the deliberate artist and toward a Lucretian world in which works of art pretty much just happen by a cultural version of particle conglomeration. Against this I hold up a picture of the author of Ruth as an artist in full command of a complex and subtle art, which art is exhibited in almost every word of the story.

X Elijah and Elisha

KENNETH R. R. GROS LOUIS

Although we certainly sympathize with him, and tend to be on his side, we often forget that Hamlet is a galling presence in the rotten state of Denmark. He is particularly galling to Claudius, of course, because he has secret knowledge of the king which others at the court do not share. Shakespeare does not tell us what the average lords and ladies of the Danish court think of Hamlet, but we can imagine their discomfort at his being there, so much in the sun. From their perspective, the king is dead, and long live new King Claudius. Hamlet is such a moody person. He dresses funereally; he casts a pall over court festivities; he says peculiar things, darkened by hints of past sins and future punishments. He plays havoc with the emotions of Polonius' daughter, mocks Polonius himself, is cold and disrespectful to his king and queen. It was not such a bad idea, these lords and ladies might have thought, to ship him off to England. The state, the political entity that is Denmark, is simply not functioning very efficiently or very effectively with Hamlet around. He represents, even more than the external enemy, Fortinbras, a real threat to the security and well-being which is the status quo. He may be dazzling in his courtliness and shrewd in his wit, he may even be right in pointing out the unfortunate gastronomical approximation between the marriage tables and the funeral baked meats. But what does he want? What secret knowledge has he brought back from his precious university?

It may seem a long way from the court of Claudius and Gertrude to that of Ahab and Jezebel. But I think in reading the narratives of Elijah and Elisha, we must be aware of their unique position, like Hamlet's, as outsiders. From the perspective of the society in which they move, they are very much in the minority. They are challenging the security of the court, and a court, we must remember, which has grown politically powerful as a result of its sins; further, they are undermining the state religion; in short, they are attacking the security and seeming well-being of the body politic, linked as it is for defensive reasons with Judah and Phoenicia, Jezebel's homeland, against the common enemy Syria. But this apparent security and strength is intolerable to Elijah and Elisha so long as the God of Israel is being passed by, so long as Baal and the Lord are worshiped as equals. These prophets, like Hamlet, "know not 'seems.'"

Consider the spiritual state of Israel at the time Elijah makes his first appearance before Ahab. Years prior to this meeting, King Solomon had set a bad precedent by building "high places" so that his foreign wives could sacrifice to and worship their strange gods, "Chemosh the abomination of Moab, ... Molech the abomination of the Ammonites" (I Kings 11:7). The Lord is angry with Solomon and, through his prophet Ahijah, divides the kingdom (vv. 30-31). So, too, in the earlier narrative, we have heard Solomon's son, surpassing his father in foolishness, reject the advice of the elders and accept the advice of his youthful followers to tell those who seek peace and compromise that "whereas my father laid upon you a heavy yoke, I will add to your yoke. My father chastised you with whips, but I will chastise you with scorpions" (12:11). We have also heard of his successor Jeroboam's sacrifice to two golden calves and the anger of the Lord in pronouncing through Ahijah the vengeance which that deed provokes: "I . . . will utterly consume the House of Jeroboam, as a man burns up dung until it is all gone" (14:13*b*). I will "give Israel up because of the sins of Jeroboam, which he sinned and which he made Israel to sin" (v. 16). The need for the Lord to avenge himself for the sins of Jeroboam hangs heavily over the narratives of Elijah and Elisha. For it is Ahab, we are told, "as if it had been a light thing for him to walk in the sins of Jeroboam . . . [who] took for wife Jezebel . . . and went and served Baal, and worshiped him" (16:31). The ghost of Jeroboam never leaves the land. Even Jehu, who carries out the destruction of Ahab's family and prophets with such savage thoroughness, "was not careful to walk in the law of the LORD the God of Israel with all his heart; he did not turn from the sins of Jeroboam, which he made Israel to sin" (II Kings 11:31).

When we first meet Elijah, then, Israel is ruled by a king who is only superficially tied to the God of Israel and a queen who worships Baal; a king who has his letters written for him by his wife, who sulks because he cannot buy a neighbor's vineyard, who is exuberant when he proves that Micaiah does indeed prophesy bad things about him; a queen who has not, like Solomon's wives, been content with high places for private worship, but who has imposed her religion on the Israelites and follows to her death a path of fanatical religious persecution of her opponents, who believes, even at the end, that by painting her face and attiring her head she can lure the vengeful agent of God to her side. The true prophets, those who have survived, are hidden in caves; and the land is experiencing physically the drought which the nation is practicing spiritually. Israel has become an actual as well as spiritual wasteland.

Elijah is one, Micaiah is one, Elisha is one ("And what is one?" Milton's Satan had asked Eve), who opposes the religious and political corruption which characterize Ahab's rule. And yet, from the perspective of those in the narrative, even those who should know better, they are, each in his turn, indeed *one*. What can they do in the face of the king's authority and his armies, in the face of 450 prophets of Baal, the 400 or so prophets who attend on Ahab and Jehoshaphat, the armies of men which come to kidnap Elisha to Syria? It is obvious that those whom Elijah and Elisha meet need to be persuaded by miracles that the Lord God is the one and only; even then, one miracle is often not enough. Elijah, for example, feeds a widow and her son for a long time from one jar of flour and one flask of oil, but when the son dies, the widow turns on Elijah and is not persuaded he is a man of God until he resurrects her son from the dead (I Kings 17:9-24). Obadiah has been loyal to the Lord of Israel since childhood, but he hesitates in carrying Elijah's message to Ahab, fearing for his life, not believing enough in Elijah's power through the Lord (18:1-16). Ahab, seizing the political moment, greets Elijah with words which seek to shift the blame for the famine to him: "Is it you, you troubler of Israel?" he says to Elijah (v. 17). The fire miracle seems to persuade the people that "the LORD, he is God; the LORD, he is God" (v. 39); but soon after, when Jezebel threatens Elijah with death, he flees (19:1-3). What has happened to the seemingly newfound faith of the people on Mount Carmel? Naboth suffers wrong at the hands of Ahab, but Jezebel persuades two of the elders of Naboth's city to testify against him and the people to stone him to death (21:1-16). The single voice of Micaiah is drowned out by Ahab's four hundred prophets, and Ahab and Jehoshaphat launch a disastrous campaign (22:5-28). Despite this accumulating evidence of Elijah's skills and of the truth in the words of the Lord's prophet, Ahab's son sends to inquire of Baalzebub the god of Ekron whether he shall recover from a sickness. "Is it because there is no God in Israel?" asks Elijah (II Kings 1:2-3). Shortly after Elijah's death, Elisha is verbally assaulted by small children, who mock him as he returns, after having divided the waters of the Jordan (2:23). Naaman the leper travels a long way to be cured of his disease of leprosy, but his initial response to Elisha's simple directions is anger, a patriotic outburst against the Jordan River. Worse still, the king of Israel suspects a trap when the request from Naaman comes, believing the Syrians are trying to start a quarrel with him. Can Elisha be so far from his mind? Elisha's own servant Gehazi is overcome with greed and follows Naaman to collect an offered reward for himself, lying twice in his master's name in the process (chap. 5). The king rends his clothes when he hears of cannibalism among his people, and instead of seeking Elisha's help, he commands a man to kill him (6:25-32). Elisha sends a young man to anoint Jehu king of Israel in the Lord's name; and Jehu's followers' initial response is, "'Why did this mad fellow come to you?' And he said to them, 'You know the fellow and his talk.' And they said, 'That is not true.'" Even Jehu's followers accuse him of deception (9:1-13). Israel is indeed a spiritual wasteland.

Elijah and Elisha are outsiders in this wasteland. From the perspective of those in authority, they represent a real though small threat to the state. From the perspective of the common people, they bring trouble, they incite slaughters; they also, however, perform miracles which can temporarily dazzle. Few in the narrative share, or share for long, Elijah's and Elisha's firm belief in the God of Israel as the only God and as the God of history; few share with them the understanding which Hamlet reaches prior to his duel with Laertes, an understanding crystallized in a single line, "There's a special providence in the fall of a sparrow." We know, from the earlier prophecies, what Elijah and Elisha know, and tend to see the narratives from their perspectives. But given their world, and seeing it clearly for what it is, our respect for them surely grows, their heroic stature as one against the many magnifies.

Given the context, we can understand why the books of Kings must delineate Elijah and Elisha in two ways. First, they must convey powerfully the force of the Lord God in opposition to the seeming force of Baal; and secondly, a much more difficult literary achievement, they must remain human while doing so. They teach, but they should also attract and delight. The first kind of characterization is the easier of the two. Many critical commentators believe that the historical sources and the folktale sources of the Elijah and Elisha narratives are confused, that some or all of the miracles may initially have been attributed to Elijah, then later shared with Elisha; or some may have been added at a later date. For our purposes, it seems that this problem is not important. What is important is to see what sense of the Lord's power is conveyed through these miracles, to ask why these particular miracles were chosen and to what purpose, to speculate on why certain miracles are repeated in the narratives of both prophets. This is the text we have, whatever its source, this is the text which has influenced literature for hundreds of years.

Consider the miracles associated with the name of Elijah. One—he causes a drought and famine to come into Israel, although he himself is fed by ravens and refreshed by a brook. Two—he feeds a widow and her son for a long time on one jar of flour and one flask of oil. Three—he resurrects a young man from the dead. Four—in the contest with Baal's prophets he causes fire to come from heaven to burn the sacrifice. Five—he brings rain to end the famine. Six—he destroys by fire two groups of fifty soldiers sent by Ahab's son to arrest him (II Kings 1:9-12). Seven—he divides the waters of the Jordan with his cloak (2:8). And, finally, eight—he ascends into heaven with chariots and horses of fire (v. 11). Now consider the miracles of Elisha. First—he divides the waters of the Jordan (vv. 13-14). Second—he provides water for the soldiers and animals of Jehoram and Jehoshaphat as they attack the Moabites (3:9-20). Third—he feeds many from twenty loaves of bread and a few fresh ears of corn (4:42-44). Four—he promises a son to a barren woman (vv. 13-17). Five—he resurrects that son from the dead (vv. 32-36). Six—he cleanses Naaman of his leprosy by having him wash seven times in the Jordan waters (5:1-14). Seven—he blinds with chariots and horses of fire the Syrians who have come to kidnap him (6:11-20). And, finally, eight—he ends a famine in Israel (chap. 7). It is obvious that the major miracles are strikingly similar. Both prophets end a famine in the land; both resurrect a man from the dead; both feed a large number of people, or several for a long period of time from a limited food supply; both make use of fire in destroying or blinding enemies; both divide the water of the Jordan; both make use of water in several of their miracles. Although some of the miracles differ in nature, they are basically the same in their execution and in the means employed. The question, of course, is why the narrative repeats the basic miracles. Whether the material comes from folk or historical sources, it is obviously repetitive when the final narrative is put together. From a literary perspective, the doubling certainly provides emphasis, as doubling provides emphasis in ballads or in lyrics, as not only the doubling but the tripling of the motif of a son avenging his father provides emphasis in *Hamlet*. Such emphasis clarifies for us the main concerns of a narrative. The effect is to reduce our attention, our concentration, on a single episode or the character involved, and to lead us to something beyond the episodes and characters. In the narrative of Kings, we see miracles performed by Elijah; but then, we see essentially the same miracles performed by Elisha. We are aware that it is not Elijah who is the powerful one, since Elisha can do the same things—either Elijah and Elisha are equal in power and magic, or their skill comes from another source. And, of course, everything in Kings points to that other source, the Lord God of Israel. Furthermore, the doubling of the account of the passing of the cloak from Elijah to Elisha reinforces this conclusion. We are told not once, but twice, that the Lord has passed on the power of prophecy and miracle-making from Elijah to Elisha. Indeed, the cloak is passed to Elisha at the command of the Lord. Beyond this, there is another explanation for the doubling of miracles in the narrative. Consider what is involved in the miracles —water, rain, fire, and lightning, corn, bread, and oil, the giving of a son to a barren woman, resurrection from the dead, ascension into heaven. The book of Kings indicates to us what, through Elijah and Elisha, the God of Israel controls. He controls fire, the symbol of civilization; he controls rain and storms, which nourish the land; he controls agriculture, suggested by the multiplication of Elisha's twenty loaves and Elijah's jar of flour and flask of oil; he controls fertility, seen both in the ending of the drought and in the son that Elisha promises to a barren woman; he controls life and death—he can heal Naaman and resurrect the two young men from the dead; he controls the heavens, where he takes his prophet's body, the body not found by Elijah's followers.

Why the emphasis in *this* particular narrative on *these* powers of the Lord—an emphasis augmented by the doubling of the miracles? If we recall the circumstances in Israel, we remember that Jezebel attempted to impose her religion upon the Israelites. And her god, Baal, was principally a god of agriculture, a god who was supposed to control storms and rain, who controlled fertility, who provided corn and oil, who, with his power over the natural cycles of the earth, was thought to control life and death, and to be capable of healing the sick. But Baal is, the narrative strongly informs us, a seeming god. His prophets cannot, after all, end the drought and bring rain; they cannot, as can Elijah and Elisha, affect fertility, agriculture, life and death, the cycles of the earth, that Baal was supposed to control. Elijah and Elisha, the prophets who "know not 'seems'," are aware of this; and it is the message that they attempt to bring to Israel, the message the narrative wishes to convey.

The more difficult literary achievement of the narrative, is the humanization of Elijah and Elisha even as they are shown to be agents of the Lord. It is good to recall what they teach, but it is even better, as Sir Philip Sidney pointed out a long time ago, to recall *them*. That the story is effective in this is attested to by the generations which have recalled Elijah and Elisha, although they may have forgotten their teachings against Baal and their roles as conveyers of the design of the Lord of history. Elisha, it seems to me, is much less interesting as a character, not only because he is less mysterious than Elijah or because he spends most of his time at home giving directions to others, but because he has so few recognizably mortal characteristics. That he is usually the offstage prompter is evident from the narrative. In the moments which *do* reveal certain aspects of Elisha, it seems to me something important is missing. When he goes with Elijah to receive his mantle, Elijah three times tells him to stay put because the Lord has directed Elijah only to Bethel, Jericho, and the Jordan. Each time Elisha insists, "As the LORD lives, and as you yourself live, I will not leave you" (II Kings 2:6*b*). We get a sense of the firmness of Elisha. He is not going to take any orders from Elijah, and he is not prepared to go into sentimental mourning over Elijah's departure. He will remain with him to the end. When they get to the river, Elijah says, "Ask what I shall do for you, before I am taken from you." And Elisha responds, "Let me inherit a double share of your spirit." Elijah rightly points out, "You have asked a hard thing" (vv. 9b-10a). It is not a humble request that Elisha makes, although not in context a proud one; but it indicates again his firmness, his certainty of what he is about to do. Later, he says to the king of Israel, "As the LORD of hosts lives, whom I serve, were it not that I have regard for Jehoshaphat the king of Judah, I would neither look at you, nor see you" (3:14). This is the kind of bluntness we come to expect from Elisha, exemplifying the supreme confidence he has in his own authority and in his own position. After he hears that the king has rent his clothes, he sends him a message, "Why have you rent your clothes? Let him come now to me, that he may know that there is a prophet in Israel" (5:8). We are struck by, "Let him come now to me." Elisha is not going to go out for anyone except his Lord. When he is offered a reward by Naaman after he has cured him, Elisha refuses it: "As the LORD lives, whom I serve, I will receive none" (5:16b). Naaman urges him to take it, but Elisha continues to refuse. He expects no reward. He knows what he has to do, he has his assignment, his mission, and he is going to carry it out. He is completely committed—it is not a time for prizes, for compromises, for making accommodations. When he hears that his servant Gehazi has deceitfully taken the reward for himself, he criticizes and punishes him—"Was it a time to accept money and garments, olive orchards and vineyards, sheep and oxen, menservants and maidservants? Therefore the leprosy of Naaman shall cleave to you, and to your descendants forever" (5:26b-27a). There is not much sympathy for others in Elisha, in part because of his enormous confidence, sense of authority and of mission. But he is wise. He tells the king of Israel, after the enemy has been defeated, "You shall not slay them. . . . Set bread and water before them, that they may eat and drink and go to their master" (6:20-22). Elisha is not excessive in his zeal, and he understands the need not to torture further or to kill a captured enemy force. All these episodes—and there are others—suggest what I believe is missing in the character of Elisha. He is certainly confident, self-assured, firm, and very impressive as a leader. But he never doubts, never questions; he is never rebuked; he never seems to have any awareness of his own position, any consciousness of the fact that he is isolated in the state; he never considers the possibility that he could be wrong. Elisha can instruct us, but we have difficulty arousing any feeling for him.

It is for Elijah that the narrative reserves its great moment, and that great moment is not, it seems to me, the contest with the prophets of Baal (I Kings 18:17-46), but the episode which follows it (19:1-18). The contest itself underlines the juxtaposition between the two scenes and prepares us for the moment. Elijah responds to Ahab's challenge that he has troubled Israel, by accusing Ahab's sinful house of being the cause of the drought. He then asks that the people of Israel, Baal's 450 prophets, and Asherah's 400 prophets, "who eat at Jezebel's table," come to Mount Carmel so that they all can see who is indeed the God of Israel. "If the LORD is God," he says to the people, "follow him; but if Baal, then follow him." They are silent. "I, even I only," he says, "am left a prophet of the LORD," emphasizing to the people that he, one man, is now going to go against many, against the 450 prophets of Baal. He suggests the kind of competition they will have, a spectacular, very dramatic one, that will prove whether the Lord of Israel or Baal is the real God. He shrewdly tells the prophets to go first, confident as he is that they are going to fail. We need to imagine the dramatic scene on Mount Carmel—the people of Israel waiting to see the outcome of the contest, hoping, more practically, for the end of the drought; Ahab, perhaps banking on Baal's prophets (and Baal) to secure his political future; the 450 prophets, chanting to their god, limping around his altar, raving throughout the day, cutting themselves to attract Baal's attention; and Elijah, biding his time, mocking them, pointing out how ineffective their prayers are. "Cry aloud, for he is a god; either he is musing, or he has gone aside, or he is on a journey, or perhaps he is asleep and must be awakened."

Nothing happens from morning to midday—"There was no voice; no one answered, no one heeded." Then Elijah says to the people, "Come near to me." We recognize the dramatic moment that Elijah has built up to. That he has a sense of the drama is indicated when he gives the people instructions: "Fill four jars with water, and pour it on the burnt offering, and on the wood." Consider what the situation is in Israel —there is famine because of the long drought, yet here is Elijah telling the people to fill four jars with water, an enormously precious commodity as we know from having been told of the death of horses and mules, and then to pour the water on the wood. And then as if not satisfied with that dramatic direction, he says, "Do it a second time. . . . Do it a third time." The people surely must carry out these instructions with foreboding and amazement. Elijah then prays to God, reminding the people of the terms of the competition—whoever can fire the sacrifice is God of Israel. "Then the fire of the LORD fell, and consumed the burnt offering, and the wood, and the stones, and the dust, and licked up the water that was in the trench. And when all the people saw it, they fell on their faces; and they said, 'The LORD, he is God; the Lord, he is God.'" The Lord answers Elijah's prayer with this spectacular display of fire, and follows it, in response to Elijah's prophecy, with a storm that brings water to the land. Elijah has triumphed. He warns Ahab to ride his chariot to Jezreel before the rain stops him, and in a final dramatic flair of his own, "girded up his loins and ran before Ahab to the entrance of Jezreel." Elijah seems secure and victorious. He has proven that even though he is one person, "I, even I only," he can, with the help of his God, defeat the prophets of Baal, cause a spectacular fire and a spectacular storm. The people seem to have been persuaded: "The Lord, he is God," they have said. Elijah must feel good. He has demonstrated the enormous power of the Lord to the wayward people of Israel; he must himself sense the enormity of that power, and the grandeur of his accomplishment.

And yet, the day after this triumph, when Elijah hears that Jezebel has ordered his death, "Then he was afraid, and he arose and went for his life." The juxtaposition is striking. Why, after he has seen the spectacular fire display, and had his belief in his God fully confirmed, should he fear vain Jezebel's threat? Following a day's journey in the wilderness, he stops to rest and asks God that he might die. We get a sense of Elijah's state of mind—he is depressed, either because he fled for his life or because his victory over the prophets of Baal seems not to have persuaded anyone. He is back where he was before—"I, even I only." "It is enough," he says, "now O LORD, take away my life; for I am no better than my fathers." Unlike Elisha, he experiences this moment of despair, of doubt, of questioning. He is no longer certain, he does not have the confidence that he had one day earlier when he challenged the prophets of Baal. An angel comes and gives him food, and tells him, "Arise and eat, else the journey will be too great for you." The journey that Elijah is physically undertaking may be difficult; but perhaps the angel is also thinking of Elijah's more important spiritual journey, his mission as a prophet. The angel's words may convey a mild rebuke to Elijah, for his despair and his sudden loss of faith.

Elijah eats and drinks and, with the strength from that nourishment, travels forty days and forty nights to a cave on Mount Horeb. The Lord says to him, "What are you doing here, Elijah?" There are several ways to read the question. If the emphasis is on *you*, then the Lord may simply be asking a question; if the emphasis is on *here*, the Lord may intend further rebuke. Why is Elijah in this cave on the mountain instead of instructing the people of Israel and opposing God's enemies? "I have been very jealous for the LORD, the God of Hosts," says Elijah, "for the people of Israel have forsaken thy covenant, thrown down thy altars, and slain thy prophets with the sword, and I, even I only, am left; and they seek my life, to take it away." Elijah repeats what he had said to the prophets of Baal and to all the people on Mount Carmel, "I, even I only, am left." The Lord tells him, "'Go forth, and stand upon the mount before the LORD.' And behold, the LORD passed by, and a great and strong wind rent the mountains, and broke in pieces the rocks before the LORD, but the LORD was not in the wind; and after the wind an earthquake, but the LORD was not in the earthquake; and after the earthquake a fire, but the LORD was not in the fire; and after the fire a still small voice. And when Elijah heard it, he wrapped his face in his mantle and went out and stood at the entrance of the cave. And behold, there came a voice to him, and said, 'What are you doing here, Elijah?'" The question is repeated in an entirely different context. The first time the question is asked, Elijah presumably has no answer, although God knows why he is there, and Elijah knows why he is there. This time the question follows the wind, the earthquake, the fire, the still small voice. After he has seen all these things, and seen them with some understanding, the Lord asks him, "What are you doing *here*, Elijah?" How could Elijah ever have been depressed, how could he have come to his present state of mind as well as to this geographical location?

In recalling the contest with the prophets of Baal, we may recognize what it is that has depressed Elijah, and indeed what he has learned here that the people of Israel have not learned. His expectation of God was adversely affected by the contest with Baal's prophets. God's presence was visually and spectacularly felt in the fire and the great storm. But here, Elijah sees a wind, an earthquake, and a fire, all without the Lord in them, and then, a still small voice. The fire miracle may have been too much for Elijah. He may have forgotten that God does not always come with spectacular displays of his power. He is not like Baal, he is not like Ahab and Jezebel with their thunderous threats. Elijah learns something about God that his very great triumph over the prophets of Baal prevented him from recognizing. God is not like earthly kings. The Lord sends him back, "Go, return on your way to the wilderness of Damascus," and gives him a series of instructions, including "Elisha . . . you shall anoint to be prophet in your place." Is this a criticism of Elijah? Or does it merely indicate that Elijah's mission is completed and that Elisha is going to take up his mantle? The last words of the Lord before he and Elijah part are: "Yet I will leave seven thousand in Israel, all the knees that have not bowed

189

to Baal, and every mouth that has not kissed him." Just a moment before, Elijah had said to God, "I, even I only, am left." And he had said the same thing the day before, "I, even I only, am left." As it turns out, he is wrong. He was never as isolated as he thought he was. He should not have made his isolation his virtue, and then that virtue his despair.

Amidst the thunderings of Ahab and Jezebel, Jehu's destruction of the house of Ahab and the followers of Baal, the chariots and horses of fire, the spectacles, the noises, the lightnings and storms and winds, the working out of the Lord's terrible vengeance, there emerges in Kings the loudest sound of all: a still small voice. In the context of their world, Elijah and Elisha are still small voices themselves, speaking of justice and righteousness to a government which seeks to assassinate them, to a people which believes only when awed by spectacular displays of power. How long before the people of Israel will learn what Elijah has learned, that God and his prophets may not operate in earthquakes and in wind and in fire, may not seek to rival the temporal power of earthly kings? How long before they realize that there is a special providence in the fall of a sparrow, that the Lord, unlike Baal and Ashtaroth, unlike Ahab and Jezebel, is also a still small voice, so still that it may make no sound at all? "Had I but time," Elijah might have said to his followers, as Hamlet says to Horatio before he dies, "O, I could tell you—but let it be."

XI The Book of Jonah

THAYER S. WARSHAW, English Department,
Newton (Massachusetts) North High School

Fact or fiction, the story of Jonah intends to teach the reader
by teaching its hero a lesson. Precisely what lesson, or lessons, it intends to teach has been debated by commentators
over the centuries, as we shall see. Nevertheless, most scholars seem to agree on at least two. One is that love, human
and divine, is more important than "law and order," as Erich
Fromm puts it.[1] A second lesson is that in the case of God
this love is, and in the case of men it should be, universal
rather than restricted to one group, whatever that group's
special relation to God.

Structure, Language, and the Theme of Mercy

The narrative clearly expresses the first theme through its
structure and, especially in the last episode, through its use
of language. Consider the events of the story, apart from
biblical and historical contexts. In the opening episode Jonah
is told to deliver what we later find to be an unconditional
prophecy of doom: for its wickedness Nineveh will be destroyed. But he is immediately aware, according to his later
complaint, that the fatal words will not prove true and that
God, being merciful, will spare Nineveh when it repents. So
he decides to evade his role in the drama of condemnation of,
and then mercy to, the wicked Ninevites.

Jonah takes passage on a ship, against which God hurls a
storm. He admits to the frantic sailors that the storm is his
fault and that they can save themselves by throwing him
overboard into the tempestuous sea. Reluctantly they do so,
and he is swallowed by a great fish. In this "whale" episode
Jonah finds himself the recipient of God's mercy. Whether or
not his psalm of submission is a later interpolation, as has

191

been argued, is irrelevant; we are dealing with the story in its present form, as it was accepted into the biblical canon. (Equally unimportant is the controversy over whether it was a "great fish," as the present story translates it from the Hebrew, or a "whale," as it is referred to in Matt. 12:40 and elsewhere. Western literary tradition takes the Christian Bible, Old Testament and New Testament, as a whole. The fish has become for us a whale, the only fish known to literal readers that looks large enough to swallow a man. We also may postpone the question of whether he is saved *from* the whale or *by* the whale.) Let us look briefly at his submissive psalm.

Jonah's prayer presents difficulties, but from the point of view of the literary critic it contains many echoes of motifs in the story that surrounds it, making it an artistic part of the whole. Our main interest here will be in what the prayer reveals of Jonah's reaction to his situation. He seems to see his physical experience in spiritual terms. The belly of the whale becomes for him the "belly of Sheol" (2:3), a kind of hell or realm of death. He realizes that he is "cast out from [the Lord's] presence" (2:4), after finding that he cannot escape "from the presence of the LORD." (1:3) He fled in a futile attempt to separate himself physically from God, but his flight, he now realizes, has caused God to separate himself spiritually from Jonah. (The RSV has Jonah saying, "the waters closed in over me" [2:5], but some older translations say "even to the soul." The Hebrew word is *nefesh*, the same word that the RSV translates as "soul" in 2:7. The earlier, now disputed, translation would reinforce Jonah's spiritualization of his experience: it might justifiably indicate his feeling that more than his body is submerged.) Jonah has fled from God and his mission; finally his soul faints within him, and he remembers the Lord and prays (2:7). In this prayer he reestablishes his position of subservience to God in an ordered universe. He is then delivered onto dry land.

The lesson of his merciful deliverance, however, is insufficiently absorbed for him to transfer it to the Ninevites. It seems to be too much for either the mind to grasp or the heart to accept in such a person as Jonah. He only learns again what he already knew, that disobedience brings punishment and that he must do his duty. On the next call he goes directly to Nineveh without protest. But, as we see from his reaction to God's sparing of Nineveh, he has not learned the main lesson, that there is a value higher than justice.

Jonah's offer to save the sailors by sacrificing himself shows less commitment to compassion than to simple justice: they have done no wrong, either to him or to God, so they should not suffer; he has disobeyed God, so it is right that he be punished. Not only is this fair and symmetrical; he has faith that God will abide by his own orderly law: having punished the guilty, he will not harm the innocent. In contrast, God's deliverance of Jonah is an instance of mercy and forgiveness to a runaway who humbly returns spiritually as he "remembers the Lord" and who is brought back physically. The act of mercy is accepted by a grateful and chastened man who has nonetheless undergone no fundamental change of values.

He preaches the word of God, Nineveh repents, and God relents. But Jonah has no sympathy for God's mercy to the Ninevites; in fact, he is exceedingly displeased. He has been made to look like a fool and a liar because his prophecy of certain doom has proved false. A man of law and order, he seems to feel that God's inexorable word, his law of retributive justice and the integrity of his order, have been broken. Undeserving people, it appears to him, have received God's mercy and love; and his harrowing experience at sea has led only to still further undesirable consequences at Nineveh.

The final episode takes place outside the city, where Jonah sits complaining bitterly. We have seen two instances of God's compassion for errant creatures: first Jonah and then the Ninevites have been spared. The third instance of God's mercy is the provision of a plant to shield the sullen Jonah from the day's heat—which God has increased in order to make the plant more welcome to Jonah. So that Jonah and the reader will not miss the message, there is a change in terminology. "You *pity* the plant." Pity! Really? One would think that the farthest emotion from Jonah's soul would be pity toward the plant. Why does God use that word?

The root of the Hebrew word translated as "pity" is *hus*, also translated elsewhere as "to spare." The translator's use of "pity" here is quite appropriate in at least one respect: neither the Hebrew *hus* nor the English "pity" has been used to describe the previous instances of God's compassion or mercy. Thus, a knowledge of Hebrew is not necessary to see the point. The new word calls attention to a new value which Jonah must learn: that mercy is not merely a capricious and negative suspension of law and order, but is an affirmative act of love. The implication is that man, made in God's image, should emulate God's compassion.

We should note the literary craftsmanship of the story. Its structure, careful plotting, and interwoven motifs reinforce the theme of the priority of mercy over retributive justice. The three examples of God's mercy interact. The disobedient Jonah prays and is released from the whale. Likewise, the wicked Ninevites repent and are saved from destruction. The third instance, like the first, favors the recalcitrant Jonah, this time with shelter from the sun—even without a prayer of submission. It is also linked to the second instance, both by Jonah and by God, but with a characteristic difference, for the edification of the reader.

Unthinking and selfish, Jonah feels the same about the two episodes, linking them by expressing his feelings in identical words. His reaction both to the deliverance of Nineveh and to the destruction of the plant is, "It is better for me to die than to live." That is not God's way of connecting the two events, however. He wants Jonah to change his perspective: to think about the word "pity," to see the real connection between the two instances of it, and to answer a question. Jonah's selfish concern for his own comfort is called, perhaps with irony, "pity" for the plant. God indulgently attributes pity to Jonah as if speaking to a small child ("You're sorry you hit your baby brother; you love him, don't you?"). This same pity is just what God says he, himself, has shown to the Ninevites (again the word root is *hus*). His final words ask Jonah the question—rhetorical to the reader, but evidently a problem to Jonah: "Should not I pity Nineveh?" The implied logic is typical of the rabbis: if pity is due the lowly plant, how much more is pity due the far more valuable and numerous inhabitants of Nineveh!

This theme of mercy accounts for the selection of the Jonah story in the Jewish liturgical calendar to be read at the climactic point of Yom Kippur, the Day of Atonement, of repentance and forgiveness. Ten days of penitence start with the New Year and end with the Yom Kippur day of penance, of prayer and fasting that begin at the previous sundown. The afternoon service, which ends this most solemn day of the year, features the reading of the book of Jonah. Its message of repentance and forgiveness is considered poignantly appropriate for the holy day.

Biblical Background, Satire, and the Theme of Universalism

The second theme of the Jonah story is that in the divine (and, by implication, human) scale of values universal love is higher than group loyalty, especially an ethnocentrism so exclusive that it leads to xenophobia. This message was clear to the thoughtful early readers or hearers of the story, who undoubtedly were familiar with the traditions that eventually became Scripture. The modern reader may need a bit of biblical background.

Jonah, the son of Amittai, was remembered as the prophet who correctly predicted Israel's expansion through conquest of neighboring Syria (2 Kings 14:25). Nineveh was immediately recognized as the capital of Assyria, which destroyed Israel (2 Kings 16:6, 18:10) and was the home of Sennacherib, oppressor of Judah (2 Kings 19:36; Isa. 37:37). It was an immoral city whose destruction was foretold by both Zephaniah (2:13) and Nahum (2:8). Nineveh was to the early audience what the Babylon of the book of Revelation became for Christians. For God to show mercy to Nineveh was an arresting suggestion. For such a nationalistic prophet as Jonah to carry a message which he knew would result in delivering Nineveh from destruction would be, to say the least, ironic. Thus Jonah does indeed become the ironic hero, protesting against the universalism that the story exemplifies and exemplifying the kind of exclusive ethnocentrism against which the story protests. The more ridiculous he is made to look, the stronger is the case against the value he represents.

Let us, then, reread the story with this new perspective, no longer accepting Jonah's words and actions at face value. Edwin Good calls the book of Jonah a satire that makes its point through many instances of the literary device of irony.[2] Jonah's name means "dove," but he is far from Noah's messenger of hope. *Ben Amittai* means "son of faithfulness" or "son of truth," but he is neither faithful to God or his calling nor eager to proclaim the truth. He says, probably reeling off the formula by rote, "I fear the LORD, the God of heaven, who made the sea and the dry land"; yet he has refused to do what his "feared" Lord commanded. Even as he says this, he is fleeing on God's sea to go to God's land of Tarshish—to get "away from the presence" of the omnipotent and omnipresent Lord. (We shall see that this is not the only case of Jonah's repeating a formula of faith whose words are belied by his actions as he speaks.) This contradiction of words by actions is typical of a voyage that is so full of ironies.

In the Bible the sea is almost invariably hostile, but Jonah assumes that it will be the helpful means of escape to a haven. Perhaps he thinks that since the sea is often represented as the chaotic opponent of the God who stands for order in the universe, it will be on his side. If so, he is wrong again. God controls the sea with his great wind and even uses its symbolic representative, the monstrous fish, as his instrument for both chastening and delivering Jonah. During the perilous storm when knowledgeable sailors are frightened, he foolishly sleeps, either in ignorance of the danger or in smug and unjustified assurance. The pagan sailors have more compassion for the man who admits he has caused the loss of their cargo and the threat to their lives than he later has for the Ninevites, who have done him no harm. Like the Ninevites, the sailors show more fear of the Lord than does the Lord's chosen prophet. Furthermore, he who started his flight from God as a paying passenger on the ship ironically ends his journey by being vomited up by a fish appointed by God, upon the "dry land" which, in his own words, God has made. And finally, the fearsome fish, which Jonah calls his Sheol, his death, is in fact God's appointed vehicle for saving his life.

The events at Nineveh seem to add up to satiric hyperbole, emphasizing the paradox of the unwelcome "success" of this reluctant spokesman of God. The city's size appears to be greatly exaggerated: "three days' journey in breadth," or diameter, would make a walled metropolis nearly as large as New York City. Its size and its reputation for wickedness make its sudden and complete repentance all the more unbelievable, and even its beasts must go without food and water, wear sackcloth, and cry mightily to God.

The climactic ridicule of Jonah comes in the episode outside the city. We are presented the picture of a prophet who sulks because of his accomplishment: with only a few words and in record time, he has just "converted" the largest and most evil city of the age. (Jonah is listed among the "minor" prophets. Minor indeed! Jeremiah, whose language echoes through the description of Nineveh's repentance, might have taken a lesson from him about effectiveness. But perhaps Jeremiah tried too hard. Jonah is the cause of the "conversion" of both the pagan sailors and the Ninevites to the fear of the true God, yet in neither case was that his intention.) Instead of rejoicing, he wants "to see what would become of the city" that has been spared; one can only infer that he hopes for the worst, a new reversal on the part of either God or the Ninevites that will result in their destruction. Presumably, he accepted his own deliverance from the whale as only natural under God's covenant with Israel; God's forgiveness of a prophet who has strayed, but then become honestly humble, is part of the contract. But wicked pagans have not strayed, they were never on the true "way"; and they are enemies of God's chosen people—doubly excluded from the terms of the covenant as he understands them.

The ironies continue. In the same breath with which he expresses his resentment at God's mercy, he petulantly acknowledges his belief that the Lord—whose voice he is privileged to hear and for whom he is chosen to speak—is a "gracious God and merciful, slow to anger, and abounding in *steadfast love" (hesed).* As with his formulaic identification of his God to the sailors, he is merely mouthing a liturgical cliché which recurs in the Bible (and in prayers) so often as to have become familiar to all early readers and to observant Jews today. Again his words are belied by his actions and his attitudes and motivation. Had Jonah consciously considered the language of the formula, he would have noticed that steadfast love, *hesed,* which is the fount from which pity *(hus)* flows, was precisely what Jonah himself was not showing toward the Ninevites. Because of his insensitivity to the implications of the word he has just used, God must shortly remind him of the true meaning of merciful acts by using that word—"pity" *(hus).*

Outside of Israel, *hus* had originally described a kind of arbitrary executive clemency beyond what is earned either by penance or penitence, a sovereign's power that goes beyond the legal confines of a judge's discretion. In the context of the biblical covenant between God and Israel, *hus* instead issued out of a relationship of *hesed,* steadfast love or loving kindness. This relationship is expressed by Nehemiah (13:22): "spare *(hus)* me according to the greatness of thy steadfast love" *(hesed).* It is the kind of unselfish, unmerited love that we also associate with the Christian concept of *agape,* as in 1 Corinthians 13. (The idea of loving pity for a plant is reminiscent of the "I-thou" relationship which Buber says a person may have with any of God's creatures, even a tree.) Early readers would connect *hus* with *hesed,* pity with steadfast love.

Further ironies link Jonah's two miraculously appointed natural shelters, the short-lived plant and the living submarine: what God could not teach Jonah by means of a fearsome sea monster he will teach him by means of a tiny worm. And Jonah misreads the role of both the whale and the plant. He sees the whale as a threat, his Sheol, whereas God has provided the great fish to deliver him from the storm onto the land. He sees the plant as a welcome relief, whereas God has provided it only so that he can deprive Jonah of its shade.

Twice Jonah whines, "It is better for me to die than to live." Twice God patiently, and ironically, replies, "Do you do well to be angry?" Does Jonah "do well" to resent the repentance and salvation of the Ninevites? Does he do well to wish to die just because a plant has withered and the heat is oppressive? (In the heat of his anger he has forgotten his booth.) Where is his sense of values? Equally ironic is God's final question: is Jonah's concern for (the loss of) the plant more appropriate than God's concern for all the dumb animals and people of Nineveh? The juxtaposing of the two cases underlines the inappropriateness of Jonah's equal distress at the destruction of the plant and the sparing of Nineveh, of which even the cattle, anticlimactically, are worth more than the plant. Jonah's objection to God's mercy to those undeserving heathens and Jonah's concern for the plant are exposed as mere self-centered irritability over his discomfiture at being proved a false prophet of doom and his discomfort at being deprived of shade from the sun.

Again the literary craftsmanship is effective. The discrepancies between appearance and reality, words and actions, meanness of spirit and magnanimity provide for the reader the distance from which to examine Jonah's actions and values critically and weigh them against those of God. We have a virtuoso exhibition of the techniques of satire, irony, and ridicule that supports the theme of universalism against a too narrow ethnocentrism.

Suspense: Why Did Jonah Flee?

At least two other examples of obviously conscious use of narrative techniques add much to the story's interest, both as a work of art and as a subject of controversial interpretation and speculation. Each enhances one of the two questions that have consistently intrigued commentators: "What is the real reason for Jonah's flight from his duty?" and "What is the real meaning of the story?"

The first question arises with the second sentence of the story. Prophets by definition proclaim God's message. Only a protestation of unworthiness is a traditionally acceptable excuse for delay in carrying out such a mission. Taken by itself as a piece of literature, as it may well have existed before being included in the canon, the story offers no immediate reason for Jonah's peculiar initial behavior. Jonah does not give his own reason until the final episode: I knew from the first that Nineveh would repent and you would forgive. The narrative technique is suspense; it urges the reader along to solve the puzzle. But there may be a more substantive reason for withholding this particular bit of information. Perhaps it is postponed so that the reader will examine it more critically and question it. Is this a valid excuse? Is it his real reason? Characterization of Jonah up to this point has been subtle but cumulative. By the time the reader reaches Jonah's own explanation, he may have already formed some opinion of his character, with which Jonah's justification of his flight does not jibe.

In this connection, we note that the exact content of the proposed message also is not immediately revealed; we do not get its full implication until we hear Jonah actually "crying out" against Nineveh. Again, the thoughtful reader may ask questions. Does this seemingly unconditional and fatal condemnation justify his reluctance? Did he get and did he transmit correctly this cruel message from a merciful God? Might there have been a promise or hint that this was only a warning of what might happen if Nineveh did not mend its wicked ways?

Indeed, some scholarly commentators have tried to explain Jonah's refusal to speak for God by speculating on the actual nature and intent of the message itself.[3] One opinion is that the words "Yet forty days, and Nineveh shall be overthrown" were intended, and rightly understood by Jonah and the Ninevites, to be conditional: repent or else. Another explanation is that God's message had originally been conditional, but that Jonah for good reason changed it to unconditional: you are doomed. A third is that the divine message was actually both verbally and intentionally unconditional, but that Jonah knew God would not fulfill it—that it was therefore untrue and false. A fourth holds that the message was unconditional and not false; it eventually came true, after Nineveh's repentance had won it a temporary reprieve (Tobit, 4:14, speaks of the future fulfillment of Jonah's prophecy). A fifth focuses on the word "overthrown" and says that it does not mean physical destruction, but implies a spiritual throwing over, a moral revolution.

Several justifications for Jonah's flight assume that the story is a lesson for sinning and stiff-necked Jews: the Ninevites believed and repented; Israel should do, or should have done, the same. One group says that Jonah refused to go, even boarded the ship so that he might be drowned rather than cause Nineveh to repent, out of loyalty to Israel, in order to protect it from the humiliation of being shown up, or the disaster of perhaps being replaced in God's favor, by the Ninevites. For this unselfish but misguided thinking, God was patient with Jonah's disobedience and subsequent rebelliousness. Or, knowing that Nineveh would repent and God grant mercy, Jonah did not want to deliver an unconditional message of certain doom and then be found a false prophet, thereby discrediting his calling, or his people, or even his God. A third kind of argument is that Jonah was reluctant to go to Nineveh because he felt he was needed more at home, as God's messenger to sinful Israel.

Others defend Jonah on different grounds. Bickerman suggests that Jonah's use of the formulaic *hesed* outside the city is quite conscious and is intended as a reproach to remind God that the "almost mechanical reciprocity between man's repentance and God's changing mind" about Nineveh is not worthy of the God of *hesed*—the God of pure, unselfish, unmerited loving kindness. (The terms of this argument would not be unfamiliar to a Calvinist.) Rauber suggests that Jonah refused the denunciatory mission because he objected to the impropriety of such a cruel threat by the God of love and would not be a party to it; Jonah was as much *mensh* as *shlemiel.*[4]

Psychoanalysis offers another tool for analyzing some aspects of literature. Fromm throws an interesting light on Jonah's character by examining the first half of the story. Jonah's external adventures symbolize his inner experiences. Wishing to escape from God, his conscience, and his obligation to his fellow man, he progressively withdraws from communication with other human beings. He seeks more and more intensive protection and isolation: "going into the ship, going into the ship's belly, falling asleep, being in the ocean, and being in the fish's belly." As with many other antisocial isolates, "escape into protective isolation ends in the terror of being imprisoned."[5] Jonah is, as he says in his psalm, in hell.

Learning by Example: What Does It Mean?

The book of Jonah, with its balance between narration and dialogue and its several dramatic events tightly packed into only 54 verses, carries one swiftly along toward the end. The story begins and ends with God's words to Jonah, in both cases making demands of him. That final question, however, asks Jonah and the reader to think not only about the specific question, but also about the story's meaning. The story has presented instances of a man and his God in action, each with different values, and asks both Jonah and the reader to draw their own conclusions from the evidence. (One may think of parables elsewhere in the Bible that follow this pattern.) Here we have another narrative (and pedagogical) technique: show, don't tell. It forces us to use our own imagination, each in his own way. It is not surprising, therefore, that commentators have come up with an array of answers to the question of the meaning of the story.

From the outset quite scholarly commentators have had an impulse toward parable, with both Jewish and Christian orientations. For some Jews the story's purpose is to explain Israel's exile: it had not followed Nineveh's example. In the same vein, another group takes its cue from Jeremiah (51:34,

44) and allegorizes the fish as Nebuchadnezzar or Babylon, with Jonah as Israel being released from captivity to carry out its universal destiny. (The dispute about the book's date, even whether it was written before or after the exile, need not concern us.) For others, its purpose is to reassure sinful Israel that it can be saved despite its prophets of doom, for God has spared even the wicked and doomed Nineveh. Still others say that the book was written to explain to Jews how it was that some prophecies, or perhaps the specific prophecies of the destruction of the gentiles, had not yet been fulfilled.

In the Gospel of Matthew (12:40, 41) Jesus likens his coming resurrection to Jonah's deliverance from the whale's belly after three days and then contrasts the repentant Ninevites with Jews who refuse to accept him. In this context Jonah's physical experience makes him a "type," a prefiguring of the Christ, as is evidenced in early Christian art. Most Christian exegetes, however, focus on God's disapproval of Jonah's lack of compassion for the pagan Ninevites. Some have gone even further, forcing this interpretation into an anti-Semitic lesson: Jonah represents benighted Judaism as opposed to enlightened Christianity; he is the typically ethnocentric and xenophobic Jew as opposed to the universalistic Christian; Judaism and the Jews object to the redemption of the "nations." (The Hebrew *goyim* and the Latin derivate "gentiles," both condescending terms to designate outsiders today, originally meant merely "nations"—parallel examples of how changing values change languages.)

This anti-Semitic interpretation has persisted from Augustine to the present day, even though opposing Christian scholars beginning with Jerome reject it because, among other things, it is inconsistent with Jesus' own words about Jonah as a type of Christ and about Israel as a favored nation. Later scholars, Christian and Jewish, also point out that if Jonah the character in the book does represent the dominant feeling in Israel when the book was circulated orally or first written down, the book of Jonah itself represents at least a minority view that was canonized by Israel.

One might also question whether universalism and group loyalty are mutually exclusive; the book of Jonah may have been trying to right a balance between the two values. In any case, the pejorative view contrasts two demonstrably false stereotypes, Jewish elitism and Christian universalism, or two others, Jewish preference for vengeance and Christian commitment to love—biased views usually proclaimed by people who do not love Jews. As Bickerman says in another context, "there has hardly ever been a tribe that was not elected by heaven";[6] and, to paraphrase him again, any monotheism—Christian, Jewish, or Muslim—is universalistic only in the sense that everyone is welcome within the fold of its own true faith.

The book itself has come in for some ridicule from various nonbelievers. Early heathens made fun of a people that could believe such a whopper as the whale. More recently, representatives of the English and French Enlightenment claimed that in their day Jonah would be sent to an institution, or that the book was an intentional satire on all prophecy. Bickerman also reports some ingenious rationalizations of the miracle of the whale: "Jonah was picked up by a ship named 'Big Fish,' or spent three nights at an inn 'At the Sign of the Whale,' or in a bathing establishment called 'The Whale'; or . . . Jonah dreamed the whole incident when, during the storm, he fell into a profound sleep."[7]

Literary Analysis: Some Considerations

Carefully wrought, the book of Jonah should be carefully read. Its structure forces the three instances of God's compassion into interaction. The contrasting language used by Jonah and by God to link the second and third instances further supports the theme that love is more important than law and order. So much is clear from a perceptive but limited reading of the story. With the addition of a little biblical background we note the irony of Jonah's call to go to Nineveh, and we look more closely for other ironies in the story. Some acquaintance with the relationship between Old Testament concepts of "pity" and "steadfast love" helps us see that Jonah himself represents those against whom the story protests: people who mouth their belief in God, the compassionate creator of all mankind, but who deny their own compassion to those of his creatures that are outside their own group. Satire points up the theme of universalism.

Beyond these readings there remains room for further speculation. Because of the story's use of suspense, the reader may question Jonah's version of both the nature of God's message and Jonah's own reason for disobeying God, neither of which is made explicit at the outset. The rhetorical final question, forcing the reader to supply his own meaning to the story, also encourages him to make imaginative use of his knowledge of human nature and of scholarly research into the historical and literary contexts of the story. Literary analysis that goes beyond the story itself and its closely related biblical background to answer the questions of Jonah's motivation and the story's meaning can be stimulating and enriching, both for the appreciation of literary values and for the enlargement of the spirit. Obviously, the biblical scholar has much to contribute that is beyond the literary critic's competence. So does the religious commentator. But there are dangers.

The characteristic role of the literary critic is to read the Bible, as he does other literature, primarily to savor it as a work of art. How does its craftsmanship work as an esthetic performance? How well do its techniques serve the work's meaning, its main idea or theme? As a rounded human being, the literary critic also hopes to find some insight into the nature of the universe or the human condition, to enlarge the reader's spirit. The biblical scholar's primary interest is to throw light on the text by examining the historical and cultural traditions out of which it came and the long history of other scholarly attempts to unlock its meaning. Again, the biblical scholar is also motivated in his scholarly pursuit to find clues to meaning for his own life and the lives of others.

The search for meaning in the universe and in human experience does not characterize the activity of the literary critic *qua* literary critic or the biblical scholar *qua* biblical scholar. In that sense, it is a secondary purpose, even though to the critic or scholar as human beings it may be most basic. For the religious commentator, on the other hand, the primary interest in the Bible is precisely this matter of discovering its message for the reader: what shall one believe and how shall one act? He also examines the techniques by which the Bible presents its message, and he does research into its historical contexts. But though he may expend even most of his time and effort on literary analysis and exegetical scholarship, these pursuits are secondary to his role as religious commentator.

Religious commentators on Jonah, whether Christian or Jewish, quite often read the story through theological glasses that color human events, making them *exempla*. Sometimes the external information and theological presuppositions or speculation that they bring to bear on these events serve only religious polemics or homiletics. In such cases the results of their efforts, however valuable for moral edification, must be carefully weighed before being accepted as helpful insights into the craftsmanship of a work of literary art.

In examining character motivation and the meaning of a story, the literary critic invites use of the imagination and familiarity with the work's contexts. He will rather err, however, on the side of reading out of the text too literally than expose himself to the charge of reading into the text too liberally. Reading the story of Jonah as a parable, with Jonah as a symbol of xenophobia, calls for close adherence to textual evidence and a very careful concern for the clear relevance of any contribution from the story's contexts.

Nor need the literary critic consider arguments over the historicity of the miracles. On the contrary, supernatural elements in a piece of literature, even in religious literature, may be considered for their literary effect. They may be seen to function, as they do in the third act of *Our Town*, so as to suggest a special perspective for quite mundane human experiences and motivations. One need not even speculate on the artistry or intent of a biblical "author"; it is the beauty and effectiveness of the literature itself that the critic examines.

This is not to deny a quasi literary defense for even al
legorical treatment of biblical literature, especially if one
believes that the Holy Spirit inspired the writing of scriptural allegories. It is to separate such a treatment from those
that depend more centrally on the usual norms and techniques of literary criticism. Nor is it to say that a religious
interpretation may not issue from a more edifying or higher
moral perspective. It is rather to suggest what is the more
appropriate activity for a public school class examining the
Bible as literature.

It would be neither unusual nor improper for a secondary
school teacher of such a class to give students an assignment
to speculate on our two main questions: "Drawing on your
own experience and imagination, why do you think Jonah
fled? and/or, What is the main point of the story? Support
your opinion by referring to the text." Among the factors
that will account for the range of responses will be the agility
of students' imaginations, their unequal knowledge of the historical and literary contexts of the story, and their differing
religious traditions or value systems. The farther these take
students away from the actual text, the more nervous a
teacher of literature should become.

Naturally, the teacher must guide students through some
acquaintance with the contexts of the book of Jonah—as our
discussion of the book's irony demonstrates. The literary
context, the Bible, is there for the reading. The historical
context is less clear because of strong differences of opinion
as to when and under what circumstances it was written.
Religious or humanistic assumptions that may affect the
reader's attitude toward the text have to be acknowledged.

The foregoing sections of the present essay are arranged
roughly in a sequence that proceeds from reading the text
without contextual information and taking it at face value;
then to a close, more sophisticated textual analysis that
draws on some literary and linguistic background; and finally
to comments that increasingly include information and speculation drawn from outside the text. Literature teachers are
urged to favor the earlier, rather than the later techniques.

XII Isaiah: Chapters 40–55

KENNETH R. R. GROS LOUIS

Although Isaiah usually appears as one book in editions of the Bible, most modern biblical scholars seem to agree that it actually consists of two distinct parts, the break coming at chapter 40 and marked by striking changes in style and attitude. Some biblical scholars argue for even a third part in Isaiah, coming after chapter 55. For reasons which I will not discuss here, I believe that chapters 40–55 do constitute a single, coherent statement. And it is this statement, introduced and controlled by the great poem of chapter 40, which I would like to describe.

Songs and poems are often written for armies going to war and for armies returning from war. The former kind tend to be didactic and public. They sketch out the conflict to come in terms of an almost universal struggle between good and evil; they outline responsibilities and duties; they are dominated by images of power and strength, of armies clashing by night; they appeal to our most public and patriotic thoughts and emotions. Songs and poems written for armies returning from war, however, tend to be less public; the personal, private reality of what has occurred constantly impinges on the universality of the struggles; the exhaustion and depression of war are pervasive; there is, of course, celebration and an occasional shout of triumph, but these always coexist with the realization that pieces need to be put back together again. The land is parched, the voice hoarse, the body weary. It is a time for renewal in the many senses of that word; man's spirit needs to be aroused and encouraged, persuaded that the war has not destroyed former beliefs and values. The major themes of Second Isaiah—the strong monotheism, emphasis on love, warnings to God's enemies, belief in God as creator and controller of history—are obviously not new themes in the Old Testament. Its images, like its themes, also are not new. What is new is the tone of celebration in chapters 40–55, a celebration the audience is asked to participate in. This is an account of a triumphant return, a rebirth, a renewal; it is a series of poems for an army returning from war, written to revitalize, to arouse and encourage by speaking comfortingly and confidently to a frustrated, religiously perplexed people.

The setting of the opening is perhaps God's council at which God's decision is announced:

> Comfort, comfort my people,
>   says your God.
> Speak tenderly to Jerusalem,
>   and cry to her
> that her warfare is ended,
>   that her iniquity is pardoned,
> that she has received from the LORD'S hand
>   double for all her sins. (40:1-3)

God implies that he is shifting to another stage in the divine plan, one in which Israel will prosper; but he also seems to acknowledge that his people have suffered a great deal; they need to be treated "tenderly." A voice carries God's announcement to earth. "In the wilderness prepare the way of the LORD,/make straight in the desert a highway for our God" (v. 3). The herald, we notice, does not speak of comfort; instead, with a double imperative—prepare and make—he announces the need for exertion. The promise held out is lofty:

> Every valley shall be lifted up,
>   and every mountain and hill be made low;
> the uneven ground shall become level,
>   and the rough places a plain.
> And the glory of the LORD shall be revealed,
>   and all flesh shall see it together,
>   for the mouth of the LORD has spoken. (vv. 4-5)

The echo we recognize from Exodus is an important one, and we will hear it throughout Second Isaiah, but of course the context is now much different. This is not to be a march of murmurings and problems, but one of triumph. The prophet responds to the herald's grand promises. "'What shall I cry?'/All flesh is grass" (v. 6a). The people have been told to prepare the way for the Lord, who will do marvelous deeds that all flesh will see and applaud. But how can this be possible, the prophet implies, how can all flesh see it together, if

> All flesh is grass,
>> and all its beauty is like the flower of the field.
> The grass withers, the flower fades,
>> when the breath of the LORD blows upon it;
>> surely the people is grass. (vv. 6b-7)

All is transitory, he suggests, all is vanity; there is no plan, everything fades away—how can all flesh see it together? Grass and flowers die, people die; "But" (an important conjunction in the poem), says the herald, "the word of our God will stand for ever." How can the gap be bridged between the changeless, permanent world inhabited by God and the changing, transitory world inhabited by humans? The contrast is enormous—God can presumably do all that he promises, his word can stand forever; *but* "the people is grass," they and their things die and are heard from no more. The promise of the herald, however, the promise of God, seems to be that the changeless and the changing, the permanent and the transitory, are somehow going to be connected, the gap between the changing world of humans and the changeless world of God is going to be bridged. Why? Because the mouth of the Lord has spoken, and his word will stand forever. Therein, perhaps in that statement of faith, lies the comfort. The doubt of the prophet is overcome by the divine reassurance.

The personified city of Jerusalem is told to "get . . . up to a high mountain, . . . lift up your voice with strength, . . . lift it up, fear not" (v. 9). The words suggest the present state of the city, presumably in ruins, its people in exile. The city is urged to get out into the open, to make some noise about its God, without being afraid of retaliation, to shout to the cities of Judah, "Behold your God!" There is no reason to be afraid any longer because the Lord God is coming with might "and his arm rules for him." "Behold," we are told for the third time, as if to emphasize the need for Jerusalem to open its eyes as well as its mouth,

> He will feed his flock like a shepherd,
>   he will gather the lambs in his arms,
> he will carry them in his bosom,
>   and gently lead those that are with young. (v. 11)

God will come in two modes: with power and strength, with an arm capable of rule, and with tenderness and love, with that same mighty arm also capable of gathering the lambs and carrying them gently in his bosom. He will come like a shepherd who can control and protect, who can also be mild and gentle. In a sense there is a union in the image of the shepherd between the infinitely great and the infinitely small, between might and mildness. The union takes us back to the contrast in the preceding verses between God's changeless world and man's changing world, and begins to bridge the gap between them.

The poem then offers a more complex statement of God's power. To this point, we have been told that the Israelites should be free of fear because the Lord is coming, that they should speak confidently to their enemies, and given one hint—that the power of God is not like earthly power, that this king is also a shepherd. Nevertheless, the Lord *is* King.

> Who has measured the waters in the hollow of his hand
>   and marked off the heavens with a span,
> enclosed the dust of the earth in a measure
>   and weighed the mountains in scales
>   and the hills in a balance? (v. 12)

Even as it describes the might of the Lord, the poem continues to work within extremes similar to those already established between God's world and man's, between a mighty king and a gentle shepherd. There is a constant expansion and contraction of the images, as if we were looking at the same subject from different ends of a telescope. We are asked to imagine all the waters of the universe—a vast image—and then told they are in the hollow of God's hand. Something enormous is compressed into something small, as if they belonged together. From the image of God's hand, the poetry explodes out into the extreme limits of the heavens, and compresses again to a measure, in which, however, all the dust of the earth is contained. For God, the mountains are in scales, the hills in a balance. On one side, we have immense things—the waters, the heavens, the dust of the earth, mountains and hills; on the other, we have minute things—a hand, a measure, scales, and a balance. But from the perspective of this God, they are the same. The magnitude of God, his immensity, is being conveyed to us. And then, the poem asks,

> Who directed the Spirit of the LORD,
>   or as his counselor has instructed him?
> Whom did he consult for his enlightenment,
>   and who taught him the path of justice,
>   and taught him knowledge,
>   and showed him the way of understanding? (vv. 13-14)

Given the power of this Lord, who can compete with him? Who might his teachers have been? With whom might he consult? Having expanded in a more complex way on the extent of God's power, the poem shifts again to the human world, following the pattern established earlier in the juxtaposition between God's eternal word and the transitoriness of human life. To this God, "nations are like a drop from a bucket." The simile has been carefully chosen, however much it may seem now a cliché, for we recall that God holds all the waters in the "bucket" of his hand and realize that the nations comprise only "one drop." They are "accounted as the dust on the scales," the same scales presumably on which God weighed the mountains. "All the nations," we are told, in as extreme a statement about the insignificance of human empires as we have been given about the potency of God, "are as nothing before him,/they are accounted by him as less than nothing and emptiness" (v. 17). Compared with the immensity of God, his infinite strength, his permanent world,

human nations are not only nothing, but less than nothing
The infinitely great dwarfs the infinitely small.

The problem posed by this enormous contrast, the same
problem raised by the prophet at the opening of the poem, is
again asked: "To whom then will you liken God,/or what
likeness compare with him?" (v. 18). How can we understand
the infinite? How can we understand God? The poem suggests that human attempts are often foolish: rich men hire
workmen and goldsmiths to create elegant idols bound in
silver chains; poor men choose wood "that will not rot" to
make images "that will not move." Why such foolishness?

> Have you not known? Have you not heard?
>   Has it not been told you from the beginning?
>   Have you not understood from the foundations of the
>   earth? (v. 21)

The lines recall for us the entire history of the relationship
between man and God, stretching back to Noah and Adam.
The answers have always been available, but man has forgotten. For the third time, the enormous differences between
God and man are described. A vast image of God, "he who sits
above the circle of the earth," is juxtaposed to a minute
image of men, inhabiting the earth "like grasshoppers." The
God who stretches out the heavens "like a curtain," spreads
them out "like a tent," also "brings princes to nought, and
makes the rulers of the earth as nothing." Like plants,
mighty rulers have scarcely taken root when God blows on
them, and they wither away. "To whom then," the poem
repeats, but this time putting the words in God's mouth, "will
you compare me, that I should be like him?" (v. 25). Given
the contrast between immensity and insignificance, between
the magnitude of God and the demagnification of human
empires, between his changeless world and man's transitory,
flowerlike life, man must "lift up [his] eyes on high and see"
who has created the world, who is its guiding intelligence.
We are asked to *remember* what we were told in the beginning; and Israel, in particular, is asked to remember. Why
should Israel say, "My way is hid from the LORD,/and my

right is disregarded by my God," when in important ways, God has been known to Israel from the beginning? "Have you not known? Have you not heard?" The repeated questions are perhaps now asked of Israel rather than of all men. One of Second Isaiah's major goals, it seems, is to help Israel remember what was once known, recall what it once heard, for in that remembering lies the comfort which God has promised to his people. God, we are told, is everlasting, he is the creator, "he does not faint or grow weary, his understanding is unsearchable." Perhaps Israel forgot because of the impossibility of understanding God's ways. Or perhaps they have never rightly understood the nature of his kingliness. They have looked for rich garments and a high throne, and have missed the shepherd always with them.

The poem returns for the fourth and last time to the differences between God and man. The first opposition was between the permanence of God's world and the transitoriness of human affairs (40:6-8), the second between the magnitude of God's activities and the insignificance of human empires (40:12-17), the third between God as controller of history and the rulers of the earth who fall before their power matures (40:22-24). The final opposition continues this narrowing-down process, which has moved from the earth to nations to princes, and sketches the relationship between God and the average individual. And for the first time, a solution is offered for man which might bridge the vast distances which have been described. The suggestion is made that it is possible for a transfer of power to take place from God to man in which the unlimited strength and being of God flows into individual men. God, it is true, "does not faint or grow weary," but "he gives power to the faint,/and to him who has no might he increases strength" (v. 29). The gap between the infinitely great and the infinitely small will be bridged because God wants to bridge it and because man cannot stand without God.

> Even youths shall faint and be weary,
>   and young men shall fall exhausted;
> but they who wait for the LORD shall renew their strength,

they shall mount up with wings like eagles,
        they shall run and not be weary,
            they shall walk and not faint. (vv. 30-31)

Everything the poem has implied about the insignificance of human endeavors is modified by two phrases which begin with the word *but*. The first phrase in verse 8 reminded us that the word of the Lord would stand forever, and his word has been that he will comfort Israel and that all flesh will see his glory. The second phrase, in the passage above, modifies man's limitations, about which we have heard so much, by indicating that those who "wait for the LORD" will share his strength. The personified city of Jerusalem, afraid and silent, has been urged in the poem to lift up its voice to announce the imminent return of God; now the promise comes that those who accept the announcement will be lifted up "like eagles." Without God, even young men will "fall exhausted." With God, they will indeed have a triumphal march, during which they will be neither weary nor faint.

The themes and images which follow in later chapters of Second Isaiah constantly echo the great poem of this chapter. In a sense the act of remembering, of recalling what has been forgotten, occurs throughout Second Isaiah in structure as well as in theme. We are asked repeatedly to recall the statement of chapter 40: that is our focal point, informing us of what we once knew, reminding us of what we have forgotten. God, we know, seeks to comfort Israel, to revive the fallen spirit of his people. A key literary question about Second Isaiah, therefore, concerns its persuasiveness. Can it rally a people? Is it successful in comforting Israel? Is it realistic in its appraisal of man's capabilities? Does it acknowledge counter-arguments? How does a poem arouse and encourage a confused nation? What themes and images does it employ which can inspire a new confidence for the future?

For Israel, a time of comfort has come, war has ended, sins have been forgiven, the word of God has promised to bridge the gap between the changing world of the finite and the changeless world of the infinite. Second Isaiah urges Israel to celebrate God's power, remembering he is the creator, the

Lord of history, the redeemer of Israel. The Israelites need courage for this renewal, this return. God is near, the book promises, and with him the Israelites can mount up with wings like eagles, move into his changeless world, away from the world of dust and fallen men and empires. But men must remember God's promises, his reward, his plan. And yet, Second Isaiah recognizes, these are difficult to remember because God's immensity is a mystery, which man can not fully comprehend, a mystery expressed symbolically in the image of the shepherd, one who seems to belong to the world of the infinitely small, but who actually can be part of the world of the infinitely great, one who protects and loves and is tender, but one who is also strong, powerful, and wise. The mystery will also be expressed in the image of the servant, who, it seems, like the shepherd, can bridge the gap between magnitude and insignificance. The unlimited strength of God can flow into man as it does into Cyrus and into the servant; but often, given man's limited perspective on history and limited understanding of God's ways, he will not recognize God's presence without courage and faith, without remembering his promises, known from the beginning. The task of these poems is to offer advice and arguments which will invigorate Israel's courage and confirm its faith.

The verbs which run through the poems—*behold, lift up, assemble, look, hear, listen, harken*—indicate that to this point Israel has been like a blind and deaf people. The Israelites are constantly reminded that God is not only present, if it would only see and hear, but also Israel's friend—"you, Israel, my servant, Jacob, whom I have chosen,/the offspring of Abraham, my friend" (41:8). God will help Israel, we are told three times in chapter 41; he will hold Israel's hand; he will punish her enemies and lead her into a new day. The key point is that God is in control of history and that his word has promised Israel redemption and peace. We are told that Cyrus the mighty king is God's servant and his shepherd; that Israel is his servant and his witness; that Babylon, in all its follies, is soon to fall; that the word to save Israel has gone out from God and that it will not return to him unfulfilled;

that Israel has suffered because God chose Israel as his special charge, chose it "in the furnace of affliction." But now that suffering has ended, and all nations will bow to Israel and lick the dust of her feet. Are these assertions persuasive? Are they supported? Can they rally a people?

The emphasis again and again is that God is the first and only God. "I, the LORD, the first,/and with the last; I am He" (v. 4). There are numerous passages reminding us of the creative power of God as well as of his divine plan and the special place in it for Israel. "I declared and saved and proclaimed" (43:12); "besides me there is no god" (44:6); "I . . . made all things" (v. 24); Cyrus "shall fulfill all my purpose" (v. 28). Passages like these run throughout Second Isaiah. The repeated concentration on God in his three-fold role as creator, controller of history, and redeemer of Israel indicates what Israel has forgotten. It is reasonable to admit that suffering has led them astray; and yet, given the knowledge they had, and the promises they were made, it is difficult not to criticize them. God says:

> From the beginning I have not spoken in secret,
>   from the time it came to be I have been there. . . .
> O that you had hearkened to my commandments!
>   Then your peace would have been like a river,
>   and your righteousness like the waves of the sea;
> your offspring would have been like the sand
>   and your descendants like its grains;
> their names would never be cut off or destroyed from
>   before me. (48:16, 18-19)

The history of the relationship between God and Israel has always been known to the Israelites. They forgot: God did not, even though it may have seemed that way. Zion said,

> "The LORD has forsaken me,
>   my *Lord* has forgotten me."
> Can a woman forget her sucking child,
>   that she should have no compassion on the son of her
>   womb?
> Even these may forget,
>   yet I will not forget you.

> Behold, I have graven you on the palms of my hands;
> your walls are continually before me. (49:14-16)

And now, Second Isaiah urges, Israel must remember, must be alert, look, listen.

> Harken to me, you who pursue deliverance,
> you who seek the *Lord;*
> look to the rock from which you were hewn,
> and to the quarry from which you were digged.
> Look to Abraham your father
> and to Sarah who bore you;
> for when he was but one I called him,
> and I blessed him and made him many." (51:1-2)

If Israel can remember, Second Isaiah promises, there will be a new day, a new Jerusalem, Israel will be renewed in body and in spirit. "Let the peoples renew their strength," chapter 41 opens, announcing the theme of renewal and rebirth which runs so powerfully through chapters 40–55. And what will God do? He will ease those who are thirsty in body and spirit:

> When the poor and needy seek water,
> and there is none,
> and their tongue is parched with thirst,
> I the LORD will answer them,
> I the God of Israel will not forsake them.
> I will open rivers on the bare heights,
> and fountains in the midst of the valleys;
> I will make the wilderness a pool of water,
> and the dry land springs of water. (41:7-18)

He will give light to those who are in darkness:

> And I will lead the blind
> in a way that they know not,
> in paths that they have not known
> I will guide them.
> I will turn the darkness before them into light.
> the rough places into level ground.
> These are the things I will do,
> and I will not forsake them. (42:16)

He will do a new thing:

> Behold, I am doing a new thing;
> now it springs forth, do you not perceive it?

> I will make a way in the wilderness
> and rivers in the desert. (43:19)

He will bring peace to the people:

> Shower, O heavens, from above,
> and let the skies rain down righteousness;
> let the earth open, that salvation may sprout forth,
> and let it cause righteousness to spring up also;
> I the LORD have created it. (45:8)

He will justify Israel's suffering:

> Behold, I will lift up my hand to the nations,
> and raise my signal to the peoples;
> and they shall bring your sons in their bosom,
> and your daughters shall be carried on their shoulders.
> Kings shall be your foster fathers,
> and their queens your nursing mothers.
> With their faces to the ground they shall bow down to you,
> and lick the dust of your feet. (49:22-23)

He will, as he promises at the opening of Second Isaiah, bring comfort to his people.

> For the LORD will comfort Zion:
> he will comfort all her waste places,
> and will make her wilderness like Eden,
> her desert like the garden of the LORD;
> joy and gladness will be found in her,
> thanksgiving and the voice of song. (51:3).

The appeal to the Israelites is very powerful. A life is sketched for them which contrasts sharply to the fear and suffering, despair and darkness which had characterized the period of their punishment.

Second Isaiah not only exhorts its audience to awaken, listen, look, remember, but also describes what will happen if it does. As if to make the point more persuasive, the account of the fate of Babylon depicts what happens to those who do not believe in the Lord as creator, controller of history, and redeemer. The images and motifs which depict Babylon's destruction are the opposites of those which describe God's "new thing." For Babylon, there will be no peace, no joy, no renewal, no song, no light. Instead of soaring into the sky like eagles, Babylon will "come down and sit in the dust. . . sit on the ground without a throne" (47:1). The city and its kings will specifically illustrate God's power to destroy the rulers of the earth, to make them like "stubble." Instead of melody and light, Babylon will "sit in silence, and go into darkness" (v. 5). Instead of rivers and flowers growing in the desert, Babylon shall suffer "disaster . . . which [it] will not be able to expiate" (v. 11). Instead of running without growing weary, Babylon will become "wearied with [its] many counsels" (v. 13). Instead of walking through the fire without being burned (43:2), Babylon's counselors will not be able to "deliver themselves from the power of the flame." Instead of being protected and well fed, Babylon will not even have a "fire to sit before" (47:14). The inhabitants of the wicked city will take the place of the Israelites before their comforting: "They [will] wander about each in his own direction"; but unlike the Israelites, "there [will be] no one to save [them]" (v. 15). Babylon will "no more be called tender and delicate," for it will be stripped to nothing. God will show no mercy because Babylon, forgetting the transitoriness of all human triumphs, showed no mercy to the conquered Israelites. The city was powerful, but it was not gentle. Man by himself cannot combine the infinitely great and the infinitely small, cannot bring God to earth or lift man to heaven. But Babylon made the prideful error of believing itself eternal. "I shall be mistress forever . . . ," it thought; "I am, and there is no one besides me" (vv. 7-8). Babylon has called itself equal to God, forgetting the enormous differences between God's permanent world and man's world of flesh and grass, between God's universal empire and man's human empires. For its sin of pride and its lack of mercy, Babylon will be ruined. The God who does not grow faint or become weary, the God of history, challenges the "wearied" prognosticators and stargazers of Babylon, "who at the new moons predict what shall befall" to save the city (v. 13). Babylon thought it was supreme, that it could control history, that it could save itself, but throughout Second Isaiah God is characterized as the only king, controller of history, and redeemer. The centrally placed chapter 47 contrasts in imagery and motif with all of the other chapters in Second Isaiah. This poem, like the poem of chapter 40, teaches and persuades through the device of contrast, this time exemplifying what befalls those who do not remember what chapter 40 contains.

But the question is still, of course, will Israel remember? Might they not forget again? Will they recall that God's ways are inscrutable but ultimately perfect? Will they recall that the shepherd and servant might reconcile greatness and smallness, the finite and infinite, the changeless and the changing? Second Isaiah, aware of man's failings, acknowledges the problem. "Who has believed what we have heard?" opens chapter 53. Will men be wise enough, courageous enough, to recognize as king the one who is also the servant? The most striking thing about the servant in all four passages (42:1-4; 49:1-6; 50:4-11; 52:13–53:12) is his anonymity—not in terms of who he might be, Israel, the prophet, a righteous remnant of Israel, a contemporary of the prophet's, the Messiah—but rather in terms of his low visibility. In the first servant passage, for example, the servant is characterized basically by his silence.

> Behold my servant, whom I uphold,
>   my chosen, in whom my soul delights;
> I have put my Spirit upon him,
>   he will bring forth justice to the nations.
> He will not cry or lift up his voice,
>   or make it heard in the street;
> a bruised reed he will not break,
>   and a dimly burning wick he will not quench;
>   he will faithfully bring forth justice.

We know that the servant has a vast mission—to bring justice to the people, but we wonder how he can fulfill it if he is silent, so silent he will not attract attention even with the noise made in putting out a candle or stepping on a reed. The servant in the second passage himself expresses that wonder. He knows the Lord has called him "from the womb" for a mission, and has endowed him with strength—his mouth "like a sharp sword," his being like "a polished arrow," and has anointed him, "You are my servant, . . . in whom I will be glorified." And yet, he is not sure what his mission is, why he has been called, when he should begin his work. "I have labored in vain,/I have spent my strength for nothing and vanity." He retains his faith in God and expects, as his remarks suggest, that he will have the honor of leading Israel back to God. His mission, however, as God tells him, is not to be so limited.

> It is too light a thing that you should be my servant
>   to raise up the tribes of Jacob
>   and to restore the preserved of Israel;
> I will give you as a light to the nations,
>   that my salvation may reach to the ends of the earth.

The servant's mission, then, is vaster than he anticipated. And yet, how can he fulfill it if he is silent and anonymous?

The third and fourth passages add to the mystery as we discover that the servant, in addition to being unknown to those around him, might also be mocked and derided by them. In the third passage, the servant again acknowledges he has been given special powers, "to sustain with a word him that is weary"; but he also recognizes (and accepts) his rejection by men.

> I gave my back to the smiters,
>   and my cheeks to those who pulled out the beard;
> I hid not my face
>   from shame and spitting.

He is confident of God's help, even though he is aware that his triumphs are to be in the future. The opening of the final servant passage better meets our expectations of what God's servant should be. He will prosper, we are told, "he shall be exalted and lifted up, and he shall be very high." He will be striking in appearance, capable of startling nations, silencing kings, teaching understanding of what has not yet been heard. But will men believe this? Our expectations of such an exalted figure have not been matched by the image of the mighty shepherd or the silent bringer of justice. It is no better matched by the servant of chapter 53. He is not attractive to look at, he is "despised and rejected by men," he has experienced sorrow and grief and humiliation. And yet, we are told through the mode of contrast, which is Second Isaiah's dominant literary device, this insignificant, infinitely small and invisible man has "borne our griefs and carried our sorrows," been "wounded for our transgressions . . . bruised for our iniquities." We do not know him, but he is saving us all:

> All we like sheep have gone astray;
>   we have turned every one to his own way;
> and the LORD has laid on him
>   the iniquity of us all.

Even as he was afflicted, "he opened not his mouth," but went to his death "like a lamb that is led to the slaughter," and was buried "with the wicked." This silent, suffering servant, however, justifies many by his death and "he shall see the fruit of the travail of his soul and be satisfied."

What is a servant? One who is subordinate, who does the bidding of the master, who has a direct, personal relationship with that master. In this case, the servant is subordinate to the power of God, he is God's instrument who carries out God's plans, he is loved by God, for God has chosen him directly and specifically for his mission. These three aspects—power, purpose, love—occur in all the servant passages. In answer to the questions: Who is the servant? Who is subordinate to God? Who is used by God as an instrument? Who is loved by God? there seems to me only one answer, and that is, everything. That, ultimately, is a major part of what Second Isaiah wants Israel to remember. Further, God's servant is not a servant in the traditional sense of that word—he is a man of power, of great authority. As the servant of God, he is a king of the peoples. And we are taken back to chapter 40 and the image of the shepherd who is mighty and strong, but also gentle and mild. We may not recognize our redeemer, as we may not recognize the servant whose suffering redeems us. The immense world of God and the nothingness of man are poetically combined in the servant and in the shepherd. This is what we must remember: that we may not recognize the reason for human suffering, we may not recognize our king. But with courage and faith in God as the creator, redeemer, and controller of history,

> Ho, every one who thirsts
> come to the waters;
> and he who has no money,
> come, buy and eat! (55:1)

Chapter 55 brings together in a simple statement much of what has preceded in Second Isaiah. We have heard throughout of water springing from rocks in the desert in the wilderness. The miracles past, we are now invited, simply: "Come, buy wine and milk/without money and without price." Urged throughout to be alert, to listen and see, the Israelites are now invited quietly by God to incline their ears, "and come to me; hear, that your soul may live" (v. 3). God recalls again the everlasting covenant that has been alluded to so many times, and states again the promise he has made.

> Behold you shall call nations that you know not,
> and nations that knew you not shall run to you,
> because of the LORD your God, and of the Holy One of
> Israel,
> for he has glorified you. (v. 5)

War is ended, Israel's sins are pardoned, a new historical time is about to begin.

> Seek the LORD while he may be found,
> call upon him while he is near:
> let the wicked forsake his way,
> and the unrighteous man his thoughts;
> let him return to the LORD, that he may have mercy on him,
> and to our God, for he will abundantly pardon. (vv. 6-7)

In a sense, these lines summarize what Second Isaiah has asked Israel to do; but the task is quietly stated. And then we are taken back to the contrasts of chapter 40, but without the extremes of those verses; the gap between God and man is stated by God simply, in an almost fatherly way, "my thoughts are not your thoughts,/neither are your ways my ways." Instead of using the vast images which so diminished man in chapter 40, God explains, "As the heavens are higher than the earth, so are my ways higher than your ways and my thoughts than your thoughts" (v. 9). This is still a statement about the immensity of God, but man is not overwhelmed by it. The gap is in the nature of things, and we have been told how it can be bridged. As the gap is natural, so God's power is natural.

> For as the rain and the snow come down from heaven,
>   and return not thither but water the earth,
> making it bring forth and sprout,
>   giving seed to the sower and bread to the eater,
> so shall my word be that goes forth from my mouth;
>   it shall not return to me empty,
> but it shall accomplish that which I purpose,
>   and prosper in the thing for which I sent it. (vv. 10-11)

The simple analogy with nature summarizes all of chapters 40–55. What God has spoken of Israel, it shall have comfort and be pardoned, and of Babylon, it shall be destroyed, will be fulfilled. And finally, as God's power is natural, so his love for his people is natural.

> For you shall go out in joy,
>   and be led forth in peace;
> the mountains and the hills before you
>   shall break forth into singing,
>   and all the trees of the field shall clap their hands. (v. 12)

God's new thing, his renewal of Israel, is condensed into two lines: "Instead of the throne shall come up the cypress; / instead of the briar shall come up the myrtle." The new thing "shall be to the LORD for a memorial, / for an everlasting sign which shall not be cut off." We are taken back to chapter 40 for the last time to remember the answer to the prophet who cried, "All flesh is grass . . . the people is grass." *But*, the herald had responded, "The word of our God will stand forever." *But*, Second Isaiah had said, "they who wait for the LORD shall renew their strength, / they shall mount up with wings like eagles."

XIII The Book of Job
KENNETH R. R. GROS LOUIS

There are a number of historical, textual, and theological problems raised by the book of Job about which biblical scholars have long debated. The problems are interesting in themselves and their solutions are important to an understanding of the place of the book in the Old Testament as a whole. But I do not think they should be of central importance to us as twentieth-century students of literature. We are presented—and stunningly—with a timeless situation: a just and upright man suffers a series of devastating blows; his friends tell him he must have sinned in some way because the good do not suffer; but he insists on his righteousness, on his guiltlessness. The issues debated by Job and his friends are still being debated, although we no longer expect, or perhaps even believe, that God will speak to any of us from a whirlwind.

The book has a simple five-part structure. It is framed by a two-chapter prose prologue and a one-chapter prose epilogue. The longest section, chapters 3–31, consists of three cycles, each cycle with six speeches, three by Job, one by each of his friends (the last cycle has only five speeches, as Zophar remains silent). There are two other speeches—by Elihu, who offers his new (but old) suggestions to Job, and by God, who answers everything while seeming to answer nothing. Whether we call the book a poem or a drama does not seem to me to matter much; what does matter is that we remember that it is a dialogue, and that we are aware of the threads which run through it.

The first thread is the discussion between Job and his friends on the problem of evil and suffering in a world supposodly ruled by a just and kind God. Job's repeated insistence on his righteousness leads us to two major and divergent conclusions about him—he is either a true saint, if indeed he is as righteous as he says he is; or he has a subtle imperfection in his character, a certain pridefulness, exemplified by the very insistence on his righteousness. His friends throughout the discussion present the underlying view of moral government and of natural conscience, and turn Job's problem into a law-and-order issue by indicating to him that if he does not accept the social and traditional view which they offer, he will be forced into a position of isolation; indeed, if other people followed Job's lead too closely, they suggest, there would be social chaos. Their mistake, as we will see, is that they delude themselves into believing what they say—that punishment comes to the wicked and prosperity to the good. Their position is not only in conflict with human experience, as Job tells them repeatedly, and as Eliphaz, the smartest of the three, seems to realize, but it also fails to cover the whole providence of God. God chastises them in the epilogue precisely because they "have not spoken of [him] what is right."

The second thread that runs through the dialogue is the shifting in Job's attitudes towards God, shifting frequently sparked by what his friends have to say. If his friends had never come, Job might well have remained in the position which he rejects when *they* advance it. At the beginning of the dialogue he seems to agree with their opinion, but their comments, rebukes, and lack of sympathy force him to consider other possibilities; two-thirds of the way through the dialogue, Job and the friends are talking about entirely different matters.

I

The narrator tells us in the first sentence that "there was a man in the land of Uz, whose name was Job; and that man was blameless and upright, one who feared God, and turned away from evil." We hear at the beginning of the book, then, the very same evaluation of Job's character that he himself will stress throughout the dialogue—he is blameless and upright, he has feared God, he has avoided evil. But we get this information from the narrator, not from Job. Given our source, and assuming that the narrator is reliable, the information will lead us to respond to Job's insistence on his righteousness differently than his friends do. Job has prospered enormously—he has ten children, a large number of animals, many servants; he obviously manages a great household; he is, in short, "the greatest of all the people of the east" (Job 1:3b). The emphasis on material success is striking, and will become more striking later when Job describes his past life without reference to his many possessions. The material emphases indicate to us that Job has not been a hermit or an ascetic, but that he has lived an active life, participated in the world and established a large estate. In this context, his goodness is even more remarkable. We recognize that his life seems to prove the congruence between goodness and prosperity, the congruence his friends will put so much faith in. Job's life also seems to achieve the perfect balance between feasting and prayer. The only possible imperfection we might detect in him is in his praying for his sons because they may have sinned. Perhaps it is presumptuous of Job to believe so strongly in his own goodness that he feels free to concern himself with interceding for the sins of others. If this is a taint on Job's character, it is indeed slight; and we conclude our introduction to Job agreeing with the narrator's opening assessment of him.

The scene then shifts to the heavenly council, where we overhear a conversation between the Lord and one of his agents who has just returned from "walking up and down" on the earth. For no apparent reason the Lord asks, in the very words of the narrator, "Have you considered my servant Job, that there is none like him on the earth, a blameless and upright man, who fears God and turns away from evil?" (v. 8). The narrator, of course, is the one who reports these words of God; nonetheless, we as readers get further confirmation of what we have already been told and have generally accepted about Job. The narrator tells us that God shares his impression of Job. Again, we are given information which Job's friends do not have access to when they challenge his insistence on his righteousness. Satan points out to God that Job has every reason to be good—given his circumstances, who would not be good? But what if you took these things away from him? Satan suggests. Would he remain righteous if he were not being handsomely paid for it? There is no clear motivation for Satan's suggestion. He seems to be cynical, in his unwillingness to believe that such a man exists (and he has recently come from earth, we remember). He may possibly be jealous because God has picked out Job and praised him to Satan's face. Perhaps his motivation is irrelevant; he may simply be playing his appointed role, conveniently serving as the foil which enables the narrator to present Job's trial. God tells Satan: "all that he has is in your power; only upon himself do not put forth your hand" (v. 12). The framework for what follows is established: God has praised the righteousness of his servant Job; Satan has pointed out that the righteousness results from Job's self-interest; God has challenged Satan's cynical theory by agreeing to test Job. Obviously, the test or trial is partly one of disinterested righteousness, but there are other issues we will need to consider during the dialogue. What is it in Job, for example, that makes him blameless and upright, as he is called by the narrator and by God? What is his strength? What might we learn from him?

In a series of hammerlike blows Job hears that everything he has, including his children and excepting only his wife, is destroyed. A messenger tells him that his oxen and asses have been killed by the Sabeans. Even while this messenger is speaking, another comes to tell him that his sheep and servants are dead. During this account, another comes to tell him that his camels have been slain. And finally, the last messenger comes to tell him that his children, feasting at the house of his oldest son, are all dead. We have no indication of Job's response as he hears each of these terrible messages. Then, however, presumably after the messengers are finished—no worse news could have come except that his wife were dead too—we are told: "Job arose, and rent his robe, and shaved his head, and fell upon the ground." These responses are not unexpected. But what Job then does seems to me stunning—he "worshiped." Considering that Job, the greatest man of the east, has heard in a matter of seconds that his personal and public world has been destroyed, his initial response is extraordinary. He worships his God: "Naked I came from my mother's womb, and naked shall I return; the Lord gave, and the Lord has taken away; blessed be the name of the Lord" (v. 21).

The scene shifts to the heavenly council where the Lord and Satan have a conversation similar to their first one. Satan, returning from walking up and down on the earth, hears God again allude favorably to Job. For the third time, we are told that Job is blameless and upright, a man who fears God and avoids evil. We have even more reason now to agree with this assessment, having seen Job unquestioningly accept the reversal of his fortune. "He still holds fast his integrity," God says, "although you moved me against him, to destroy him without cause" (2:3b). (We will remember the phrase, "without cause," when Job's friends later accuse him of wrong-doing.) Job holds fast his integrity, God says—why does he not say his "faith," or his "loyalty," or his "righteousness"? Is it his integrity that Job is preserving or trying to preserve? Is this what is being tested? What does the word mean? Should we understand it in its primary medieval and Renaissance meaning of wholeness, the state of being complete or undivided? The word frequently occurs with this connotation, for example, in criticism on *King Lear* and *Hamlet*, and is applied to what Hamlet and Lear seek to recover. They are torn apart in some way, and they want to be brought back together again; they want their integrity, their wholeness. If Job is analogous to them, of what does his integrity consist?

Satan is not persuaded. Again cynically, perhaps enviously, he suggests that Job's goodness is still a result of self-interest. Job has not been injured personally, Satan tells

God; he has lost everything that he loves and everything that he owns, but his body is still healthy. God responds to this challenge, "Behold, he is in your power, only spare his life" (v. 6). Do anything you want to Job, in other words, but keep him alive. "So Satan went forth from the presence of the LORD, and afflicted Job with loathsome sores from the sole of his foot to the crown of his head. And he took a potsherd with which to scrape himself, and sat among the ashes" (vv. 7-8).

Job's wife tempts him to take the simple way out: "Do you still hold fast your integrity? Curse God, and die" (v. 9). Job responds, again surprisingly, "You speak as one of the foolish women would speak. Shall we receive good at the hand of God, and shall we not receive evil?" (v. 10). Given his circumstances, his reply is again extraordinary. We should also note that it is essentially what the comforters are going to say before they start accusing him of sins, of blasphemy in particular. If the comforters had never come, it is reasonable to assume that Job would have maintained this attitude. He had received good from the Lord, and now he was receiving evil from the Lord, and that was that. But as we will see, the comforters without realizing it suggest other alternatives to Job, which lead him ultimately to his repeated request that God appear to him in some way, that God notice him as an individual, and acknowledge his integrity.

II

Job's three friends arrive to "condole with him and comfort him." These are good men presumably, and wise, or they would not be Job's friends. They are enormously sympathetic, they weep and tear their clothes, they sit with Job for seven days and seven nights without saying a word. However much we may criticize their suggestions and observations during the dialogue, we must remember these facts so that we take what they say, representing the accumulated wisdom of Job's community, very seriously.

Job begins the dialogue in a way which indicates how much he despairs of his life.

> Let the day perish wherein I was born,
> and the night which said,
> "A man-child is conceived."
> Let that day be darkness!
> May God above not seek it,
> nor light shine upon it. (3:3-4)

He curses even the night of his conception "because it did not shut the doors of [his] mother's womb" (v. 10). Given the normal human love of life, the sealing up of a mother's womb is a terrible curse. While Job clearly longs for death, here and elsewhere in the dialogue, he never thinks of suicide. It may be that Job does have a sense of his dignity and the dignity of all life. It may also be that he has an underlying faith in his God, not faith that he will get everything back again, but simply faith that there is a reason for his present suffering, that God has something in mind for him.

We learn other things about Job from this initial cry of despair. He seems to believe he knows what life and death are—life is light and death is darkness, he implies over and over. He balances his longing for death, its peace and restfulness, with his outrage at having been brought into the light. Job's neat equations will come back to us when God speaks to him from the whirlwind and reminds him, and us, that death may not be darkness, life may not be light. We get a good sense in this opening speech of Job's priorities in regard to material wealth and earthly power. He has no illusions about their permanence or their value. Death comes to all, kings and servants, the wicked and the good, and equalizes them.

> The small and the great are there,
> and the slave is free from his master. (v. 19)

His despair has nothing to do with what he has lost, but more with the frustrations he feels, the perplexity of life itself which is given to him when he no longer wants it, when, indeed, he never wanted it. His material wealth, which was emphasized by the narrator, is barely mentioned by Job. He sees his life in other terms. He is certainly depressed here, but we begin to wonder whether despair is not too strong a word for his mood. It is striking, for example, considering his situation, considering that he wonders why he was born, longs for death, meditates about what happens after death, that he turns, as he so often does, to a series of questions that seem to be more than mere rhetorical complaints.

> Why is light given to him that is in misery,
>   and life to the bitter in soul,
> who long for death, but it comes not,
>   and dig for it more than for hid treasures;
> who rejoice exceedingly,
>   and are glad, when they find the grave?
> Why is light given to a man whose way is hid,
>   whom God has hedged in? (vv. 20-23)

Job, it seems, is not really ready to die after all, because he has some questions that need to be resolved. His energy remains, his integrity remains, he insists that he himself remains, and there are some questions that he wants to ask about his God. He has neither ease nor rest, and he will not be quiet.

The first comforter, Eliphaz, offers Job a conventional consolation. He is, like the other friends, sympathetic to Job and concerned about his well-being. At this point, he seems to understand Job's agitation and truly wants to comfort him, as gently and as quietly as possible.

> If one ventures a word with you, will you be offended?
>   Yet who can keep from speaking?
> Behold, you have instructed many,
>   and you have strengthened the weak hands.
> Your words have upheld him who was stumbling,
>   and you have made firm the feeble knees.
> But now it has come to you, and you are impatient;
>   it touches you, and you are dismayed. (4:2-5)

The sentiment Eliphaz expresses is basically what Job had said to his wife. "Shall we receive good at the hand of God, and shall we not receive evil?" Eliphaz reminds Job that he had advised and helped others when they were suffering and points out that he should now follow his own advice. Job needs to pull himself together.

> Is not your fear of God your confidence
> and the integrity of your ways your hope? (v. 6)

And then, very gently, Eliphaz implies that Job has sinned.

> Think now, who that was innocent ever perished?
> Or where were the upright cut off?
> As I have seen, those who plow iniquity
> and sow trouble reap the same. (vv. 7-8)

The statement is a general one, but Job surely recognizes its intended applicability to him. Eliphaz is suggesting that Job is being punished for doing wrong. The solution, then, is to ask God's pardon. As if to frighten Job, Eliphaz explains the might of the Lord which was conveyed to him in a vision (Eliphaz is always seeing visions, receiving information secretly or stealthily in the night).

This particular vision concerns the enormous gap which exists between man and God, a gap which Job would not be surprised to hear about, but not the gap that God himself will describe when he speaks from the whirlwind. A spirit appeared to Eliphaz.

> It stood still
> but I could not discern its appearance.
> A form was before my eyes;
> there was silence, then I heard a voice:
> "Can mortal man be righteous before God?
> Can a man be pure before his Maker?
> Even in his servants he puts no trust,
> and his angels he charges with error;
> how much more those who dwell in houses of clay,
> whose foundation is in the dust,
> who are crushed before the moth." (vv. 16-19)

Compared with the perfection of God, Eliphaz is arguing, all creatures, even God's own angels, are imperfect. And if God's angels are imperfect, then what of man, a creature of the dust? The point is being made gently, but not too subtly, that Job is mistaken if he thinks he is guiltless. Eliphaz is no fool—he recognizes, more than do Bildad and Zophar, that the good do not always prosper. Life itself is trouble.

> Man is born to trouble
> as the sparks fly upward. (5:7)

Yet for the sake of social order, it is useful to argue that the good prosper and the evil suffer. To reject this view, as Job may seem to Eliphaz on the verge of doing (Eliphaz is right), could lead to chaos. As he speaks, and without realizing it, Eliphaz is, however, giving Job an idea he did not have earlier when he chastised his wife for not acquiescing in the reversal of his fortunes. Eliphaz asks if mortal man can be righteous before God. "Call now; is there any one who will answer you?" (v. 1). If Eliphaz were Job, he suggests, "I would seek God,/ and to God would I commit my cause" (v. 8). What Eliphaz means is that Job should admit his sins and ask for God's pardon. What Job envisions, however, as he begins to consider the idea of "seeking" God, is a personal confrontation with God, not as equal to equal, but as man to God. One of Job's strengths is surely that he always recognizes that he is a man and that God is God; he knows there are distinctions between them. At the same time, Job's God is less remote and mysterious than Eliphaz's; for Eliphaz, God "does great things and unsearchable," he gives rewards and punishments, not answers and explanations. Job is going to reject that word *unsearchable;* he will admit that God does unsearchable things, but in relation to *his* life and *his* situation, there should be answers.

Eliphaz offers a second reason why Job should be comforted. "Behold," he says,

> Happy is the man whom God reproves;
> therefore despise not the chastening of the Almighty. (v. 17)

Job's suffering, in other words, can be educational. God's afflictions are not only given to the wicked, but occasionally to the good, to educate them, strengthen them, correct them, make them stronger for the future. What Job needs, Eliphaz concludes, is faith in God.

> He will deliver you from six troubles;
> in seven there shall no evil touch you.

> In famine he will redeem you from death,
>   and in war from the power of the sword.
> You shall be hid from the scourge of the tongue,
>   and shall not fear destruction when it comes.
> At destruction and famine you shall laugh,
>   and shall not fear the beasts of the earth.
> For you shall be in league with the stones of the field,
>   and the beasts of the field shall be at peace with you.
> You shall know that your tent is safe,
>   and you shall inspect your fold and miss nothing.
> You shall know also that your descendants shall be many,
>   and your offspring as the grass of the earth.
> You shall come to your grave in ripe old age,
>   as a shock of grain comes up to the threshing floor in its
>   season.
> Lo, this we have searched out; it is true.
>   Hear, and know it for your good. (vv. 19-27)

Eliphaz's statement is powerful, and yet it depends heavily on conventional sentiments which somehow fail to acknowledge the position that Job is in. "The beasts of the field shall be at peace with you," Eliphaz argues, but Job is, as he will soon say, "a brother to jackals and a companion of ostriches." Eliphaz tells Job his descendants will be many and his "offspring as the grass of the earth," but only a week has passed since Job's ten sons and daughters were killed. How comforting can Eliphaz's words be under the circumstances? He tells Job he will come to his grave in a ripe old age, but Job sits in front of him covered with loathsome sores from head to feet. The gap between the sentiments and the reality suggests that conventional sentiments are sometimes going to be absurd. We have all mouthed them or sent cards which express them, but how comforting are they to the person who is experiencing the pain and loss? Essentially, Eliphaz is saying to Job that his sons and daughters are not gone, they are just away. Job presumably had said the same kind of thing to others, but, as he now tells Eliphaz, he was not they, and Eliphaz is not he. He knows that there is truth in what Eliphaz says, but he has great trouble apprehending it at this particular moment, with his sons and daughters dead and his own body covered with sores.

The arrows of the Almighty are in me}
my spirit drinks their poison;
the terrors of God are arrayed against me. (6:4)

He sees no consolation in Eliphaz's remarks—if God would
grant his desire and crush him, however, "This would be my
consolation" (v. 10). "What is my strength," Job says in
direct reply to Eliphaz, "that I should wait?"

And what is my end, that I should be patient?
Is my strength the strength of stones? [a word
Eliphaz has used a moment ago]
or is my flesh bronze? (vv. 11-13)

Job insists that an outsider cannot understand and comfort
someone in his position. He expresses surprise, in fact, that
Eliphaz is not more sympathetic, surprise because he knows
Eliphaz is trying to be sympathetic, because perhaps he
himself had said the same things when he thought he was
comforting others. "He who withholds kindness from a
friend/forsakes the fear of the Almighty" (v. 14), Job says
somewhat sarcastically to Eliphaz.

Have I said, "Make me a gift"?
Or, "From your wealth offer a bribe for me"?
Or, "Deliver me from the adversary's hand"?
Or, "Ransom me from the hand of oppressors"?
Teach me, and I will be silent;
make me understand how I have erred. (vv. 22-24)

Job is willing to consider the possibility of sinfulness, but he
wants specifics to support Eliphaz's vague suggestion. He
does not, given his present circumstances, need to be chastised.

Do you think that you can reprove words,
when the speech of a despairing man is wind?
You would even cast lots over the fatherless,
and bargain over your friend. (vv. 26-27)

Job urges his friends to look at him, to consider his position,
to listen carefully to his insistence on his righteousness. He
knows the difference between right and wrong, but he may
have overlooked some flaw which his friends can point out to
him.

And yet, even as he speaks, Job may be growing aware that they cannot comfort him, that, as he has already implied, this is a matter between him and God. Job is becoming conscious of the primacy of individual experience, the primacy of individual response. An outsider cannot know what he feels or help him get in touch with God. He accepts Eliphaz's basic premises—that man has "hard service" on earth, that his days are "like the days of a hireling," that his "flesh is clothed with worms and dirt" (7:1, 5). But he also is urging Eliphaz and his other two friends to look at him and consider his situation.

> The eye of him who sees me will behold me no more; . . .
> As the cloud fades and vanishes,
>   so he who goes down to Sheol does not come up;
> he returns no more to his house,
>   nor does his place know him any more. (vv. 8a-10)

Death is the end for Job, and death is darkness. "Therefore," says Job, "I will not restrain my mouth;"

> I will speak in the anguish of my spirit;
> I will complain in the bitterness of my soul. (v. 11)

Since death is the end, and Job believes himself to be righteous, he must seek justice now. By the end of his speech, Job is no longer speaking to Eliphaz, but to God.

> If I sin, what do I do to thee, thou watcher of men?
>   Why hast thou made me thy mark?
>   Why have I become a burden to thee?
> Why dost thou not pardon my transgression
>   and take away my iniquity?
> For now I shall lie in the earth;
>   thou wilt seek me, but I shall not be. (vv. 20-21)

Job subtly hints that God may be unjust. Job's replies to his comforters follow the basic pattern of this reply to Eliphaz. He begins by answering something they have said, but soon he is talking to God; indeed, his point increasingly is that this is a matter between only him and God.

Bildad offers the same kind of general view advanced by Eliphaz. No one before Job, Bildad will suggest, has ever rejected religious comforts. Who is Job to reject them? Who is Job to challenge the attitude that has kept society together? "How long will you say these things?" asks Bildad.

> Does God pervert justice?
> Or does the Almighty pervert the right? (8:2)

Bildad seems to realize what Job is thinking, and attempts to divert him from it.

> If your children have sinned against [God],
>   he has delivered them into the power of their trans-
>   gression.
> If you will seek God
>   and make supplication to the Almighty,
> if you are pure and upright,
>   surely then he will rouse himself for you
>   and reward you with a rightful habitation. (vv. 4-6)

If Job were *really* righteous, if he were *really* good, says Bildad, he would not be suffering. He advises Job to seek God and, as Eliphaz had suggested, to ask his pardon. Job is attracted by the notion of seeking God, but he wants to ask him for explanations, not for forgiveness. "For inquire, I pray you," Bildad continues, not realizing what he has planted in Job's mind, "of bygone ages,/and consider what the fathers have found." Unlike Eliphaz, who relies heavily on his visions and revelations, Bildad relies on authority and tradition, on the various explanations and comforts that have been handed down from generation to generation. "For we are but of yesterday," he says, "and know nothing,/for our days on the earth are a shadow." Bildad, of course, presumes to know something. He is more prideful than Job, who will accuse all three friends of interpreting what they themselves claim is inexplicable. Bildad tells Job what he knows from bygone ages:

> Will they not teach you, and tell you,
>   and utter words out of their understanding?
>
> Can papyrus grow where there is no marsh?
>   Can reeds flourish where there is no water?
> While yet in flower and not cut down,
>   they wither before any other plant.

> Such are the paths of all who forget God;
> > the hope of the godless man shall perish. (vv. 10-13)

Bildad hopes to persuade Job by using a particular kind of metaphor. As the papyrus and reeds will not grow without water, so too man will not grow without nourishment from God. Bildad's analogy, as we will see, becomes very important to Job and to Job's thinking. Bildad concludes by telling Job that everything is just. Again, we recognize that the gap between the conventionality of the sentiments and Job's situation is enormous. The final verses are almost painful:

> He will yet fill your mouth with laughter,
> > and your lips with shouting.
> Those who hate you will be clothed with shame,
> > and the tent of the wicked will be no more. (vv. 21-22)

Bildad's remarks, like those of Eliphaz, illustrate the great difficulty of understanding another's experiences from the outside. The three comforters never really do get inside Job.

Job begins his response, as he often does, by acknowledging the general truth in what Bildad has said, "Truly I know that it is so." Job has something else on his mind, too.

> But how can a man be just before God?
> If one wished to contend with him,
> > one could not answer him once in a thousand times. (9:2-3)

Job is not on the same wavelength as his friends. He is talking about *contending* with God; they, on the other hand, are telling him to make supplication to God. Job is well aware of God's enormous power. "He is wise in heart, and mighty in strength . . . he . . . removes mountains . . . [he] shakes the earth out of its place" (vv. 4-5). His disagreement with his friends is not over God's might; indeed, what he says foreshadows what God will say of himself from the whirlwind. Nor is his disagreement over how difficult it is for man to question God. He becomes particularly aware of this as he considers how little time man has to understand the ways of God. Job knows that he cannot comprehend God, that he cannot really question him, that he cannot expect answers.

He is, however, looking for some indication that God cares
for him, some indication, perhaps, that God is his friend.
"Behold," he says, "he snatches away; who can hinder him?"

> Who will say to him, "What doest thou?"

> God will not turn back his anger;
>   beneath him bowed the helpers of Rahab.
> How then can I answer him,
>   choosing my words with him?
> Though I am innocent, I cannot answer him;
>   I must appeal for mercy to my accuser. (vv. 12-15)

The comforters' suggestion that he seek God has not only
sparked Job to the thought that he might get a response from
God but has also led him to a metaphor which they did not
intend—the metaphor of a courtroom, of a trial. God is now
his "accuser," Job will "summon" him to present his "appeal."
But the spark of hope dims.

If it is a contest of strength, behold him!
  If it is a matter of justice, who can summon him?
Though I am innocent, my own mouth would condemn
    me;
  though I am blameless, he would prove me perverse. (vv. 19-20)

We wonder if Job really believes what he is saying—he has
insisted on his blamelessness, and will continue to do so. Is he
then being perverse? He seems to vacillate between the hope
the law-court metaphor gives him, and the realization that he
cannot contend with God, both because God is mightier and
because God is accuser, judge, and executioner. What kind of
trial can there be?

> For he is not a man, as I am, that I might answer him,
>   that we should come to trial together.
> There is no umpire between us,
>   who might lay his hand upon us both. (vv. 32-33)

Job is working out in his mind some of the metaphors that
have been planted there by his comforters. He is jolting them
a bit, too. "It is all one," he asserts, "therefore I say,/he
destroys both the blameless and the wicked." As far as the
comforters are concerned, the statement is outrageous. Job

knows that, presumably, but he wants to make them realize that indeed he is taking a position much opposed to theirs. We might ask whether he is also trying to jolt God. Is he already beginning to contend with God? Job is always questioning.

> I will say to God, Do not condemn me;
>   let me know why thou dost contend against me.
> Does it seem good to thee to oppress,
>   to despise the work of thy hands
>   and favor the designs of the wicked?
> Hast thou eyes of flesh?
>   Dost thou see as man sees?
> Are thy days as the days of man? (10:2-5)

"Thou knowest that I am not guilty," Job insists,

> and there is none to deliver out of thy hand[.]
> Thy hands fashioned and made me;
>   and now thou dost turn about and destroy me. (vv. 7-8)

Job's insistence may seem an act of pride; but in the context of what he is suffering, and according to the terms of the dialogue set by the comforters, a charge of pride seems excessive. Job has not directly alluded to his great material and personal losses; he has a more critical concern, one sparked by what the comforters have said: Is God his friend, or is God his enemy? "Thou hast granted me life and steadfast love," he says to God,

> and thy care has preserved my spirit.
> Yet these things thou didst hide in thy heart;
>   I know that this was thy purpose.
> If I sin, thou dost mark me,
>   and dost not acquit me of my iniquity.
> If I am wicked, woe to me!
> If I am righteous, I cannot lift up my head. (vv. 12-15)

Job is perplexed. Is God his friend or not? Has he sinned or not? He is no longer sure. He knows that God, who is all-powerful, hunts him "like a lion," works "wonders" against him, renews "witnesses" against him, increases his "vexation" towards him. But why, Job wonders, "Why didst thou bring me forth from the womb?" (v. 18). Job might never have asked the question had his friends not come. They have suggested to him that he is suffering because he has sinned. He does not believe it. Still, what is the purpose of his life? Of his suffering? Job, remember, believes death is the end. He asks his friends to leave him alone, "before I go whence I shall not return,/to the land of gloom and deep darkness" (v. 21). Job wants some understanding of his life before he dies, before he leaves the light.

Zophar, the third comforter, picks up in chapter 11 the pattern established by Eliphaz and Bildad. He is, however, a little more indignant. "Should a multitude of words go unanswered,/and a man full of talk be vindicated?" (11:2). Zophar seems to realize, as the others have not, that Job has in mind a real contact with God, that he seeks explanations, not pardon.

> For you say, "My doctrine is pure,
>   and I am clean in God's eyes."
> But oh, that God would speak,
>   and open his lips to you,
> and that he would tell you the secrets of wisdom!
>   For he is manifold in understanding.
> Know then that God exacts of you less than your
>   guilt deserves. (vv. 4-6)

The comforters are getting angrier. Their remarks are having no effect on Job, and they begin to grow harsher, pointing out more explicitly that he must have sinned. "Can you find out the deep things of God?" questions Zophar, as if in response to the implications of Job's suggestion that perhaps he can reach God. Zophar mocks this hope.

> Can you find out the limit of the Almighty?
> It is higher than heaven—what can you do?
>   Deeper than Sheol—what can you know? (v. 8)

Zophar tells Job that he is being foolish, that he cannot reach God. The best thing to do is to submit, and all will be well. Zophar, like Eliphaz, tries to picture for Job what his life will then be like, but again, the description seems inappropriate under the circumstances.

> And your life will be brighter than the noonday;
>> its darkness will be like the morning. (v. 17)

Job may believe this, but he cannot, at this time, accept it. The conventional sentiments are not consoling to him.

His friends have not only not told him anything new, but they are becoming condescending and patronizing to him.

> But I have understanding as well as you; [Job says]
>> I am not inferior to you.
>> Who does not know such things as these? (12:3)

And yet, as Job points out, he also knows from his experience that "the tents of robbers are at peace, and those who provoke God are secure" (v. 6). He knows the conventional wisdom about prosperity and suffering, that they result from good and evil actions. But he is blameless, he insists, and still he is a "laughing-stock." His friends' explanation—one he perhaps has given in the past—is accurate. He too can recite the accepted text describing God.

> With him are strength and wisdom;
>> the deceived and the deceiver are his.
> He leads counselors away stripped,
>> and judges he makes fools.
> He looses the bonds of kings,
>> and binds a waistcloth on their loins.
> He leads priests away stripped,
>> and overthrows the mighty.
> He deprives of speech those who are trusted,
>> and takes away the discernment of the elders.
> He pours contempt on princes,
>> and looses the belt of the strong.
> He uncovers the deeps out of darkness,
>> and brings deep darkness to light.
> He makes nations great, and he destroys them:
>> he enlarges nations and leads them away. (vv. 16-23)

All of this is for the benefit of Job's friends, to whom he now repeats,

> Lo, my eye has seen all this,
>> my ear has heard and understood it.
> What you know, I also know;
>> I am not inferior to you. (13:1-2)

At the same time, he has come to a different conclusion:

> But I would speak to the Almighty,
>   and I desire to argue my case with God. (v. 3)

His friends, he charges, are being of no comfort to him whatsoever. They are even presumptuous in their attempts to explain God's ways. Perhaps they, and not he, should stop talking.

> Oh that you would keep silent,
>   and it would be your wisdom!
> Hear now my reasoning,
>   and listen to the pleadings of my lips.
> Will you speak falsely for God,
>   and speak deceitfully for him?
> Will you show partiality toward him,
>   will you plead the case for God? (vv. 5-8)

Who are Job's friends to explain his suffering to him, to define the logic of his experience? Job has heard Eliphaz report his secret visions and Bildad describe human traditions and authority and Zophar dogmatically assert his sense of the truth. But none of them is Job, none of them is God. Job insists on his integrity, on his individual relationship with God.

> Let me have silence, and I will speak,
>   and let come on me what may.
> I will take my flesh in my teeth,
>   and put my life in my hand.
> Behold, he will slay me; I have no hope;
>   yet I will defend my ways to his face. (vv. 13-15)

Job is not asking to contend with God as an equal, but to present his case before his God, in whom he has faith, and in whose ultimate justice he has trust. "Behold, I have prepared my case;/I know that I shall be vindicated" (v. 18). In opposition to his comforters, Job is not trying to guess God's position; he is rather trying to find out what God's position is, confident as he is of his own.

This brief moment of optimism falters, however, when Job again thinks of death and of the grave. "Man that is born of a woman is of few days, and full of trouble" (14:1; Eliphaz, we recall, had said the same thing).

> He comes forth like a flower, and withers;
>> he flees like a shadow, and continues not. (v. 2)

Job cannot forget death and the darkness he associates with it. The analogy between man's life and a flower may well be in his mind as a result of Bildad's earlier metaphor of nourishment: as reeds need water, Bildad had said, so man needs God. Job extends the metaphor:

> For there is hope for a tree,
>> if it be cut down, that it will sprout again,
>> and that its shoots will not cease. (v. 7)

He agrees with Bildad that plants and trees need nourishment in order to grow; but, he wonders, suppose a tree is cut down, might it not, if properly nourished, grow again? And he begins to ponder: Is it possible, then, for being, for existence, to continue after death?

> Though its root grow old in the earth,
>> and its stump die in the ground,
>> yet at the scent of water it will bud
>> and put forth branches like a young plant. (vv. 8-9)

Job, on the verge of a new insight, at this point rejects the extended metaphor.

> But man dies, and is laid low;
>> man breathes his last, and where is he?
> As waters fail from a lake,
>> and a river wastes away and dries up,
>> so man lies down and rises not again. (vv. 10-12*a)*

Job concludes that man, unlike the tree, will not sprout again. He lapses back into partial despair as the thought of death and the grave overwhelms him. What he has experienced does indeed seem to be all that there is of life.

III

Job's friends are obviously angry with him in the second round of the dialogue. They came to console him, they gave him thoir bost advice, and he has rejected it. The time for repentance, they seem to believe, is now past. Their emphasis is increasingly on Job's wickedness, implicitly when they describe the fate of sinful men, explicitly when they charge Job with blasphemy. Eliphaz begins the attack: "Your own mouth condemns you, and not I;/your own lips testify against you" (15:6). Eliphaz knows that Job has been insisting on the primacy of individual experience, on the primacy of *his* relationship with God and *his* need to get in touch with God. Ironically, of course, Eliphaz's own private visions have presumably led Job to his insistence on *his* vision. But Eliphaz is unaware of the connection. He considers Job's position dangerously antisocial and egocentric, one which can only lead him into total isolation. If Job alienates himself from society, he will be alone; if all men agreed with Job, society's rules and traditional mores would be ineffectual. Eliphaz wants Job to recognize that he is part of society.

> Are you the first man that was born?
>   Or were you brought forth before the hills?
> Have you listened in the council of God?
>   And do you limit wisdom to yourself?
> What do you know that we do not know? (vv. 7-9)

Eliphaz remembers that Job has pointed out that he knows what they know and wants to remind Job that the reverse is also true. He is not about to let Job get the upper hand with that argument. Nor will he permit Job to forget that they speak for many and that many before him have endorsed their wisdom.

> Both the gray-haired and the aged are among us,
>   older than your father.
> Are the consolations of God too small for you,
>   or the word that deals gently with you? (vv. 10-11)

Job, from Eliphaz's perspective, is simply being obstinate in turning his spirit against God and speaking as he has. He gives Job a picture of what happens to the wicked and throughout emphasizes that God is so perfect that man, by comparison, is nothing. What Eliphaz has "seen" in another of his visions is clearly meant to apply to Job, to terrify him into submission because he, like the wicked man whose painful life Eliphaz depicts, "has stretched forth his hand against God, and bids defiance to the Almighty" (v. 25). In his harsh account, Eliphaz makes extensive use of the plant-tree metaphor—the wicked man will not "strike root in the earth," the "flame will dry up his shoots," "his branch will not be green." Job, as we know, is pondering another possibility for this metaphor. He has agreed that trees and men need nourishment, but he has also noted that trees, once cut down, might be nourished to grow again. Earlier he had rejected this hope for man; but does Eliphaz unknowingly reawaken it?

For the moment, it seems not. Job, getting angry himself, calls all three of his friends "miserable comforters."

> I also could speak as you do,
>   if you were in my place;
> I could join words together against you,
>   and shake my head at you.
> I could strengthen you with my mouth,
>   and the solace of my lips would assuage your
>   pain. (16:4-5)

Job reminds his friends that they came to comfort him, not to attack him. If he were they, he implies, he would be doing a better job. He then turns to Eliphaz's social argument, seeming to recognize what Eliphaz's concern for him is, that he will become isolated. He points out to Eliphaz that he already *is* isolated and alienated. He has lost everything, he is covered with loathsome sores, men gape at him, strike him on the cheek, "mass themselves" against him. He is already an outcast; Eliphaz's warning comes too late. Worse, Job says, God has

> set me up as his target,
>   his archers surround me.
> He slashes open my kidneys, and does not spare;
>   he pours out my gall on the ground. (vv. 12*b*-13)

What society does Eliphaz think Job belongs to?

> My face is red with weeping,
>> and on my eyelids is deep darkness. (v. 16)

Even at this low point, however, Job insists, maintaining his integrity, "my prayer is pure." Even at this low point, Job retains his faith.

> . . . Behold, my witness is in heaven,
>> and he that vouches for me is on high.
> My friends scorn me;
>> my eye pours out tears to God. (vv. 19-20)

Once he has told Eliphaz that the social argument is irrelevant for him because he is already alienated and isolated by his very situation, Job recognizes that he needs God more than ever. His tears are directed solely to his God. His very isolation has forced him to come into closer contact with God than he was when he platitudinously instructed his wife: "Shall we receive good at the hand of God, and shall we not receive evil?" And yet, Job's leap of faith again falters, and for the same reason that it did before. "The grave is ready for me" (17:1), he thinks.

> If I look for Sheol as my house,
>> if I spread my couch in darkness,
> if I say to the pit, "You are my father,"
>> and to the worm, "My mother," or "My sister,"
> where then is my hope?
> Who will see my hope? (vv. 14-15)

Bildad ignores Job's questions and gives him another picture of the lot of the wicked. He clearly feels, like Eliphaz, that all hope for Job is past, that the time for repentance is past. All he can try to do now is to jolt Job out of his mood by terrifying him with descriptions of what might happen to him. He is also annoyed with Job's stubbornness.

> How long will you hunt for words?
>> Consider, and then we will speak.
> Why are we counted as cattle?
>> Why are we stupid in your sight?
> You who tear yourself in your anger,
>> shall the earth be forsaken for you,
>> or the rock be removed out of its place? (18:2-4)

Bildad is being sarcastic in asking if Job expects a special thing to happen to him. He, along with Eliphaz and Zophar, knows all the traditions; they have had visions, studied philosophy and past authorities. Can Job seriously believe he can go against all of this knowledge? "Yea," says Bildad smugly, "the light of the wicked is put out,/and the flame of his fire does not shine" (v. 5). Bildad's depiction of the wicked's fate is extremely harsh, and seems close to home at times: "By disease his skin is consumed" (v. 13). But again, without knowing it, the comforter sparks Job's imagination. The roots of the wicked, says Bildad, "dry up beneath, and his branches wither above" (v. 16). That, Job may think, is what has happened to him. He also may think, however, of the cut-down tree, whose roots may again be nourished, whose branches may again be green.

During his response to Bildad, Job reaches the climax of his spiritual agony, the point at which his own sufferings fade. By the end of his remarks, he firmly believes that he will personally be declared innocent, and he is no longer concerned with his own pain. In his further speeches, he moves to the question of the seeming paradox between an all-righteous God and the prosperity of the wicked on earth, while his friends continue to talk about him. "How long will you torment me," he says to Bildad and the others, "and break me in pieces with words?" (19:2). He reminds them again of his situation and of his depression—his hope, he says, God "has pulled up like a tree." As he says this, surely Job remembers his earlier observation that "there is hope for a tree, if it be cut down, that it will sprout again." Job reviews his present position. Everyone has turned away from him.

> My kinsfolk and my close friends have failed me;
>   the guests in my house have forgotten me;
> my maidservants count me as a stranger;
>   I have become an alien in their eyes.
> I call to my servant, but he gives me no answer;
>   I must beseech him with my mouth.
> I am repulsive to my wife,
>   loathsome to the sons of my own mother.

Even young children despise me;
  when I rise, they talk against me.
All my intimate friends abhor me,
  and those whom I loved have turned against me.
My bones cleave to my skin and to my flesh,
  and I have escaped by the skin of my teeth. (vv. 14-20)

He is, in other words, totally alone, isolated, alienated, despised. And he says to his friends, most reasonably,

Have pity on me, have pity on me . . .
  for the hand of God has touched me!
Why do you, like God, pursue me?
  Why are you not satisfied with my flesh? (vv. 21-22)

Job seems to separate himself from his friends; their opinions are nothing compared to Job's more important audiences—us and his God. He has confidence in us, "Oh that my words were written!/Oh that they were inscribed in a book!" And he has, this time without faltering, confidence in his God.

For I know that my Redeemer lives,
  and at last he will stand upon the earth;
and after my skin has been thus destroyed,
  then from my flesh I shall see God,
whom I shall see on my side,
  and my eyes shall behold, and not another. (vv. 25-27a)

At this climactic moment Job insists on the primacy of the individual consciousness—*he* will see God, *his* eyes will behold him. As he has held throughout, the experience is his, the problem is his, the solution will be his.

Zophar recognizes that Job has achieved a happy moment, and it makes his rebuke all the harsher.

Do you not know this from of old,
  since man was placed upon earth,
that the exalting of the wicked is short,
  and the joy of the godless but for a moment?
  (20:4-5)

What can Zophar be referring to except the look of joy on Job's face when he says "I know that my redeemer lives"?

Zophar, like Bildad and Eliphaz, then offers another elaborate picture of what happens to the wicked, implying throughout that this is what is being reserved for Job, an implication which, in a few moments, will kindle Job's review of his past life. His friends are now furious at what they interpret as his willfulness, arrogance, and self-righteousness. "He swallows down riches and vomits them up again," says Zophar of the godless man.

> God casts them out of his belly.
> He will suck the poison of asps;
>   the tongue of a viper will kill him.
> He will not look upon the rivers,
>   the streams flowing with honey and curds. (vv. 15-17)

We might imagine that Zophar's violent images here and in the remainder of his outburst would anger Job; but Job, in his response, pays only minimal attention to them.

"Listen carefully to my words," Job says, "and let this be your consolation." (How the tables have turned!) "Bear with me, and I will speak,/and after I have spoken, mock on" (21:2-3). Essentially, Job dismisses his friends. What he is about to say will shock them, he knows; but his words are for God, not for them.

> Look at me, and be appalled,
>   and lay your hand upon your mouth.
> When I think of it I am dismayed,
>   and shuddering seizes my flesh.
> Why do the wicked live, reach old age,
>   and grow mighty in power? (vv. 5-7)

Job is no longer concerned with himself—the issue of his righteousness or wickedness will be decided by God and by future readers; he now questions the underlying assumptions of his friends' account of God's government of the universe. The wicked are not, he asserts, always punished.

> They send forth their little ones like a flock,
>   and their children dance.
> They sing to the tambourine and the lyre,
>   and rejoice to the sound of the pipe.

> They spend their days in prosperity,
>   and in peace they go down to Sheol.
> They say to God, "Depart from us!
>   We do not desire the knowledge of thy ways.
> What is the Almighty, that we should serve him?
>   And what profit do we get if we pray to him?"
> Behold, is not their prosperity in their hand?
>   The counsel of the wicked is far from me.
>
> How often is it that the lamp of the wicked is put out?
>   That their calamity comes upon them? (vv. 11-17*a)*

From experience, says Job, we can see that death does not result from the quality of one's life, that goodness does not lead to prosperity or wickedness to suffering.

> One dies in full prosperity,
>   being wholly at ease and secure,
> his body full of fat
>   and the marrow of his bones moist.
> Another dies in bitterness of soul,
>   never having tasted of good.
> They lie down alike in the dust,
>   and the worms cover over them. (vv. 23-26)

The quality of life makes no difference. One man can be in full health, at the peak of his life, and he dies. Another can die at a moment of great bitterness, at the moment when he is blaspheming God. But there is no pattern, no logic. Job is quiet here. He believes in ultimate justice, he has his faith again, the integrity which enabled him to respond so well to his sudden losses. He also has his perplexed questions, however, to which answers may not be available. Demands for death, which so dominated his earlier responses, have faded. While he still hopes for some indication of God's concern for him, some proof that God is his friend, he is confident that he will one day be justified for he knows that he will see his redeemer with his own eyes.

IV

The third cycle in the dialogue confirms the positions now held by Job and his friends and pushes Job to his life review in chapters 29–31. Eliphaz accuses Job of specific sins which Job will deny.

> You have given no water to the weary to drink,
>   and you have withheld bread from the hungry. . . ..
> You have sent widows away empty,
>   and the arms of the fatherless were crushed. (12:7,9)

From all we know of Job, these charges are preposterous, and for Eliphaz to suggest them indicates how much his friendship with Job has decayed during the discussion. Eliphaz still wants Job to give in, to surrender: "Agree with God, and be at peace; . . . humble yourself, . . . lift up your face to God. . . . God abases the proud, but he saves the lowly" (vv. 21, 23, 26, 29). Job, as he has before, points out in chapter 23 his willingness to seek God, not however, to abase himself, but to present his case. He wavers between believing that this is not possible: "Would he contend with me in the greatness of his power?" and affirming his faith in its possibility.

> No; he would give heed to me.
> There an upright man could reason with him,
>   and I should be acquitted forever by my judge. (23:6-7)

He seeks God everywhere—forward, backward, to the left, to the right—but he cannot see him. No matter, Job says, he will come. Insisting again on his righteousness, Job tells his friends that God "will complete what he appoints for me." At the same time, the seeming moral chaos of the world troubles him. Why, he wonders, if God is just, does he permit so much suffering to be unalleviated, so much wickedness to be unpunished?

> From out of the city the dying groan,
>   and the soul of the wounded cries for help;
>   yet God pays no attention to their prayer. (24:12)

Bildad, in his very short answer in chapter 25, offers Job one explanation. God is so mighty, says Bildad, that

> . . . even the moon is not bright and the stars are not clean
>   in his sight;

how much less man, who is a maggot,
and the son of man, who is a worm! (25:5-6)

These are the last words spoken by Job's friends, and they are the logical extension of what they have said throughout the dialogue. Man, from their perspective, can find peace and security only when he acknowledges that he is, compared to God, a maggot and a worm. Job refuses to accept their depressing conclusion. The language of his first words in response to Bildad underlines his view of man. Even in his position, surrounded by the shambles of his life's achievements, covered with loathsome sores, he speaks of man's potential dignity.

How you have helped him who has no power!
How you have saved the arm that has no strength!
How you have counseled him who has no wisdom. (26:2-3)

Job admits that he is at man's minimal level of existence, but he still seeks help to recover his power, strength, and wisdom. Until he dies, Job insists, he will not speak as deceitfully of God as his friends have, in their suggestion that God's special creation is wormlike.

Far be it from me to say that you are right;
till I die I will not put away my integrity from me.
I hold fast my righteousness, and will not let it go. (vv. 5-6)

To let it go at this point, Job may feel, would be to agree with Bildad. Instead, he argues, let us assume that the wicked suffer and that good men perform marvelous feats. Even so, asks Job,

. . . Where shall wisdom be found?
And where is the place of understanding? (28:12-13)

It is not in the earth or the sea, it cannot be bought, it is hidden from the eyes of the living and from the birds of the air, death has "heard a rumor of it." And Job then answers his own question.

> God understands the way to it,
>   and he knows its place.
> And he said to man,
>   "Behold, the fear of the LORD, that is wisdom;
>   and to depart from evil is understanding." (vv. 23, 28)

Job has presumably said this quietly and softly to his friends. He is alone with his God now; the comforters have nothing more to say. He reviews his past life and attempts to prove that he is, as the narrator and God told us at the very beginning, "A blameless and upright man, who fears God and turns away from evil."

What Job says in chapters 29–31 would have seemed extremely prideful had he said it earlier. Considering all that has preceded, however, the account of his former happiness (chap. 29), of his present position (chap. 30), and of his ethical standards (chap. 31) are not statements of pride; they represent his justification. He is, at last, contending with God; this is his case that he has wanted to present before God for so long. Job begins by recalling the time when God was indeed his friend.

> Oh, that I were as in the months of old,
>   as in the days when God watched over me,
> when his lamp shone upon my head,
>   and by his light I walked through darkness;
> as I was in my autumn days,
>   when the friendship of God was upon my tent;
> when the Almighty was yet with me,
>   when [a particularly painful phrase] my children
>   were about me. (29:2-5)

We recall that the narrator at the beginning of the book gave us a picture of Job which stressed his material wealth; but Job, in his own life review, barely mentions his possessions. What seems more important to him is the quality of life. Perhaps there was a time when Job, like King Lear, was impressed by the quantity of things and servants and animals he had as "the greatest of all the people of the east." His isolation, however, may have put the past in a different perspective for him. He now knows that possessions can be easily destroyed. Job recites his good deeds:

> . . . I delivered the poor who cried,
>   and the fatherless who had none to help him.
> The blessing of him who was about to perish came
>   upon me,
>   and I caused the widow's heart to sing for joy.
> I put on righteousness, and it clothed me;
>   my justice was like a robe and a turban.
> I was eyes to the blind,
>   and feet to the lame.
> I was a father to the poor,
>   and I searched out the cause of him whom I did
>   not know. (vv. 12-16)

He thought in those years, Job tells us, that he would die peacefully, that his "roots [would] spread out to the waters, with the dew all night on [his] branches" (v. 19). He was respected, a chief and king among the people, like one, he says perhaps for the benefit of his friends, "who comforts mourners." The metaphor of the tree is still much on his mind. He had expected that in his final days he would be nourished by God and that his children, the ten now dead, would extend his heritage like roots. But he has, like a tree, been cut down.

"But . . ." chapter 30 opens, as Job shifts from a review of his past to an account of his present condition,

> But now they make sport of me,
>   men who are younger than I,
> whose fathers I would have disdained to set with
>   the dogs of my flock. (30:1)

He had been chief among the people, and now, he is rejected and despised by even the vilest men of the land.

> They abhor me, they keep aloof from me;
>   they do not hesitate to spit at the sight of me.
> Because God has loosed my cord and humbled me,
>   they have cast off restraint in my presence. . . .
>   My honor is pursued as by the wind,
>   and my prosperity has passed away like a cloud. (vv. 10-11, 15)

257

The affliction and pain Job experiences have made him become, he says, "like dust and ashes." Job's account of his present condition suggests one of the problems with the traditional view presented by his comforters. If his friends argue that the good prosper and the evil suffer, how do they explain Job's biography? How can a man who has in the past done the good things Job describes come into Job's present situation, isolated, alienated, cut off from others, abhorred by others?

> I am a brother to jackals,
>   and a companion of ostriches.
> My skin turns black and falls from me,
>   and my bones burn with heat.
> My lyre is turned to mourning,
>   and my pipe to the voice of those who weep. (vv. 29-31)

Following the review of his past life and account of his present situation, Job offers his oath of purgation, an oath carefully constructed around conditional clauses. Job does not assert that he followed this code, and should therefore be rewarded, but rather *if*:

> If I have walked with falsehood,
>   and my foot has hastened to deceit;
> (Let me be weighed in a just balance, and
>   let God know my integrity!)
> if my step has turned aside from the way,
>   and my heart has gone after my eyes,
>   and if any spot has cleaved to my hands;
> then let me sow, and another eat;
>   and let what grows for me be rooted out.
>
> If my heart has been enticed to a woman,
>   and I have lain in wait at my neighbor's door;
> then let my wife grind for another,
>   and let others bow down upon her. (31:5-10)

The same construction continues throughout. Job is saying that if he has done these things, then he deserves his punishment. The implication, of course, is that he has followed a high ethical code. But he is not as affirmatively confident of his righteousness as he was earlier. The standard he had set for himself was lofty. He believes that he listened to his servants' complaints, that he fed and clothed the poor and fatherless, that he raised orphans as his own children, that he avoided the lure of gold and possessions, that he was never vain, that he prayed for his enemies, that he opened his doors to all who came to him, that he openly acknowledged his own failings and sins, that he cared for his land and for those who cultivated it. If he has not done these things, he recognizes, he has no case before God, he cannot face God's majesty. If he has done them, Job concludes, "I would give him an account of all my steps;/like a prince I would approach him" (v. 37). Job's case is before the court. His life, he argues, has been based on the highest ethical standards, not because he expected to be paid, but because it was his nature, his integrity, to be blameless and upright, fear God, and avoid evil. Even though great suffering has come to him, he maintains the integrity of his position. He believes that he will be justified, that man is no maggot or worm, but a creature capable of improving himself and the lives of those who need him.

V

Job's friends say nothing. A young man appears rather suddenly, apparently angry at Job for seeking to justify himself and at his friends because they could not persuade Job that he was wrong. With propriety Elihu had waited to speak until the older men had had their say. Many commentators believe that Elihu's speech is a later addition to the text of the book. Certainly, the poetry is less good, although perhaps very appropriate to Elihu's youthful, blunt, straightforward remarks. He is extremely confident of his position which, it turns out, does not differ much from that of Job's friends. It may be that Elihu's remarks are included to suggest how alienated Job is. The "wisdom" offered to him by his friends is not simply society's old-guard, conservative position; brash Elihu, potentially the young radical, agrees with it. Job is not, in other words, an old leader of a young movement. "Behold," says Elihu to Job, "you are not right" (33:12) to insist on your righteousness. God is greater than man. Man's lot is to suffer. God's justice is not perverse. He is not available for court-hearings. What he does, he does. And what does it matter to God, says Elihu, whether Job is wicked or righteous? Sincere requests to God are not rejected, but requests made in pride "he does not answer" (35:12). We have heard these arguments before although, ironically, Elihu constantly draws attention to himself as one who has the answer—"truly," he says immodestly, "my words are not false; one who is perfect in knowledge is with you" (36:4). He repeats the comforters' warnings; he reasserts the punishment of the wicked; he describes the magnitude of God. Elihu challenges Job to explain God's mysterious ways, in words very similar to God's from the whirlwind; yet, the great difference, we come to realize, is that Elihu is not God and his challenge is therefore arrogant. "The Almighty," Elihu confidently concludes, "we cannot find him. . . . he does not regard any who are wise in their own conceit" (37:23-24). And then, as if in answer to Elihu, and in justification of Job, "the LORD answered Job out of the whirlwind" (38:1).

VI

> Who is this that darkens counsel by
>   words without knowledge?
> Gird up your loins like a man,
>   I will question you, and you shall declare to me.
> Where were you when I laid the foundation of the
>   earth? (vv. 2-4)

The tone is forceful and direct. God asks Job to act "like a man," a phrase he will soon repeat, and yet to be a man is to be unable to answer God's questions. He asks Job where he was at the beginning of time. Who determined the measurements of the earth, says God almost sarcastically echoing the tone of Job and the comforters, "Surely you know?" If not, he implies, who is Job to contend with God? And what is Job's power over nature?

> Have you commanded the morning since your days began,
>   and caused the dawn to know its place,
> that it might take hold of the skirts of the earth,
>   and the wicked be shaken out of it? (vv. 12-13)

What does Job know of the sea, of death, of darkness? "Declare," says God again challengingly, "if you know all this." Job, we know, has declared many things. He had, for example, equated life with light, death with darkness. But now God asks him,

> Where is the way to the dwelling of light,
>   and where is the place of darkness,
> that you may take it to its territory
>   and that you may discern the paths to its home? (vv. 19-20)

God seems to be answering Job after all. Job had told his friends that he was going into darkness, away from light, but God points out that Job does not know what light and darkness are—how, then, can he say that he is going into darkness? Perhaps, God suggests, again sarcastically, Job does know. "You were born then, and the number of your days is great!" (v. 21). With each jab, Job must feel increasingly battered and overwhelmed.

If Job thinks it is logical for death to be in darkness, he is forgetting that God, from man's perspective, is not always logical. Job and his friends throughout have been alluding to the nourishment for the land provided by rain and snow, praising the goodness of God in helping food grow for man, as though God's acts were to be measured by their value for man. But God asks Job to tell him who brings "rain on a land where no man is, on the desert in which there is no man" (v. 26). How can Job explain this? In a series of metaphors from nature, God reminds Job that he was not present at the beginning, that he has no understanding of nature, that he is unaware of some of the seemingly illogical activities of God.

And can Job do what God has done? "Can you bind the chains of the Pleiades?" Or can he undo what God has done?—"or loose the bands of Orion?" (v. 31). What animals does Job control? Is he willing to provide food for man's enemy? "Can you hunt the prey for the lion, or satisfy the appetite of the young lions?" (v. 39). Not only does God do things that do not help man (causes rain in the desert), he does things which may be harmful to man (sustain lions). Can Job understand this?

God surveys the animal world (chap. 39), implying to Job that he does not know the habits of animals. The powerful suggestion is building that God cannot be judged by man's standards. God will sharply rebuke the three comforters for precisely this error. Their revelations, their traditions, their dogma—all are insufficient as means of understanding and judging God. Job, of course, made the same mistake by trying to contend with God in terms of a law-court analogy. God asks:

> Who has let the wild ass go free?
>   Who has loosed the bonds of the swift ass,
> to whom I have given the steppe for his home,
>   and the salt land for his dwelling place?
> He scorns the tumult of the city;
>   he hears not the shouts of the driver
> He ranges the mountains as his pasture,
>   and he searches after every green thing. (39:5-8)

Some of God's creatures live where Job would not go; some exist on food that Job would not touch. The earth, God is telling Job, is not only for men. The operations of the animal world, like those of nature, do not follow the logic of men. The ostrich has proud wings, says God, but she is foolish.

> For she leaves her eggs to the earth,
>   and lets them be warmed on the ground,
> forgetting that a foot may crush them,
>   and that the wild beast may trample them. (vv.
>   14-15)

Like rain in the desert, the actions of the ostrich seem inexplicable, perhaps to men even cruel. But, says God, "she has no fear; because God has made her forget wisdom,/and given her no share in understanding" (v. 17). God tells Job that he takes care of the foolish ostrich—he has his logic; he also has his gifts. "When she rouses herself to flee,/she laughs at the horse and his rider" (v. 18). The ostrich has no wisdom, she has no understanding, she does foolish things with her eggs, but she is faster than man, faster even than the horse which means so much to man. And, continues God, what of the horse? Man can use him, train him, control him; but can man create him? "Do you give the horse his might?/Do you clothe his neck with strength?" (v. 19). God then describes the power and importance of the horse which man uses, but cannot create. After this awesome account of the enormous gap between man and God, God returns to the request Job has made throughout the dialogue, and asks Job, "Shall a faultfinder contend with the Almighty?/He who argues with God, let him answer it." And Job, overwhelmed, seems to accept Bildad's position: "Behold, I am of small account; what shall I answer thee? I lay my hand on my mouth" (40:2-4). God, surprisingly, speaks again from the whirlwind and again commands Job, "Gird up your loins like a man." God has just described for us his magnificence, but he has also described the great variety of existence on earth, much of which man does not understand. When he says, "Gird up your loins like a man," might he not mean that this variety is for man to find out about, for man to study and to enjoy? Man might not be able to answer God's questions, but he can fulfill his own being, he can have his own integrity. Perhaps man's job in girding up his loins is to question and investigate the differences and vastness in God's universe. In a sense, that is exactly what Job has done, and perhaps that is why God is speaking to him.

> Have you an arm like God,
>   and can you thunder with a voice like his?
> Deck yourself with majesty and dignity;
>   clothe yourself with glory and splendor. (vv. 9-10)

Job had said a moment ago that he would appear to God "like a prince." God tells him he can have princely robes if he wishes, get all the power he wants, abase the proud, but "Then will I also acknowledge to you,/that your own right hand can give you victory" (v. 14). It is not Job's power or his glory or his wealth that matters, but the way he lives, that will justify him. God describes Behemoth and Leviathan (40:15-41), two enormously powerful creatures. (Even if these are later additions to the text, surely the editor had something in mind in including the passages.) Both of them, we notice, are much greater than man; yet they were, as God points out, created by God. Man cannot harness them; he cannot feed them; he cannot tame them; he cannot use them. If there is such a gap between the Leviathan and the Behemoth and man, God is saying, consider then what a gap there is between man and God. Will the Leviathan, asks God, "make many supplications to you?/Will he speak to you soft words?/Will he make a covenant with you?" (41:3-4). The Leviathan is so great that man might be tempted to worship him, but he is under God's control and, as God reminds Job, only God can make a covenant with man. God created the Leviathan to remind man of the dangers of pride.

> He beholds everything that is high;
> he is king over all the sons of pride. (v. 34)

God's entire speech from the whirlwind, an account of his immensity, must be overpowering to Job. And yet, that very immensity and the fact that God describes it, provides an answer to Job's question. Throughout the dialogue, Job has wanted to know, he has sought proof, that God is interested in him as an individual, that God is interested in his integrity. The very appearance of God, the very sound of his voice speaking to Job is the proof Job has been seeking. That God's power is immense emphasizes the wonder, the uniqueness, of God's coming to Job, to one man. If there is such a gap between man and God, what a wonder it is that God should speak to man at all. Job has the answer to his personal problem—God is his friend. Job cries:

> I have uttered what I did not understand,
>> things too wonderful for me, which I did not know.
>
> . . .
>
> I had heard of thee by the hearing of the ear,
>> but now my eye sees thee. (vv. 3, 5)

His faith has been justified—he has, as he demanded, to his friends' outrage, seen God with his own eyes. That sight presumably answers Job's second problem—the question of the suffering of the innocent. Having seen God, Job has no further questions. "I despise myself," he concludes, "and repent in dust and ashes" (v. 6). During the earlier account of his present condition, Job had said he had "become *like* dust and ashes." He is now prepared to repent *in* dust and ashes; once cut down, he is ready for nourishment and new growth. God criticizes Job's friends for not speaking of God what was right, and returns to Job, in greater abundance, everything that he had before.

VII

The book of Job develops many themes and concerns:

It tests disinterested righteousness, disinterested obedience to God, for which patience and integrity are needed. Man must learn, the dialogue suggests, to serve without being paid.

The book is also concerned with the suffering of the innocent—we can either resign ourselves to it or have faith in God's ultimate justice, Job's faith, based on the analogy of the tree which may be cut down, but properly nourished, may also grow again.

We are made aware of the limitations of religious dogma. We recognize from the errors of the comforters that man cannot explain by himself, with his limited understanding, the entire operation of divine providence, and that it is self-deluding to think that we can, as indeed Job's friends are self-deluded to think that they can. Analogies which attempt to define man's relation to God, such as the trial metaphor, are not always successful. Man cannot really contend with

God because of the enormous gap which exists between them.

God is inscrutable in Job, and hence, from man's perspective, unpredictable, as God illustrates, for example, with his account of the ostrich. God cannot be measured by man's standards; he does not act only for man's benefit. The view of Job's friends, which sees God in terms of rewards and punishments, is too limiting. Instead, we see that God is also a God whose justice may be difficult to perceive. The good may suffer, the evil may prosper. The metaphors which describe God are active, often violent—metaphors of the hunt, of armies, of storms. And yet, paradoxically, God is hunting man because he loves him, because he is man's friend.

There is, finally, Job himself—either he has a subtle imperfection in his insistence on his righteousness, or he is, as I believe, a true saint whose testing reveals that man cannot expect happiness no matter what he does. Man should not, therefore, concentrate on his career, whatever it might be, as lawyer, as physician, as teacher, but he should, as Job has done, concentrate on his calling, as a being whom God loves. The view of man presented by the three comforters is depressing—man is a vile creature, a maggot, a worm. Job's desire, on the other hand, to have God as his friend, his insistence on the reality of individual experience, his belief in an individual relationship between man and God, saves and dignifies him, and also, by extension, dignifies us. To be like a man, as God says to Job, is not necessarily to be able to answer the ultimate questions, but it is to gird up one's loins, to be upright, fear God and turn away from evil as a matter of personal integrity.

XIV Ecclesiastes
KENNETH R. R. GROS LOUIS

Ecclesiastes, like so much of the wisdom literature in the Old
Testament, is concerned both with the dignity of the individual and the pursuit of human happiness. This may seem at
first a strange statement to make about Ecclesiastes, considering the bulk of criticism on the book which emphasizes its
cynicism and pessimism, its rationalism and agnosticism. The
Dartmouth Bible editors, for example, call it "a classic out-
pouring of the skepticism and disillusionment experienced in
many epochs and civilizations." And indeed the abridged text
which follows this introduction in The Dartmouth Bible
strongly suggests such a view, leaving out as it does the more
optimistic verses of Ecclesiastes. What the Preacher has to
say about life is likely to find a sympathetic response among
many contemporary readers, even though the Preacher himself we may find less appealing. In a century of almost constant war, during a time when the dehumanization of the
individual is of concern to so many, when the credibility gap
widens between the government and the governed, when
simple justice seems so overwhelmingly complex, when work
and play are becoming separate and unrelated activities as
we conceive of Monday to Friday as time to think and only
Saturday and Sunday as time to feel; much of what is in
Ecclesiastes, with or without its underlying faith and belief
in a divine being, strikes responsive chords. The Preacher's
failure to respond actively to the injustice and the tyranny he
describes, however, may seem to us a flaw. We wonder if he
might not have done some good with his wealth and wisdom.
Could he not have made things better? Why does he not seek
reform? Or does he? And if so what mode does the reform
take?

A passage written by Walter Pater in the early 1870s as part of a conclusion to his series of essays on the Renaissance is useful in several ways, I believe, in beginning a study of Ecclesiastes. Although Pater is writing towards a different end and from the perspective of an entirely different world view, he provides us with a possible guide to what the Preacher is doing and suggesting. "The service of philosophy," Pater writes,

of speculative culture, towards the human spirit, is to rouse, to startle it to a life of constant and eager observation. Every moment some form grows perfect in hand or face; some tone on the hills or the sea is choicer than the rest; some mood or passion or insight or intellectual excitement is irresistibly real and attractive to us, for that moment only. Not the fruit of experience, but experience itself, is the end. A counted number of pulses only is given to us of a variegated, dramatic life. How may we see in them all that is to be seen in them by the finest senses? How shall we pass most swiftly from point to point, and be present always at the focus where the greatest number of vital forces unite in their purest energy? To burn always with this hard, gem-like flame, to maintain this ecstasy, is success in life. While all melts under our feet, we may well grasp at any exquisite passion, or any contribution to knowledge that seems by a lifted horizon to set the spirit free for a moment, or any stirring of the senses, strange dyes, strange colors, and curious odors, or work of the artist's hands, or the face of one's friend. Not to discriminate every moment some passionate attitude in those about us, and in the very brilliancy of their gifts some tragic dividing of forces on their ways, is, on this short day of frost and sun, to sleep before evening. With this sense of the splendor of our experience and of its awful brevity, gathering all we are into one desperate effort to see and touch, we shall hardly have time to make theories about the things we see and touch. What we have to do is to be forever curiously testing new opinions and courting new impressions, never acquiescing in a facile orthodoxy.

"Vanity of vanities, vanity of vanities! All is vanity," says the Preacher wearily, as he begins his carefully worked out argument against the theistic view, his manifesto of skepticism and naturalism, his firm rejection of the orthodox. The second verse of Ecclesiastes states what seems to be the final position of the speaker, at least in regard to his search for happiness and pleasure and contentment, and what follows supports the statement with evidence drawn not from dogma and authority, but from fact and experience. From these first words which represent a kind of universal statement on the vanity of human activity in general, the Preacher moves to a more personal question: "What does man gain by all the toil at which he toils under the sun?" Not only is the universe full of vanities, but the individual man receives no gain from his own labors. The word *gain* perhaps jumps out at us as unusual in this context. What kind of equation is the speaker looking for? A cause and effect relationship is implied—man does his work in order to *gain* something, things exist because presumably they *do* something—the speaker in a moment will ask of pleasure, "What use is it?" Such questions may suggest the Preacher's limited understanding.

Following his general and personal opening remarks, the Preacher then describes for us a cyclical theory which operates on many levels. "A generation goes, and a generation comes, but the earth remains for ever." There are two parts to this verse, and there will be two parts to the verses which follow. The first part boldly states the coming and going of generations; the second part explains what makes such cycles so depressing to the speaker: there are things around him —in this instance the earth—which seem to endure "for ever." There is order, in other words, there is a pattern, there is permanence, but they do not involve man. We should recall that this very concept of cycles, of the great rhythms of the world and of history, are seen in some of the psalms as a source of delight and of comfort, that a stress upon continuity and succession is what helped Israel endure as one generation passed away and was replaced by another. To the Preacher, however, the cycles tend to be oppressive. "The sun rises and the sun goes down, and hastens to the place where it rises." Like human generations, the sun comes and goes, but unlike generations, it returns to the place where it came from and, more depressingly, it will come again. There is order here, and permanence; there is nothing for the man who lives in light and then goes into darkness. "The wind blows to the south, and goes round to the north; round and round goes the wind." The wind, like man, seems constantly in flux, but again unlike man, returns to its sources. The wind comes back, man does not. "All streams run to the sea, but the sea is not full; to the place where the streams flow, there they flow again." There is also order and permanence in the activities of the waters. "All things are full of weariness; a man cannot utter it"; the Preacher is surrounded by movement, energy, vitality, and yet, he is depressed because he is insatiable: "the eye is not satisfied with seeing, nor the ear filled with hearing." There can be no satisfaction, no enjoyment, because "what has been is what will be, and what has been done is what will be done; and there is nothing new under the sun." The repetition that the Preacher sees ultimately bores and disgusts him. "Is there a thing of which it is said, 'See, this is new'? It has been already, in the ages before us." There is no progress, nothing is advancing. The rhythms of history, like those of nature, are unceasing. "There is no remembrance of former things"—man's memory is not sufficient to recall what former men have done, and man's intellect is therefore limited. "Nor will there be any remembrance of later things yet to happen among those who come after"—as we can not remember all the things that past men have done, so future men will not remember the things that we have done. We not only have limited intellects, the speaker suggests, we also have limited potential. And that is why the Preacher is depressed, why for him, "all is vanity."

It is easy enough, then, to document the pessimism and the despair of Ecclesiastes. We should be conscious, however, that the voice which says: "The words of the Preacher, the son of David, king in Jerusalem," may not be the speaker in the narrative, that that voice may be presenting to us a speaker who is identified as the son of David, king in Jerusalem. There may be a difference, in other words, between the voice (I will call him the "author") and the Preacher himself. There are sound literary reasons for the author to create this persona. For one thing, the words of Solomon, a symbol of wisdom, give the text authority and more immediate respect. Further, the words of a *king* (and not a poverty-afflicted prophet) save the text from being charged with presenting a sour grapes attitude towards life and towards experiences; presumably, as king, Solomon has had every material thing he desired. Finally, the words of one specifically identified as "king over Israel in Jerusalem" enable the text to comment from the inside, as it were, and not from the perspective of an outsider who might not be expected to understand Israel's history and Israel's religion; Solomon should understand them very well. The Preacher may, then, be a created character with a life and experiences of his own. There may be a distance between the author of Ecclesiastes and the Preacher himself; their biographies might differ, and the author's interpretation of the Preacher's life might not be the same as the Preacher's. We need to be alert to ironic possibilities and internal inconsistencies as the Preacher proceeds to summarize his life.

The Preacher announces that it had been his intention "to search out by wisdom all that is done under heaven." He has indeed seen everything that is done under the sun, he tells us, and "Behold, all is vanity and a striving after wind." Reform does not seem possible—what is crooked, in both a metaphorical and literal sense, cannot be made straight; basic needs cannot be filled, "what is lacking cannot be numbered." We can neither reduce the wickedness which abounds in the world nor satisfy the many wants of the people. The Preacher is puzzled; he had acquired "great wisdom," indeed he had surpassed all who came before him in Jerusalem. He had experienced wisdom and knowledge. Yet even as he says this, surely he must recall his own statement of verse 9: "What has been is what will be, and what has been done is what will be done." In what sense, then, can he have surpassed those who came before him? And how can he be confident of such a claim, considering his own statement that "there is no remembrance of former things"? So he applied his mind, he says, "to *know* wisdom and . . . madness and folly." He attempted to translate the wisdom he had gained into feeling, into emotion; he wanted to respond to it in a personal way instead of studying it and analyzing it. But he

271

quickly perceived that this also failed: "in much wisdom is much vexation, and he who increases knowledge increases sorrow." The more he learned, the more he knew of man and of life, the less satisfied he became. And therefore, he turned away from wisdom and knowledge and said to himself, "Come now, I will make a test of pleasure."

He shifts philosophical ground, in other words, abandoning contemplation, meditation, Stoicism, mental exertion, intellectual inquiry—call it what you will—in favor of activity, Epicureanism, laughter, material pleasures. But this life-style also turns out to be vanity. Earlier, the Preacher had asked what "gain" came from a man's labor, now he wants to know what "use" pleasure has: such passages may underline the gap between the author of Ecclesiastes (the "voice" of verse 1) and his character. It may not be proper to ask about the function or end of human activity before considering the value of the activity itself. The Preacher tried to cheer himself with wine, to "lay hold on folly," so that he might see "what was good for the sons of men to do under heaven during the few days of their life." He wanted, simply, to find out what made a man happy. The Preacher then describes in a passage of great vitality and energy all the great things he did, all his great works—he built houses and planted vineyards, he made gardens and orchards, he planted fruit trees, made pools, bought slaves. Much time passed, so much time that he had slaves who were born of slaves in his house. His flocks became numerous, he accumulated silver and gold, "the treasure of kings and provinces"; he hired singers and collected concubines. "So," he concludes, "I became great and surpassed all who were before me in Jerusalem." Our first response might be that he has deluded himself, that his greatness consists only of transient material things; but he also tells us, "my wisdom remained with me." He was now great in material wealth, and in wisdom and knowledge, knowledge of all the works that had been done under the sun. He seems to have achieved the human ideals of physical comfort and intellectual brilliance. He denied himself nothing: "Whatever my eyes desired I did not keep from them; I kept my heart from no pleasure." Because of his wisdom and his wealth, he tells us, anything he wanted was his.

But then, he says, "I considered all that my hands had done and the toil I had spent in doing it, and behold, all was vanity and a striving after wind." What has gone wrong? Why did all these works and all this knowledge fail to bring happiness? The Preacher considers his position and realizes that he has in a real sense set the limits: "What can the man do who comes after the king? Only what he has already done." Here I am, he thinks, and what can any man do after me, what progress or advances can be made—and the answer he gives himself is "nothing." But then he must recall his own earlier conclusion that "there is nothing new under the sun," and, in a moment of shattering self-awareness, must recognize that what he has done was done before him. He had thought that he had experienced moments unique to him, that he had burned with a "hard, gem-like flame." But he has not, after all, set the limits; he has simply achieved the limits already set. What then is *his?* How can he define his unique individuality, his unique happiness, when all he has accomplished is a repetition of the accomplishments of others? He has learned something; he sees that "wisdom excels darkness." At least he has the awareness, as a result of his wisdom and of his searching, that everything that he has, others have had before him and others will have after him. For a brief moment he is willing to accept this insight as the end of his search.

But then he shifts position again, by taking his conclusion one step further. It is true, he admits, that the wise man lives in the light and the fool in darkness; but it is also true "that one fate comes to all." He is wise, he has more awareness than the fool, he understands the limits of human activity; but he also, like the fool, will die. "What befalls the fool will befall me. . . . Why then have I been so very wise?" The Preacher acknowledges that everything he has achieved, intellectually and materially, is doomed; he will be forgotten, his works will be forgotten or worse, they might go into the hands of another he does not even know. "So," says the Preacher, at his lowest point in the narrative, "I hated life." In Deuteronomy 30:15 Moses had spoken to the people of Israel: "I have set before you . . . life and good, death and evil. . . . Therefore choose life." The Preacher at this moment seems to choose death.

Believing that his works have brought him no gain or profit, the Preacher, with uncharacteristic pettiness, becomes concerned that they might bring pleasure to others. He has turned his back on life, and yet, ironically, he is still enough attracted to life to be envious of those who will come after him. "I hated all my toil in which I had toiled under the sun, seeing that I must leave it to the man who will come after me." This seems a strange concern for someone who is supposedly wiser than all others and suggests again the ironic distance between the author and the Preacher. The Preacher is annoyed to think that someone else—a wise man or perhaps a fool—will be master of his houses and lands and slaves. The objects themselves seem to mean more to him than the functions they can perform, the pleasures he can derive from them. He falls into despair, jealously imagining another man enjoying the results of his labor, like a miser who will destroy his hoard before seeing it make someone else happy. The only solution seems to be for him to enjoy what he has while he has it: "There is nothing better for a man than that he should eat and drink and find enjoyment in his toil." Eat, drink, and be merry, the Preacher advises. But surely there is bitterness in this advice, considering that the Preacher had already concluded that pursuit of pleasure is also vanity. He is advocating a kind of hedonism that reflects his despair that life has nothing else to offer except a full belly. This is the gift of God, he says ironically, "For to the man who pleases him God gives wisdom and knowledge and joy; but to the sinner he gives the work of gathering and heaping, only to give to one who pleases God." Such an orthodox statement about God's system of reward and punishment conflicts sharply with human experience, as the Preacher has already pointed out (a fool might inherit his estate), and as he will point out repeatedly during the remainder of his meditation.

Having turned ironically to orthodoxy to counter his despair, the Preacher at the beginning of Chapter 3 takes us back to his opening words in order to flesh out the cycles within the larger cycle of generations coming and going. The human limits he had achieved, he now seems to recognize, were accomplished within the frames provided by larger limits, limits which in turn provide justification for the Preacher's Epicurean advice that we should enjoy life, eat and drink, and have a good time; "For everything there is a season, and a time for every matter under heaven." There is "a time to plant, and a time to pluck up what is planted"—these are the limits of nature. There is "a time to kill, and a time to heal; a time to break down, and a time to build up"—these are the limits of destruction and creativity. In a series of parallel phrases, the Preacher defines the coordinates of human life. Man moves between life and death, planting and harvesting, killing and healing, destroying and building, tears and laughter, mourning and dancing, forgiveness and anger, love and hate, searching and losing, hoarding and giving, tearing and patching, silence and talk, war and peace. Between these extremes man moves like a shuttle, his life being woven into patterns beyond his control. The desire of the Preacher to seek out wisdom, to see everything, to experience everything, has led him only to disillusionment, weariness, and despair. He suffers no outward or inward injury. He is not in the perplexed situation of Job. For the Preacher, it is the setting of life itself that is so painfully disappointing.

We hear less in what follows of the Preacher's biography, framed as it is by the general statements of the transitory nature of human experience in 1:2-11 and by the more detailed presentation of the main coordinates of human experience at the beginning of chapter 3. We also are less aware of the thought processes which led the Preacher to his conclusion, "All is vanity." Instead, we are given a combination of autobiographical recollections and reflections, brief narratives, maxims and parables, proverbial sayings, even, in chapter twelve, a short allegory. If we assume that the author maintains his use of the fictionalized speaker throughout, of someone who is at a distance from him and who is being manipulated by him towards self-revelation, then it seems that he is exploring, through the Preacher, various possible approaches to the problem of human happiness. The Preacher recalls more and more the anomalies he has seen, the depressing conclusions his experience and knowledge have led him to. He cites proverbs as if they might provide consolation. He offers maxims to bolster his sagging faith. He creates parables and brief narratives in order to look at the problems from different perspectives. He writes an allegory to consider life from yet another perspective. The Preacher constantly seems to be looking for some explanation which can provide comfort and open up the possibility of human happiness. Such a reading, which imagines the Preacher as separate from the voice of 1:1, is supported both by the biographical information we get about the Preacher in chapters 1 and 2, and also, strangely, by the inconsistencies of the text.

The inconsistencies are many. The Preacher's conclusions would seem to lead him toward thoughts of suicide, but that he never contemplates; instead, the meditation ends affirming life and even in the most pessimistic sections we seem to hear an energetic voice which is thinking out loud, exploring the possibilities for happiness. In chapter two, for example, he seems to reject a life of wisdom as vanity and unprofitable; and yet in chapter eight he will tell us, "A man's wisdom makes his face shine." At the beginning of chapter nine he informs us, "One fate comes to all, to the righteous and the wicked, to the good and the evil, to the clean and the unclean"; but shortly before in chapter eight he had pointed out that "though a sinner does evil a hundred times and prolongs his life, yet I know that it will be well with those who fear God, because they fear before him; but it will not be well with the wicked, neither will he prolong his days like a shadow, because he does not fear before God." On the one hand, to be evil or good seems not to matter; on the other hand, God seems very watchful of those who perform evil or good. In chapter four he praises "the dead who are already dead more . . . than the living who are still alive," and goes on to assert that the most blessed of all are those who have not been born. But then in chapter nine he tells us that "a living dog is better than a dead lion." These are only a few of the many inconsistencies in the text. Has the author nodded? Some of the inconsistencies might be explained away as later interpolations, or as indications of several hands being involved in the original compilation. But we are not dealing here with *War and Peace*. Ecclesiastes is a short collection of a few hundred verses and it is hard to believe that the priestly interpolators or editors were so bad that they could not straighten out the numerous contradictions.

If the Preacher is seen as a consistent literary creation throughout, however, then the seeming inconsistencies are part of his reflections, not a result of the author's incompetence. The author has created someone who confronts the contradictions and inconsistencies of human experience and draws on all his wisdom in an attempt to understand them. The Preacher muses on his own experiences and compares them with the formal learning he has obtained from various sources, and he discovers that the two do not complement each other very well. Proverbs and maxims, anecdotes and narratives simply do not always accurately reflect human experience. The Preacher is aware of the relative value of proverbs and maxims, as he is aware of the relative value of philosophies and orthodoxies. A good proverb timely introduced can suit almost any circumstance. A respectable philosophy can be unearthed to justify almost any decision. This does not mean that the Preacher is any less pessimistic; he may be pessimistic, however, for reasons other than the one normally assumed—that he believes life is meaningless. Certainly in the biographical passages he offers good reason for pessimism. He has digested all knowledge and wisdom and discovered that the righteous suffer and that the evil prosper. In addition, his brief narratives pick up and emphasize the statements of the opening: that God is inscrutable, that man cannot change the world, that our efforts and energies are a waste of time, that goodness does not lead to happiness. And what, after all, did the Preacher want? What was he searching for? He wanted justice; he wanted to be remembered; he wanted to have faith in men; he wanted to feel a sense of progress and of permanence in human affairs; he wanted to perceive a moral order. And he was disappointed in all his desires. Realist that he is, he boils everything down to two great realities, to the essentials—death and chance.

The concepts are linked many times and form a prominent and depressing pattern which runs throughout Ecclesiastes. Because of chance and death, the quality of a man's action has no final meaning; "one fate comes to all . . . . As is the good man, so is the sinner." Even man's potential is limited; he is not preeminent over the beasts, "for the fate of the sons of men and the fate of beasts is the same; as one dies, so dies the other." What man and beast have in common is more crucial than their trivial differences. Man's actions, therefore, mean nothing. He is moving towards the same end as the beasts over which he has no preeminence. Even the time between the coordinates of birth and death provides no comfort: "the race is not to the swift, nor the battle to the strong, nor bread to the wise, nor riches to the intelligent, nor favor to the men of skill; but time and chance happen to them all."

This is all very somber and pessimistic when stated in summary fashion. Yet, it does not seem to capture the flavor of Ecclesiastes as a whole. Nor does the consolation which runs throughout Ecclesiastes seem to capture that flavor either. We first hear of the consolation in chapter two when the Preacher says that there is nothing better for a man than that he should eat and drink and find enjoyment in his toil. The same sentiment is expressed often enough in later chapters to constitute an important secondary theme to the Preacher's primary emphasis on human vanity. We hear it in chapter three: "It is God's gift to man that every one should eat and drink and take pleasure in all his toil," and again in chapter 5, "Behold, what I have seen to be good and to be fitting is to eat and drink and find enjoyment in all the toil with which one toils under the sun." We are reminded of the consolation in chapter eight: "I commend enjoyment, for man has no good thing under the sun but to eat and drink and enjoy himself," and again in chapter 9: "Go, eat your bread with enjoyment, and drink your wine with a merry heart." Finally, chapter 11 opens with the advice, "Cast your bread upon the waters, for you will find it after many days," and goes on to commend the instinctive natural life. Essentially, the advice of the Preacher in these passages is for man to enjoy himself while he can from moment to moment without planning too far ahead; to avoid grand schemes, to be moderate, cautious; to accept things as they are; to ignore reform, ignore what is predetermined and a matter of chance anyway; to enjoy being alive without theorizing about life; to enjoy work without worrying about the profit to be gained; to enjoy moments of happiness or pleasure for their own sake.

How far is this consolation from the purely aesthetic and amoral world of Walter Pater? Pater argues that the end of life is not the fruit of experience, but experience itself. "With this sense of the splendor of our experience," writes Pater, "and of its awful brevity, gathering all we are into one desperate effort to see and touch, we shall hardly have time to make theories about the things we see and touch." There is a kind of consolation here, in Pater as in Ecclesiastes, and yet it does not seem to satisfy a modern sensibility, as perhaps it did not satisfy the author of Ecclesiastes' sensibility either. At best such a view of life is hedonistic and epicurean; at worst, it is amoral and selfish. It cuts us off from being concerned about other people, sensitive to their needs and their aspirations. It takes us away from the complexity of life and shields us by concealing from us the control of chance, the opposite poles of life and death, happiness and sadness, creativity and destruction, between which our lives, shuttle-like, are woven. At the same time, the evidence from Ecclesiastes is that the Preacher seems to have adopted this principle himself. He tried pleasures and found them wanting. He achieved wisdom and found it vanity. The gifts of God are surely to eat and drink and toil; but, as he asks repeatedly, are these God's only gifts?

The very tone of Ecclesiastes, however, works against his apparent consolation, against the principle he appears to have adopted. He is himself much involved, he loves to question, to theorize, to criticize. He takes delight in working up his case. He loves to go against the grain, denying what everyone else accepts. But his remarks are also full of unbounded vitality. The work as a whole denies his assertion, "I hated life," filled as it is with activity and exertion, and enjoyment in the activity and in the exertion.

Throughout Ecclesiastes the Preacher balances images of light and darkness, life and death, sun and shadow, day and night, and he comes down strongly on a preference for light. By light, however, he does not mean simply life lived in awareness; he means life lived without self-deception, without despair, life lived in full questioning awareness. We cannot be smug or complacent, Ecclesiastes is reminding us. We must look anew at everything—naturally, instinctively, consciously. We begin to realize that his main purpose in these somber meditations on death is to give additional zest and sparkle to life itself. We must remember, he tells us repeatedly, what old age and death really are. "Remember also your Creator in the days of your youth," he says at the opening of chapter 12, "before the evil days come, and the years draw nigh, when you will say, 'I have no pleasure in them'; before the sun and the light and the moon and the stars are darkened and the clouds return after the rain." We should appreciate the heavens while we can still see them. We should experience the sensation of touching another object or person before "the day when the keepers of the house tremble" and we are bent with age. We should savor our food and drink before "the grinders cease because they are few." We should enjoy what is around us before "those that look through the windows are dimmed," before we are blind, "and the doors on the street are shut" as the funeral processions of friends pass by. We should eat to surfeit, before "the sound of the grinding is low," before our strength wanes. We should listen while we can hear and are alert, before we rise up "at the voice of a bird, and all the daughters of song are brought low." The time will come when we will be beset with fears, "afraid . . . of what is high, and terrors . . . in the way." The time will come when age will be a burden, when "the almond tree blossoms," and we cannot smell it, when the grasshopper announces the coming of spring, but "drags itself along and desire fails," when we near our eternal home, "and the mourners go about the streets." The time will come when all our senses will fail us, when we cannot see, cannot touch, cannot taste, cannot hear, cannot smell. Even simple everyday tasks will elude us, "the silver cord is snapped, or the golden bowl is broken, or the pitcher is broken at the fountain, or the wheel broken at the cistern." And then, writes the Preacher, concluding his allegory of dying, "the dust returns to the earth as it was, and the spirit returns to God who gave it."

Ultimately, there is no pessimism here. There is bluntness and honesty, and painful self-awareness. The author who created the Preacher has no answers, although he has the Preacher survey many possible ones; he has no final consolation, although he knows man should fill his life, according to his individual capacities, remembering that his reach will always exceed his grasp, that good will never be attained proportionate to his yearnings for it. The Preacher, in his exploration of proverbs and maxims, anecdotes and allegory, autobiographical recollections, philosophical systems, religious positions and dogmas, opens up the many ways in which a man might find happiness. But no way, he suggests, is better or worse than another; like the proverbs, they are relative, and a man must find those which best suit his nature and his instincts. "What we have to do," the voice which introduced the Preacher would agree with Pater, "is to be forever curiously testing new opinions and courting new impressions, never acquiescing in a facile orthodoxy." "Truly the *light* is sweet," the light of full consciousness. Man may be the shuttle, moving between the coordinates of birth and death, happiness and sadness, creativity and destruction, but the shuttle makes a pattern, a fabric is woven, and the movements culminate in a finished garment. "Man is the shuttle," wrote the seventeenth-century poet Henry Vaughan,

> to whose winding quest
> And passage through these looms
> God ordered motion, but ordained no rest.

XV The Two Kingdoms in Matthew's Gospel

JAN WOJCIK, *Department of English, Purdue University*

The best way to read any narrative text is to consider it so closely that the author seems to be reading it directly to us. All the emphasis that the author wanted the reader to catch becomes obvious. In some narratives the author seems to intrude into the work to address the reader directly. In many narratives the author emphasizes the story more subtly. The composition of the work—the way scenes fit together, the way character personalities conflict and resolve their differences, the way the book ends—creates a pattern of emphasis. This pattern can have an almost magical effect. Through it a consciousness beyond the story signals a presence to the reader and, at the same time, shows the reader the meaning of the work. This pattern works in Matthew's Gospel. It makes Jesus' message about the two kingdoms, preached throughout the Gospel, seemingly shape the very narrative which carries the message.

We begin with a passage which opens a window onto the significance and artistry of Matthew's Gospel. The passage is Matthew 14. Imagine what effect the juxtaposition of the two scenes which begin the chapter might have been intended to have for the early audience.

(Scene One) For Herod had seized John and bound him and put him in prison, for the sake of Herodias, his brother Philip's wife; because John said to him, "It is not lawful for you to have her." And though he wanted to put him to death, he feared the people, because they held him to be a prophet. But when Herod's birthday came, the daughter of Herodias danced before the company, and pleased Herod, so that he promised with an oath to give her whatever she might ask. Prompted by her mother, she said, "Give me the head of John the Baptist here on a platter." And the king was sorry; but because of his oaths and his guests he commanded it to be given; he

sent and had John beheaded in the prison, and his head was brought on a platter and given to the girl, and she brought it to her mother. And his disciples came and took the body and buried it; and they went and told Jesus.
(Scene Two) Now when Jesus heard this, he withdrew from there in a boat to a lonely place apart. But when the crowds heard it, they followed him on foot from the towns. As he went ashore he saw a great throng; and he had compassion on them, and healed their sick. When it was evening, the disciples came to him and said, "This is a lonely place, and the day is now over; send the crowds away to go into the villages and buy food for themselves." Jesus said, "They need not go away; you give them something to eat." They said to him, "We have only five loaves here and two fish." And he said, "Bring them here to me." Then he ordered the crowds to sit down on the grass; and taking the five loaves and the two fish he looked up to heaven, and blessed, and broke and gave the loaves to the disciples, and the disciples gave them to the crowds. And they all ate and were satisfied. And they took up twelve baskets full of the broken pieces left over. And those who ate were about five thousand men, besides women and children. (14:3-21)

Both these scenes are often commented on separately, especially the second scene, which becomes a prefiguration of the Last Supper, or of the institution of the Eucharist, or a type of the Passover. But what is the impact of the two scenes taken together? It is implicit, I think, in the contrasts. Both are scenes of a party and a meal. In the first the aristocracy entertain themselves with an erotic dance. This leads to Herod's serving up on a dish a horribly sterile meal—the head of a man—that can only nourish the darkest appetites of the soul. In the second a great multitude of the common people are nourished with good words and then with a miraculously fruitful meal.

The implicit lesson of the two scenes would be very obvious if you saw them juxtaposed in a movie. In fact, the first time it occurred to me that this might have been an intentional coupling of scenes was in viewing Pasolini's film, *The Gospel According to Saint Matthew*. What makes the gospel so easy to transfer almost literally to the screen, as Pasolini did, is that it is already very cinematic in its composition. Both in the book and in the film the significance of the contrasting scenes is given

In silence with no explicit attention drawn to it. The reader or viewer himself is invited to draw the meaning from the silence.

There is another silent gesture made here, I think. The contrast in scenes dramatizes a contrast to which Jesus draws attention in his preaching: the opposition between the kingdom of evil and the kingdom of heaven in the world. Consider how devils haunt this Gospel with images of evil. Possessed pigs rush off a cliff at one place, in many others sick people writhe in the possession of Satan. In every scene which Jesus shares with devils he takes the opportunity to emphasize the existence of two opposed kingdoms in the world which his presence and the presence of the devils signify. "It is only by Beelzebub, the prince of demons, that this man casts out demons," say the Pharisees when Jesus cures one possessed person. Jesus responds that if the devil's kingdom were ordered against itself it would fall. The true division is between the devil's kingdom and the kingdom of God by whose spirit he casts out devils (12:22-28). In two other similar situations Jesus uses the confrontations as an opportunity to describe the distinguishing quality of "faith" which those in the kingdom of heaven have and those without do not. A Canaanite woman's daughter is exorcised because of her great faith (15:21-28). He tells the disciples that they have failed to cast the devil out of an epileptic "because of [their] little faith" (17:14-20). He makes the same contrast when Peter says that he will not permit Jesus to suffer execution. Jesus replies, "Get behind me, Satan! You are a hindrance to me; for you are not on the side of God, but of men" (16:21-24). When we bring these scenes together it seems that "being on God's side" means having faith, which means being a member of the kingdom of heaven. The necessity of faith suggests that the kingdom of heaven is a state of mind rather than a political estate.

We can find out more about this state of mind if we gather together what Jesus says about it in parables. We proceed tentatively for at one place Jesus rightly calls parables "the secrets of the kingdom of heaven"; they suggest only an elusive definition even when taken together. These definitions begin with a statement that "the kingdom of heaven is like this," and then follow with a story of some decisive action. A man sows a mustard seed which grows into a large tree (13:31-32). A woman takes yeast and leavens flour (13:33). These two parables suggest that the state of mind is something that grows greatly after a small beginning. Other parables suggest that the state of mind develops through or is manifest in generosity to others. A king forgives the debt of a servant. Later he discovers that the servant does not forgive another servant in his debt. The king punishes his servant (18:23-35). A landowner pays all the laborers in his vineyard, even those who came last, the same wage (20:1-16). Taking these parables together with the scenes of exorcism, we see that the kingdom seems to be a state of mind with which one chooses to believe in God and to be generous with one's neighbor.

It should be noted that I have started using another kind of analysis with these scenes and parables than the kind with which we started. We consider these scenes and parables out of the sequence in which they occur. This is done because the way Jesus is shown to teach seems to require it. There does not seem to be any progressive development of definitions or ideas in Jesus' preaching. Rather he uses each occasion to make a certain point. Taken together, the cumulative defini-tions of the two kingdoms are suggestive, rather than pre-cise, and seem to invite further investigations. Jesus defines "kingdom" in Matthew much as Paul defines "law" in the Epistle to the Romans, or again as John's Jesus defines "world" after the great discourse. The word recurs each time with a slightly different meaning attached to it. The reader is drawn to compare the definitions and to construct a signifi-cance that is not given explicitly in the text.

Again, the narrative gestures in silence to meanings which the reader must corroborate to derive. Perhaps this is an aspect of the genius of didactic literature in the Scriptures. Often the narrative implicitly invites the reader to gather together the seeds of its meaning. Matthew invites two kinds of analyses: the first is thematic, the second structural. The reader who can grasp what the opposition of kingdoms means in Jesus' preaching can perhaps better appreciate Matthew's extension of this idea in the very composition of the Gospel, as in the scenes of the two meals. Taken together, thematic and structural analyses underlie a literary reading of the gospel. The text is used to interpret itself.

But before considering again the compositional emphasis Matthew gives to the theme of the two kingdoms, we should look at two more parable-given definitions of the kingdoms. We can discover, I think, a subtle and important idea about the kingdoms which Jesus emphasizes and to which Matthew gives subtle emphasis compositionally. A man sows his field with good seed. An enemy sows weeds in the field. Both spring up together. The man decides to separate the plants only at harvest time (13:24-30). Another parable presents this idea in another form. A net is thrown into the sea and brings up good and bad fish (13:47-50). When taken together both these parables suggest that the people of both kingdoms live together until a harvest time, that both kingdoms inhabit the same world at any point in time. One has to choose in which state of mind one will live until some future time when the states of mind will become truly separate estates.

The structure of one passage towards the end of the gospel emphasizes this notion of the cohabitation of the two kingdoms. Now we take up again the first kind of analysis —looking for an imitation of the theme or an emphasis on the theme in the composition of a narrative. The passage begins chapter 26. Its first scene presents the disciples at table:

When Jesus had finished all these sayings, he said to his disciples, "You know that after two days the Passover is coming, and the Son of man will be delivered up to be crucified." (26:1-2)

This scene immediately dissolves into another; Jesus' enemies are plotting the execution he has just prophesied:

Then the chief priests and the elders of the people gathered in the palace of the high priest, who was called Caiaphas, and took counsel together in order to arrest Jesus by stealth and kill him. But they said, "Not during the feast, lest there be a tumult among the people." (26:3-5)

The indefinite words for the time—"when" and "then"—suggest that both scenes occur simultaneously, the two kingdoms operate contemporaneously, and once again we see the activities of both contrasted through a scene shift.

The scene then shifts to the house of Simon the leper. The action is picked up in the middle of a party, in order, it seems, to emphasize again that Jesus is preparing for the execution that his enemies are supposedly planning in secret. Their plots are merely necessary adjuncts to a providential pattern Jesus seems to control:

Now when Jesus was at Bethany in the house of Simon the leper, a woman came up to him with an alabaster flask of very expensive ointment, and she poured it on his head, as he sat at table. But when he disciples saw it, they were indignant, saying, "Why this waste? For this ointment might have been sold for a large sum, and given to the poor." But Jesus, aware of this, said to them, "Why do you trouble the woman? For she has done a beautiful thing to me. For you always have the poor with you, but you will not always have me. In pouring ointment on my body she has done it to prepare me for burial. Truly, I say to you, wherever this gospel is preached in the whole world, what she has done will be told in memory of her." (26:6-13)

The narrative has involved the reader in a conspiracy of knowing. The reader shares the narrator's point of view and is privy to Jesus' superior point of view as well. All of us can see, as no one directly in the story can see, that Jesus goes to his death ritually and consciously. It is no mistake. We see all this from heaven as it were, from the perspective of the kingdom of heaven. Something else in the narrative presentation suggests as well that everything Jesus does is premeditated; the placement of the scene here seems obviously to be premeditated as well. Again the time is left indefinite. There might have been days or weeks between the Last Supper and this incident. Indeed, this scene could well have happened prior to the last days, and have been inserted here strictly because of it appropriateness. But even if it did occur in sequence with the scenes between which it occurs in the narrative, the focus on just the climactic and significant moment at the party demonstrates how much control over the material the narrative has. Its control parallels Jesus' control of his destiny.

The next scene consists of a fleeting glance of Judas Iscariot caught at the moment of betrayal:

Then one of the twelve, who was called Judas Iscariot, went to the chief priests and said, "What will you give me if I deliver him to you?" And they paid him thirty pieces of silver. And from that moment he sought an opportunity to betray him. (26:14-16)

Judas' momentary scene dissolves once again into a scene dominated by Jesus. And as it does, the pattern we have been following culminates. Both Jesus and an enemy are at the same place. Notice how the camera-like eye telling the scene zooms in at the end for an intense close-up of Jesus and Judas speaking. Only the reader can overhear the dialogue spoken across the frontiers of the two kingdoms. The scene has three parts: the preparation, the meal, and the close-up:

Now on the first day of Unleavened Bread the disciples came to Jesus, saying, "Where will you have us prepare for you to eat the passover?" He said, "Go into the city to a certain one, and say to him, 'The Teacher says, My time is at hand; I will keep the passover at your house with my disciples.' " And the disciples did as Jesus had directed them, and they prepared the passover.

When it was evening, he sat at table with the twelve disciples; and as they were eating, he said, "Truly, I say to you, one of you will betray me." And they were very sorrowful, and began to say to him one after another, "Is it I, Lord?" He answered, "He who has dipped his hand in the dish with me, will betray me. The Son of man goes as it is written of him, but woe to that man by whom the Son of man is betrayed! It would have been better for that man if he had not been born."

Judas, who betrayed him, said, "Is it I, Master?" He said to him, "You have said so." (26:17-25)

The parables now have a realistic dramatization. Here are the wheat and the weeds in the same field, the good and bad fish in the same narrative net. The reader can become involved in a rich pattern of cross referencing, drawn on only by the materials of a single Gospel.

We have considered an essential part of this Gospel. The variety of the ways in which Jesus teaches about the two kingdoms indicates its importance to him. The narrative or compositional echo of the theme indicates that the evangelist learned well from Jesus. The artful contrivance of scenic composition of the theme indicates to the reader how important it is that the reader also understand the theme. A reader who has made these kinds of discoveries is now on solid enough ground to proceed in a number of directions. The most valuable one would be a personal reflection on the significance discovered. What does the text mean to me? Do I believe the ideas its story and narrative composition emphasize? This kind of questioning need not be the next step in reading, but whenever it occurs, it can be untainted by excessive subjectivity with a solid understanding of the text as it is in hand.

We have so far simply correlated the theme of the two kingdoms with what seems to be a structural or compositional echo of the theme. Our method has not required heavy scholarly apparatus. I have suggested that its worth is in its simplicity. With this method a student could confidently read a text well, for only the text and an acute reading is needed for appreciation of literature. Any good reader could do it, even on a bus. Good teachers strive to make themselves gradually superfluous by showing students how they might handle texts on their own. This method needs no teacher after it is grasped, although its users could enjoy the company of other readers sharing insights.

Now let us consider how valid the method is in itself as an honest appraisal of a scriptural narrative or of any narrative. I would like to use two approaches. The first is to ask of the text the question, How much conscious literary craftmanship is there in this echoing of the theme in the narrative composition? Is this structural echo merely a fortuitous coincidence or part of the intention of the gospel? After all, we are trying to hear the gospel as it was composed purposefully. The second approach is to compare our method with other methods traditionally used to interpret narratives.

Initially, it might seem that this gospel is not necessarily making conscious structural echoes of Jesus' preaching. The two sets of scenes we have considered in Matthew occur in the other Synoptic Gospels of Luke and Mark in the same order and in roughly the same places in the story. The juxtapositions of the scenes seem to be an inherited or shared form handed around intact. Mark has been given credit by many scholars for first giving the materials in the Synoptic Gospels their shape. But, perhaps even Mark inherited the scenes set up in this way. At any rate the Gospel of Matthew cannot be given credit for originating the scenes as narrative echoes.

A close comparison of the rest of Luke and Mark with Matthew, however, shows that only Matthew stresses the theme of the two kingdoms. This suggests that the Gospel of Matthew uniquely links this set of inherited scene shifts with the unique theme of the two kingdoms in Jesus' preaching. So, this gospel's originality, perhaps, resides in finding a theme to echo the narrative forms. This is a fascinating reversal of our normal expectations if it is true.

We might find evidence that the gospel of Matthew was consciously correlating the theme of two kingdoms with the narrative technique of juxtaposing scenes if we consider one narrative structure that *is* unique to this Gospel. Let us look at the ending of the Gospel, or I should say, the two endings, one for the adherents of each kingdom, each state of mind. The first "ending" occurs in chapter 29, verses 8-10 and 16-20. Taken together these verses read as follows:

So they departed quickly from the tomb with fear and great joy, and ran to tell his disciples. And behold, Jesus met them and said, "Hail!" And they came up and took hold of his feet and worshiped him. Then Jesus said to them, "Do not be afraid; go and tell my brethren to go to Galilee, and there they will see me." (28:8-10)

Now the eleven disciples went to Galilee, to the mountain to which Jesus had directed them. And when they saw him they worshiped him; but some doubted. And Jesus came and said to them, "All authority in heaven and on earth has been given to me. Go therefore and make disciples of all nations, baptizing them in the name of the Father and of the Son and of the Holy Spirit, teaching them to observe all that I have commanded you; and lo, I am with you always, to the close of the age." (28:16-20)

We find sandwiched between these two segments of the same scene another scene which features the activities of Jesus' enemies:

While they were going, behold, some of the guard went into the city and told the chief priests all that had taken place. And when they has assembled with the elders and taken counsel, they gave a sum of money to the soldiers and said, "Tell people, 'His disciples came by night and stole him away while we were asleep.' And if this comes to the governor's ears, we will satisfy him and keep you out of trouble." So they took the money and did as they were directed; and this story has been spread among the Jews to this day (28:11-15)

Matthew gives the reader a choice between endings just as Jesus challenges his hearers to a choice between kingdoms. We can see another aspect of this technique of juxtaposition as it is used in this passage, in the John the Baptist/Multiplication of Loaves passage, and in the Last Days passage; that is, that the Jesus scene or the kingdom of heaven scene is always a much more attractive scene than its counterpart. The sterile meal is nothing to compare with the nourishing one; the plotters do not have as much control over the situation as their victim; the authorities' explanation of Jesus' disappearance from the tomb is dry and dull compared with the wonderful belief of the disciples. One is encouraged by the narrative contrasts to see the value of the state of mind of the believers in the good kingdom.

We could conclude from this textual validation that there does seem to be a conscious literary artistry inviting us to see the profound convictions to be gained from correlating the forms of the Jesus story with the themes of the Jesus story. Therefore our method which has ferreted out this artistry in the narrative of the story is on sound ground. We have made a simple validation of a simple method. We have only gone as far afield as the other Synoptic Gospels to find some confirmation of the value of what we are doing with Matthew's Gospel, reading it by itself. Now let us consider how our purely literary method holds up against more familiar scholarly methods of interpretation.

The first thing that could be said is that an acute, appreciative reading should accompany any type of analysis of a literary text. A good professional interpreter, interested in a literary text as a symptom of extraliterary thought, social practice, or the personal development of a writer, usually gets to know the text intimately, as an integral object, in the process of using the text as a source for whatever kind of knowledge being pursued. A moderately perceptive reader in the sense used here has simpler interests—to understand the text in all its thematic and compositional complexity, but the beginning point for the ordinary and the professional reader is the same. For excellent examples of a professional reading, see Erich Auerbach's essays on the Abraham-Isaac story and the story of Peter's denial in Mark's gospel (Erich Auerbach, *Mimesis: The Representation of Reality in Western Literature*, trans. Willard R. Trask (Princeton, New Jersey: Princeton University Press, 1968)). Auerbach traces an evolution in literary and social perceptions by means of a sensitive integral analysis of literary texts.

To define our method in comparison to a close cousin, we could say that it is a literary-aesthetic analysis, much like the analysis the New Criticism makes of poetical texts. The text is viewed as a complex unity whose parts relate to one another to form a whole, special kind of discourse. But the method as demonstrated here stops short of evaluating the text critically in comparison with others of its type, as New Criticism readings often do. If we did go so far, we might condemn Matthew's Gospel for not sustaining its compositional commentary. Only occasionally do such windows illuminate the Jesus story. The text is a rough collection of sayings and events without much obvious significant order. On the other hand, we could praise the lack of narrative order as an invitation to the reader to compose an order himself. Matthew's Gospel subtly involves the reader in discovering the shape of its significance. The structural echoes provide occasional clues. Thus the Gospel is good didactic literature and not simply poorly organized narrative art. Using our literary method, however, one does not need to make such judgments. The ordinary reader reads in order to see the text as part of a conversation with the writer of the story.

The real question to be put to this method is, how clearly present is the author in the pattern of emphasis in the story? Form criticism of the Bible has been used to treat forms as colder phenomena—evidence of the pressure of changing dogmatic opinions to include, exclude, or alter materials in a text as it is passed down. Original collections of sayings and descriptions of events are shaped one way and then reshaped according to differing concerns of different communities at different times. Much New Testament criticism has been an attempt to identify layers of composition and redaction much as a geologist identifies the strata of a hill. It could be argued that any method such as the "literary-aesthetic" method which warms the narrative shape of a Gospel into a human indication of how the significance of the story is to be understood is sentimental. It anthropomorphizes the effects of dogmatic evolution of a text, effects whose causes are not completely known, and which might have been more random, less purposeful, than a holistic reading makes them seem.

The response to the question is to concede that our purely literary interpretation is a limited, anthropomorphic interpretation, but that there are good reasons for using it. The most important is that it can be a means to an honest, unexcessive analysis of how a text actually does hold together; the end justifies the means. Students can be led to see what is actually there if permitted to entertain a fiction that minds much like theirs made the text to be self-explanatory. Whatever remains that does not fit into what one sees to be a whole design can be understood as similar to the shadows of mystery which accent any manifestation of human motivation.

It can also be argued that the long life Matthew's Gospel has had in its present shape adds some authority to the idea that it deserves to be read as it stands. It is the way it is, and means as it means in the present idiosyncratic shape it is in.

But what I think is the most interesting defense of our method can be derived from a practice prevalent in much modern criticism of novels and narratives—the practice of treating the implied narrator of a narrative as an artificial construct, as a kind of character made up by the actual author to do the telling. The narrator is not to be considered a ventriloquist dummy for its author-creator. In Matthew's gospel, this narrator is composed of all the decisions, errors, revisions, inspiration, and quirks of history that made the text what it finally becomes. What we hear when we read is a narrator as repetitious and garrulous as Pickwick. The narrative shifts from lists of sayings to a jumble of events without ever losing sight of its purpose and sometimes clarifying that purpose brilliantly. For all that, the narrator is a trusted guide into the world of the text.

One final thought. This purely literary method will most likely be used with translations in unspecialized studies of the Scripture. This does not necessarily mean that students need to be warned that they are interpreting only a shadow image of the original text. The method relies on an acute observation of narrative structures—scene shifts, contrasts, narrative point of view, etc.—which translate in prose narratives without serious loss from one language to another. What is lost in translation, of course, is the poetic and allusive quality of language, which highlights, but does not shape the substance of prose narratives. Perhaps, as intended, the Bible is substantially accessible to confident, acute, ordinary readers.

XVI The Gospel of Mark

KENNETH R. R. GROS LOUIS

Our students come to the study of the New Testament as literature with the same disadvantages that we bring to it in teaching it as literature. We all know the plot and many of the characters and incidents of the story, many of its phrases and parables; we are probably aware, also, of the traditional meaning and significance of the narrative. We are expected, in other words, to analyze and interpret as literature a piece of writing which comes to us already fully interpreted. It is most important, therefore, even more so perhaps than in the Old Testament, for us to separate what we know about the life of Jesus from the Gospel of Mark, to approach the book as much as possible as if we had not seen it before, as if this were a work that was new to us.

My intention is to look closely at the opening four chapters of Mark and attempt to analyze them as freshly as possible. Following this analysis, we will consider the development of the major themes in Mark (all of them introduced in the opening chapters) and the use of parables in the text. How do the parables function in relation to the whole? For what purposes are they used? What do they contribute to the narrative? What do we learn from them that we would not learn from straightforward narration? Consideration of the parables will lead us to a third concern—the arrangement of scenes in the narrative. Why do certain details, stories, foreshadowings, digressions, appear where they do? Do we get any sense of purposeful structural and thematic designs? Finally, as another means of demonstrating the literary achievement of the gospel, we will consider what the story might mean to us as twentieth-century students of *literature*.

I

"The beginning of the gospel of Jesus Christ, the Son of God. As it is written in Isaiah the prophet, 'Behold, I send my messenger before thy face, who shall prepare thy way; the voice of one crying in the wilderness: Prepare the way of the Lord, make his paths straight.'" Why does the text take us back to earlier biblical prophecy? The key is perhaps in the phrase "as it is written." A pattern is being established, a pattern with a long and known history: as Isaiah is understood to have announced the coming of John, so John announces the coming of Christ, and so Christ will announce the coming of the new kingdom. From the very beginning of the narrative we know that it will depict the culmination of historical events in which Old Testament prophets, John, and Christ have taken or will take part. We are given as well a sense of preparation for something which is coming, for Christ's teachings, as it will turn out, which are themselves a preparation for something else. This is the "beginning" of the gospel of the Son of God. "Prepare the way of the Lord, make his paths straight," it has been written. What does it mean to us that the Lord will come? What is he going to bring? What is he like? How will he be described? The questions are similar to those we might have asked about the nature of God in Genesis; but here, after the long traditions of the Old Testament, the questions have many echoes, many reverberations. "John the baptizer appeared in the wilderness [a connection is made to Isaiah, both verbally (the "wilderness") and in the terms of the event (the preparation)], preaching a baptism of repentance for the forgiveness of sins. And there went out to him all the country of Judea, and all the people of Jerusalem." Many believers (hyperbolically, "all the people") come to John, indicating to us the circumstances of his time: there seems to be eagerness to believe this herald in the wilderness who is proclaiming a baptism of repentance; and yet, of course, as we will soon see, the eagerness is not universal. John will be arrested. "They were baptized by him in the river Jordan, confessing their sins. Now John was clothed with camel's hair, and had a leather girdle around his waist, and ate locusts and wild honey."

Why does the narrative emphasize these details about John? Some readers might recall the description of Elijah (II Kings 1:8), but there is no particular reason for us, as first readers, to know anything more about John than that he is a messenger, the messenger announced in Isaiah (we might not even know who Isaiah is), that he is proclaiming a baptism, that he is announcing the coming of the Lord. But the description informs us that he is a man of the desert. He wears camel's hair, a leather girdle, and he feeds on locusts and honey. And yet, in what is for us a paradox, this rough desert man is also a "herald," and one who is preparing the way of the Lord. Even more strikingly, John announces: "After me comes he who is mightier than I." Since John has just been described as a man of the desert, wearing a rough coat, feeding on locusts and wild honey, in what sense is he mighty? And in what sense then can the "he" who is coming be mightier? But John continues, "I am not worthy to stoop down and untie" his sandals. If John's role as herald seems puzzling, the might of the one who is coming is more mysterious. Obviously, he is not going to be mighty because of great wealth, power, or influence. "I have baptized you with water," says John, "but he will baptize you with the Holy Spirit." We may not know what baptism or the Holy Spirit are, but we are certainly aware that there is a striking difference between John and the one who comes—the one whose way he is preparing—not only in the degrees of their might, but in the fact that the one who comes will "baptize" in a way, John suggests, which is superior to his.

We then hear that Jesus has come from Nazareth and has been baptized by John. "And when he came up out of the water, immediately he saw the heavens opened and the Spirit descending upon him like a dove; and a voice came from heaven, 'Thou art my beloved Son; with thee I am well pleased.' " There are a number of signs—the Spirit descending, the heavens tearing open, the voice speaking from heaven—signs which presumably suggest who this person is and where he comes from. We have been told he is the Son of God, but those in the narrative do not share our information. They must wonder: Is he the one? What do the signs mean? They know that there is a difference between John and Jesus, and yet John himself—there is no reason to think otherwise, except that he is a "herald"—is not very impressive according to conventional standards. Will this Jesus be more impressive? "The Spirit immediately drove [Jesus] out into the wilderness [a further narrative link in that Isaiah had announced the voice crying in the wilderness, John had appeared in the wilderness, and now Jesus goes into the wilderness] and he was in the wilderness forty days, tempted by Satan." No explanation is given of what "tempted by Satan" means, but it opens up enormous imaginative possibilities and enlarges on the mystery of Jesus. "He was with the wild beasts; and the angels ministered to him." The seemingly paradoxical situation in which the wild beasts surround Jesus and yet angels wait upon him, recalls the suggested differences between baptism by water and by the Holy Spirit as well as the basic distinction between John, the man of the desert, and one who, in some sense, is mightier than he.

The ministering angels seem to confirm the signs about Jesus; but then, suddenly, we hear that John has been arrested. Why? There is no indication of any wrongdoing on his part; indeed, from what we have been told of John, he seems to be well received by the large number of people who flock to him for baptism. And yet, he has been arrested. All is apparently not well; the atmosphere in which Jesus moves is perhaps less friendly to him than we might have thought. If John, the herald announcing the coming of Jesus, has been arrested, does the same fate await Jesus? "Jesus came into Galilee, preaching the gospel of God." The pattern suggested in the opening is nearing completion—Isaiah proclaimed the coming of John, John prepared for the coming of Jesus, now Jesus preaches the gospel of God, that the kingdom of God is coming. Jesus becomes the herald in John's place, and the focus of the narrative shifts to him. John's story is, for a time, put aside. Why are the details of John's arrest and subsequent fate withheld? Why will they be given only later as a flashback, breaking the chronology of the narrative?

"The time is fulfilled," says Jesus, "and the kingdom of God is at hand." Given our religious heritage, we might nod understandingly and pass over the words quickly; and yet, as part of a literary narrative, the statement is mysterious. We do not know what it means. Certainly those in Jesus' world do not know what he means, as we will see repeatedly. The people he speaks to, even his disciples, have great difficulty understanding what he is talking about. "Repent," he says, "and believe in the gospel"—believe, that is, in the message of the very book we are reading. Jesus walks along the shores of the sea of Galilee and sees two fishermen, Simon and Andrew. "Follow me and I will make you become fishers of men," he says to them, "and immediately they left their nets and followed him." The invitation by itself is not going to attract two fishermen to leave their nets, their livelihood, to follow a stranger. The mystery of Jesus grows. There is something about him, the way he looks, the authority with which he speaks, that leads two grown men to leave their work behind and follow him. The mystery is underlined when a similar invitation given to James and John is quickly accepted. They not only leave their important work mending the nets, but, the text tells us, they leave their father as well. Obviously, Jesus has some strange power to attract people simply by speaking to them. He also seems to know exactly what he is doing, even if those around him in the narrative have difficulty understanding.

He goes with his four followers to Capernaum, "and immediately on the sabbath he entered the synagogue and taught." The kind of details we expect in narrative are left out. We have no description of the town, no explanation of why Jesus goes there, of how he knows where the synagogue is, of what he teaches. We know, however, the response he receives: the people "were astonished at his teaching, for he taught them as one who had authority." The explanation of their astonishment is vague, but we are inclined to believe it because we have seen the "authority" which has attracted four men to leave their work and follow Jesus. "There was in their synagogue a man with an unclean spirit; and he cried out, 'What have you to do with us, Jesus of Nazareth? Have you come to destroy us? I know who you are, the Holy One of God.'" Jesus rebukes him. The unclean spirit's question is, however, well worth asking under the circumstances, although it may be illuminating to us that only the spirit recognizes the source of Jesus' authority. Those in Jesus' world are confronted by a man whose coming has been proclaimed by someone recently arrested—certainly the people know that John has been arrested—and he begins to teach them, telling them that the kingdom of God is upon them, that they need to repent and believe the gospel. It is reasonable to ask what Jesus wants. The question will be asked repeatedly not only by those with whom Jesus comes into contact, but by the Pharisees plotting behind his back, and by his own family when they believe he is mad and want to protect him. He responds to his synagogue questioner by driving out his unclean spirit, an act which amazes the people. "What is this?" they say. "A new teaching! With authority he commands even the unclean spirits." The mystery of Jesus' "authority" expands. He commands unclean spirits as easily as he had controlled the wild beasts in the wilderness.

Jesus and his followers leave the synagogue for Simon and Andrew's house. "Now Simon's mother-in-law lay sick with a fever, and immediately they told [Jesus] of her. And he came and took her by the hand and lifted her up, and the fever left her." This is the second kind of curing Jesus has performed and it begins to expand our understanding of him, as well as the knowledge of those in the narrative. He cures the physical illness of Simon's mother-in-law as, in the synagogue, he had cured a man of an unclean spirit. He can cure physically; he also seems to cure spiritually. It is the latter power, as we will see, that the people have most difficulty accepting, most difficulty being attracted to. They are constantly fascinated by his ability to cure physical illness, but they tend to downplay, much to Jesus' annoyance, his ability to cure spiritually. Recognizing both powers, however, the people bring him the sick and those "possessed with demons." The whole city gathers outside the door. Knowledge and understanding of Jesus begins to spread for us as readers and for those *in* the narrative.

The next morning Jesus, wanting to be alone, rises before dawn and goes out to pray. But Simon and others "pursued" him and told him that everyone was looking for him. We assume they are eager to observe him perform more miraculous cures. What else do they understand at this point? Jesus has told them little (and the text has told us little) about his mission, about what he has come for. That he has a mission becomes clear, however, in his response: "Let us go on to the next towns, that I may preach there also; for that is why I came out." The mystery of Jesus is increased. He knows what he is doing; there is some purpose, some plan that he is following, although it is not revealed to us nor is it revealed to the people in the narrative. He cures a leper, but sternly charges him, "See that you say nothing to anyone; but go, show yourself to the priest." The man, like everyone else Jesus asks to be secretive, tells everybody about his cure. Why should Jesus want to keep his miracles secret? He seems eager to preach his message to a variety of people, and he has implied that he is on a clearly defined mission. Why not have his presence known and advertised? Does he want the people to see him themselves? Does he want to deemphasize his curing of physical afflictions? Does he realize his charge of secrecy will add incentive for the man to advertise him? Is he thinking of John's arrest, concerned that he too will be arrested before his mission is completed?

People begin to come to Jesus "from every quarter." They crowd around him as he preaches "the word to them." We do not yet know the extent of that "word"—in a sense, the mystery of Jesus is maintained longer for us than it is for those in the narrative. Only gradually is the "word" revealed to us, only slowly, like the metaphors which will describe it, is the concept of the kingdom of God developed for us. The excitement of the people is conveyed in the account of the paralytic cured by Jesus who, because of the press of the

crowd, has to be brought to him through an opening cut in
the roof. Not all eyes watching Jesus are favorable, however.
"Now some of the scribes were sitting there, questioning in
their hearts, 'Why does this man speak thus? It is blasphemy! Who can forgive sins but God alone?'" Like the
questions in the synagogue, these are not unreasonable questions under the circumstances. The scribes, protectors of
traditions, storehouses of past wisdom, see a man who claims
to be able to forgive sins as well as cure physical illness. Is
this not blasphemy, they ask? We remember, too, that John
has been arrested. By these scribes? Are they to be the
source of opposition to Jesus and his "new teaching"? Unknowingly, the scribes add to the mystery of Jesus by assert-
ing that only God can forgive sins. The people have seen that
Jesus can drive out "unclean spirits." Is he then God? Jesus,
perceiving the scribes' thoughts, challenges them and then
amazes them by curing a paralytic. The people agree, "We
never saw anything like this!" referring as much perhaps to
Jesus' rebuke to the scribes as to his cure of the paralytic.
Jesus' "authority" is again demonstrated when he persuades
Levi to come with him simply by saying, "Follow me."

The narrative begins to expand on Jesus' "new teaching." To
this point, we know that he speaks with "authority," that
large crowds gather to hear him, that he can cure men, and
that he has warned men to repent because "the time is
fulfilled." We also know that the man who prepared his coming
has been imprisoned and that there are scribes questioning
him "in their hearts." We now hear of Jesus in a new role:
"As he sat at table in his house, many tax collectors and
sinners were sitting with [him] and his disciples; for there
were many who followed him. And the scribes of the
Pharisees, when they saw that he was eating with sinners
and tax collectors, said to his disciples, 'Why does he eat with
tax collectors and sinners?' And when Jesus heard it, he said
to them, 'Those who are well have no need of a physician, but
those who are sick; I came not to call the righteous, but
sinners.'" What Jesus is doing, presumably, is breaking a
social custom. The scribes criticize him because he is doing

what—from their perspective, from the human standards that they have established, the human conventions as they have defined them—is improper. He is in some way rebelling, in some way thumbing his nose at their social, perhaps moral, code. Such activities of Jesus become common practice for him in the narrative. Once, when "John's disciples and the Pharisees were fasting; and people came and said to [Jesus], 'Why do John's disciples and the disciples of the Pharisees fast, but your disciples do not fast?' . . . Jesus said to them, 'Can the wedding guests fast while the bridegroom is with them? As long as they have the bridegroom with them, they cannot fast. The days will come, when the bridegroom is taken away from them, and then they will fast in that day.'" The passage opens up many things. It confirms the rule-breaking nature of Jesus' mission, here seen in terms of the lack of fasting of his disciples at a time when the Pharisees and even John's disciples are fasting. It also introduces a further mystery about Jesus. Presumably he refers to himself in alluding to a bridegroom, but who then is the bride? In what way is Jesus a bridegroom? And when will Jesus, the bridegroom, be taken away? By whom? Under what circumstances? The passage also touches on a topic, marriage, which will be picked up several times in the narrative. We will hear of it, of course, in the story of Herod (6:14-29), and it will come up again when Jesus is asked whether it is lawful for a man to divorce his wife (10:2-12). "No one sews a piece of unshrunk cloth on an old garment," continues Jesus. "If he does, the patch tears away from it, the new from the old, and a worse tear is made. And no one puts new wine into old wineskins; if he does the wine will burst the skins, and the wine is lost, and so are the skins; but new wine is for fresh skins." These sayings interrupt a series. We have just heard that Jesus' disciples have broken a religious rule and that Jesus himself has broken a social rule. In the verses that will follow (2:23-3:5), Jesus and his disciples again break rules. Jesus, in the passage which is centrally placed among these four instances of rule breaking, makes very clear that his mission involves not only breaking rules, not only making minor reformations, but total change. He is coming with both "new wine" and "fresh skins." His is not to be a mere patchwork job, as the first metaphor suggests, which will lead to a worse tear; he has come to effect a total revision, "new wine is for fresh skins." The phrase will haunt us as it opens up imaginatively during the narrative: the fresh skins, we already may recognize, are Jesus' new teaching; the "new wine," we do not yet know, will be his blood.

The passage is followed, as it was preceded, by two instances of Jesus and his disciples shocking the Pharisees. The disciples are challenged for doing "what is not lawful" by picking heads of grain on the sabbath. Jesus is watched by the Pharisees to see whether he will unlawfully attempt to heal a man on the sabbath. In each instance, Jesus answers them, the second time "with anger, grieved at their hardness of heart." But we recognize that Jesus, however rightly, is repudiating the authorities; they sit silently, seeking a charge to bring against him, the same kind of charge, presumably, that has already been brought against John. They begin to plot: "The Pharisees went out, and immediately held counsel with the Herodians against him, how to destroy him." This is our first allusion to "Herodians," our first notion that Herod is somehow going to be a critical character in the narrative. Only later do we find out that Herod is the one who had arrested John. Although we do not yet know anything about Herod, the allusion to "Herodians" reminds us that John has been arrested, that Jesus has said that the bridegroom will be taken away, and that the Pharisees have already charged Jesus with blasphemy. We have learned more of the opposition to Jesus, and that knowledge foreshadows for us what is to come. In 3:19, at the end of the list of Jesus' disciples, comes the name Judas Iscariot, "who," the text tells us bluntly, "betrayed him." Even on a first reading of the Gospel, we would be aware early in the narrative of what is to come, so that when it did come, it would really be no surprise to us.

The crowds following Jesus become "a great multitude" as

305

his reputation spreads. The unclean spirits call him "the Son of God," but again, desiring secrecy, "he strictly ordered them not to make him known." "He went up on the mountain, and called to him those whom he desired; and they came to him. And he appointed twelve, to be with him, and to be sent out to preach." Consider how this appears to the Pharisees and the Herodians of the story. Instead of one man, speaking with "authority," gathering crowds to him, they must now contend with a band of men. For the opponents of Jesus and John, this is becoming a serious matter. They see Jesus beginning to expand and increase his power; they now face thirteen rebels, each with "authority to cast out demons." The allusion to Judas Iscariot, however, "who betrayed [Jesus]," reminds us that Jesus is not going to triumph, at least not in the traditional sense of the word. The suspense of the narrative is in part undercut for us, but suspense is also increased because we do not know how Judas will betray Jesus; we do not know why, or how, or when it will be described. As there is a mystery about Jesus, in other words, so too the text is creating mysteries for us by planting these foreshadowings which will only be revealed later in the narrative.

We hear for the first time of Jesus' family, which attempts to "seize him, for people were saying, 'He is beside himself.'" Their concern is not unreasonable—indeed it is very realistic—considering what Jesus has said and done and the fact that he has now formed a band of men. Their concern also, of course, suggests the lack of belief that surrounds Jesus; even his family does not understand him. Or do they simply fear for him? They know that John has been arrested. They have perhaps heard that the Pharisees and the Herodians are beginning to think of charges that they might bring against Jesus. Before his family arrives, Jesus answers the scribes who say that he is "possessed by Beelzebul," and that "by the prince of demons he casts out the demons." "How can Satan cast out Satan?" asks Jesus. "If a kingdom is divided against itself, that kingdom cannot stand. And if a house is divided against itself, that house will not be able to stand."

The exchange, occurring presumably as Jesus' family is coming to "seize" him, perhaps mildly rebukes their lack of faith in him (his house should not be divided) and at the same time attempts to assuage their doubts. They want to take charge of him, as we know, because they think he is mad. The scribes' accusation seems to confirm their worst fears. Jesus, in his response, not only ridicules the scribes' logic; he also suggests, adding to his mystery, that Satan is under his control. "And his mother and his brothers came; and standing outside they sent to him and called him." The crowd tells Jesus his family is asking for him. "And he replied, 'Who are my mother and my brothers?' And looking around on those who sat about him, he said, 'Here are my mother and my brothers! Whoever does the will of God is my brother, and sister, and mother.'" The mystery of Jesus grows even as we gain more knowledge about him. We have seen him expand his authority and reputation, increase the size of his band by appointing twelve disciples, and he now enlarges his charge to include all believers as his mothers, sisters, and brothers.

The narrative gives us more specific information about Jesus' teaching. Enormous crowds gather, so large that Jesus must get into a boat and sit in it on the sea. He relates a parable about a sower and his seeds, concluding it with: "He who has ears to hear, let him hear." Jesus will constantly tell his disciples and others to *hear* if they have ears, to *see* if they have eyes. He cannot mean hearing and seeing in the physical sense, since the content of his parables cannot be literally heard or seen and understood. What he is describing, the kind of message he is bringing, he seems to suggest, is not going to be seen or heard without intellectual effort. Those about him question him about the parables. "To you," he tells them, "has been given the secret of the kingdom of God, but for those outside everything is in parables." Strangely, the first thing that Jesus announced in the narrative, that the kingdom of God was at hand, has become a "secret," as Jesus' power and "authority" are themselves mysterious, although their source has been revealed at least to us—he is the Son of God (which is itself a mystery). The

LITERARY INTERPRETATIONS OF BIBLICAL NARRATIVES

secret will gradually be revealed during the narrative, but Jesus' remark creates for us narrative suspense in that we realize that the gospel needs not only to be believed, but also understood. And we need to see and hear in unusual ways, unlike those, Jesus says, who "may indeed see but not perceive . . . hear but not understand."

Following his explanation of the parable of the sower (which we will consider below), Jesus, for the first time, reveals a reason for his desire for secrecy: "Is a lamp brought in to be put under a bushel, or under a bed, and not on a stand? For there is nothing hid, except to be made manifest; nor is anything secret, except to come to light." The statement may explain why Jesus has urged silence on those he has cured. Nothing remains secret or hidden long, he suggests, perhaps because it is human nature to explore and reveal such things; perhaps, because at the right time, all secrets will be known. Jesus' statement reverberates throughout the narrative, in reference to the kingdom of God, the gospel itself, the message that Jesus brings, his parables, who or what he himself is, his desire for secrecy. The narrative brings to light (as all narratives do?) the secrets and mysteries of its opening chapters. Jesus begins here to reveal the secret of the kingdom of God. It is, he says, like a seed which sprouts and grows, "first the blade, then the ear, then the full grain . . . . When the grain is ripe . . . the harvest has come." Or, he adds, it is like a grain of mustard seed which, "the smallest of all the seeds on earth . . . grows up and becomes the greatest of all shrubs." Both parables describe the growth from something small to something large; the first includes a hint of an ending, "the harvest," the second a hint of peaceful rest, "the birds of the air can make nests in [the shrub's] shade." The kingdom of God, like the seeds, is presumably future oriented, small now, but with the promise of great growth, and of harvest, and of rest. Most of those to whom Jesus preaches have great difficulty accepting a future triumph; they expect their rewards, their rest and harvest, in the present. "With many such parables he spoke the word to them, as they were able to hear it; he did not speak to them without a parable, but privately to his own disciples he explained everything."

If he did explain everything to his disciples, they seem to have "heard" little. Chapter four ends with Jesus and his disciples tossed about by a storm at sea. The disciples wake him, "Teacher, do you not care if we perish?" Jesus rebukes the wind, orders the sea to be still, and turns to his disciples—"Why are you afraid? Have you no faith?" And even the disciples, the chosen twelve, those to whom everything has been explained, do not understand. "Who then is this," they say to one another, "that even wind and sea obey him?"

II

The opening four chapters identify many of the major themes of the Gospel of Mark. It is important, I think, to stand back somewhat from our close analysis of these chapters and attempt to answer some of the questions which they have raised. Certain conflicts have been suggested, our interest in the character and mission of Jesus has been aroused, the expanding nature of Jesus' authority and reputation has been established. And yet, we have seen even his disciples wondering who he is, a question which has been asked, implicitly or explicitly, by the people he has cured, by the crowds which press upon him wherever he goes, by the scribes, by his own family. We as readers have been told he is the Son of God; but we do not know what that means. We know he will be betrayed, but not how or where or why. Given a complex narrative such as this, it will not be possible to describe fully the development of every theme suggested in its first four chapters. In some instances, therefore, I will point out what seems to me the beginning and ending point of a theme whose development is fairly self-evident; in other instances, I will describe the full development. Any of these themes could easily provide material for a lengthy essay or discussion on the Gospel.

A first theme is the mystery of Jesus, the mystery prepared for by the prophet Isaiah and by John and elaborated on in Jesus' first words: "the time is fulfilled, and the kingdom of God is at hand; repent, and believe in the gospel." He whose way has been prepared has come, but he seems to be himself preparing the way for something else. The people in the synagogue in 1:27 recognize that he brings a "new teaching," and throughout chapters 1–4, we have seen Jesus amazing and confounding his followers as well as his opponents. The mystery of Jesus is opened up for us in two ways. First, we gradually find out more about who he is. The questions we might be asking (what does it mean to be the Son of God?) are asked for us in a different form by those in the narrative. At the opening of chapter 6, for example, many who are astonished by his words say, "Where did this man get all this? What is the wisdom given to him?" These are the kinds of questions the narrative, any narrative, must answer.

Our first piece of concrete information about Jesus comes in 6:3: "Is not this the carpenter, the son of Mary and brother of James and Joses and Judas and Simon, and are not his sisters here with us?" He is a carpenter, then, known to the people, whose family is also well known; he does not come from some distant city or foreign territory. That Jesus *is* one of them adds to their sense (and our sense) of his mystery because they know all about his family (they can name their names). Our confirmation of who Jesus is culminates in the narrative, as we might expect, during his trial when the high priest asks (14:61): "Are you the Christ, the Son of the Blessed?" and Jesus answers, "I am; and you will see the Son of man seated at the right hand of Power, and coming with the clouds of heaven." The high priest, of course, charges Jesus with blasphemy; but nevertheless, from the perspective of those in the narrative, this exchange solves the mystery created by the coming of Jesus.

The mystery of Jesus is opened up in a second way by the gradual explanation of the phrase he uses when he first speaks: "the kingdom of God," he says, "is at hand." The revealing of the nature of this kingdom clarifies who or what Jesus is as Christ or Messiah. Both words mean anointed (i.e., king) and imply deliverer or savior. As the kingdom is defined, spiritually and theologically, the nature of the Messiahship is also defined spiritually. The disciples' question, "Who then is this?" is also our question, even though they know him personally and we have been told he is the Son of God. The phrase is initially mysterious, however, to those inside the narrative (and to us) because we do not know what it means. Clearly, the people have misconceptions about it. Most of them seem to believe that it is going to come in their lifetime, that they are actually going to "see" it. The word "kingdom" gives them notions of glory, of a triumph of some kind; they may be correct, but not in the ways they anticipate. This is why Jesus' announcement to his disciples (8:31) that he is going to be tortured and killed is so stunning to them, and why Peter then "rebukes" Jesus and takes him aside presumably to offer him the disciples' protection. For the disciples, as for the people, Jesus' "kingdom" is not what they expected, his "triumph" not the glory they awaited. During the narrative, we become aware that "the kingdom of God," whatever it might be, is not earthly and present, but nonearthly and future. We have seen the first hints of this in the two seed parables in chapter 4. The seeming future orientation of the kingdom is explicitly elaborated on in the account of Judgment Day (13:4-37). "Tell us," four of the disciples ask, "when will this be, and what will be the sign when these things are all to be accomplished?" "The end is not yet," Jesus replies; and he describes the chaos that will come, the suffering of his followers, the false prophets who will arise, the darkening of the sun, the gathering of God's elect "from the ends of the earth." Whether this passage is a later addition or not, it completes, for us, our knowledge of "the kingdom of God." What is surprising about the explanation of the phrase is not only that the kingdom is in the future (those in the narrative expected otherwise), but that it is a kingdom which will involve arrests and pain, not glory and triumph in conventional, human standards. There is, therefore, irony in the development of this theme. What was originally announced by Jesus was misinterpreted by his followers; their human perspective proved wrong or limited. Throughout the narrative, Jesus will point out the gap which may exist between human standards or human conventions and the truth of God. Man's rules, concepts, standards, he will suggest, are not necessarily God's.

A second theme begun in these first four chapters and developed in the narrative involves the healing powers of Jesus, already demonstrated in his various miracles. Jesus, we have seen, cures physical diseases and forgives sins. The pattern of the theme is marked by a gradual deemphasis of Jesus' curing of the physically afflicted and a corresponding increase in emphasis on his cleansing or absolving the spiritually afflicted. That, at least, is the pattern of the narrative. Ironically, however, the people in the narrative stress Jesus' powers as a healer of the physically ill. Most of them are certainly aware of his other power, and some come to him to be forgiven their sins; but what fascinates and attracts the crowds, what increases Jesus' reputation, is his ability to heal the blind and deaf, those with fever and palsy. His more important power, from the perspective of the narrative, is increasingly overlooked, even by his own disciples. As Jesus hangs on the cross, he is mocked because he seems powerless to end his own physical suffering: "He saved others," the chief priests say to one another. "He cannot save himself." The narrative seems to run in ironic counterpoint to those in the narrative, expanding on the spiritual healing of Jesus as the people cry for more spectacular physical cures.

A third theme established in the opening chapters of Mark is the concept of the secrecy of Jesus. In only one instance (5:19) does Jesus tell a man he has cured: "Go home to your friends, and tell them how much the Lord has done for you." Part of Jesus' reason for secrecy is given in the parable about the lamp (4:21-22). What is hidden, he had said, is hidden to be disclosed. Gradually during the narrative, however, Jesus becomes less concerned about secrecy. His earlier concern, then, may reflect his knowledge of the atmosphere in which he moves; he knows that John has been arrested. The need for secrecy disappears entirely when Jesus gets to

Jerusalem, when he has reached the geographical location and the point in time where his mission is about to be completed. He enters Jerusalem openly and publicly (earlier in 7:24 he had gone to Tyre and Sidon "and would not have anyone know it"). The manner of his entrance delights his followers: "Hosanna!" they shout. "Blessed is he who comes in the name of the Lord! Blessed is the kingdom of our father David that is coming!" Their enthusiasm mounts as Jesus becomes a more public figure, presumably because they believe his triumph is near. The need for secrecy has passed. John's death (it has occurred by this time) may seem to have marked only an interlude in the conflict. Jesus, they may believe, is ready for open confrontation. All their thoughts are, of course, correct; but the end of secrecy, the new information to come about the kingdom of God, will lead to a triumph—the crucifixion—which will, for all but a very few, be a disappointment.

The fourth theme established in the opening chapters and then expanded in the narrative is of Jesus as a breaker of rules, an overturner of traditions, a revolutionary as far as the authorities are concerned. The emphasis indicates why those who follow Jesus and who hear his words seem to shift back and forth between believing him and not believing him. They are being pressured, perhaps, or threatened by the authorities; they are concerned about what the authorities are going to do, not only to Jesus, but to them. Jesus' rebelliousness may explain why the disciples desert him when he is arrested; they know what has happened to John, that he has been arrested and executed. It is not safe to be one of Jesus' followers because Jesus is constantly attacking tradition and human interpretations of Scripture. In 7:9, the Pharisees ask him why his disciples ignore "the tradition of the elders" by eating with defiled hands. "You have a fine way," responds Jesus, "of rejecting the commandment of God, in order to keep your tradition!" He gives them another illustration of their misreading of Scripture and tells them that they make "void the work of God through . . . tradition . . . . And many such things you do." The "many such things" are delineated in Jesus' subsequent clashes with various authorities, with the scribes, the Pharisees, and Pontius Pilate. If there is any tension in Mark, any potential for dramatic conflict, it comes in these various clashes. There are many of them, and the theme of Jesus as a breaker of rules dominates them all. In the exchanges, Jesus becomes more forceful in his attacks on tradition, on human traditions which masquerade as God's traditions, as he emphasizes how the authorities have perverted God's word for their own gain and their own ends. The repeated confrontations between Jesus and the authorities underline Jesus' passive nature. What seems to puzzle the authorities is that he does not respond angrily, even when he is tortured and tormented by soldiers. From their human perspective, Jesus should defend himself, lash out at his accusers, rally his band of disciples, start a political revolution. Pilate cannot understand—he "wondered"—why Jesus does not respond to the charges brought against him. The rebellion he leads seems somehow to end in a paradox, a triumphant crucifixion.

A fifth theme touched upon in the opening chapters is of Jesus as bridegroom. The allusion he makes in 2:19-20 had raised many questions. Who is Jesus' bride? What marriage is to take place? What does the marriage promise? On the one hand, Jesus alludes to "wedding guests" and a "bridegroom," implying festivities; on the other hand, he tells the people the bridegroom will be taken away. We suspect, of course, that Jesus will be taken away by the authorities when he is, like John, arrested. What we do not expect is that he also, in a sense, takes himself away, that the "marriage" he infers takes place as he hangs from the cross, that his death is necessary to consummate the marriage. There is again irony for those in the narrative because they expect a different kind of wedding feast, as they had expected a different kind of triumph. The narrative helps us understand the paradoxes, but those in the narrative are justifiably puzzled.

A sixth theme we have already seen is the lack of understanding of the people who hear Jesus speak (we will leave the disciples aside for a moment). Their lack of understanding leads to numerous misconceptions and ultimately to almost total denial. The theme is brilliantly conveyed in the narrative, perhaps because it epitomizes one of the overriding concerns of the gospel: to indicate the differences between the standard that Jesus brings and the standards and conventions established by the authorities and adhered to by the people. In 11:27 the chief priests and the scribes and the elders, representatives of different kinds of knowledge and authority, ask Jesus, "By what authority are you doing these things, or who gave you this authority to do them?" "I will ask you a question," Jesus responds. "Answer me, and I will tell you by what authority I do these things. Was the baptism of John from heaven or from men?" The scholars argue among themselves: "If we say 'From heaven,' he will say 'Why then did you not believe him?' But shall we say 'From men?'—they were afraid of the people, for all held that John was a real prophet. So they answered Jesus, 'We do not know.' And Jesus said to them, 'Neither will I tell you by what authority I do these things.'" The very questions asked of Jesus suggest the difference in perspective between him and those with whom he comes into contact. Essentially, the elders, scribes, and priests want to see Jesus' credentials. Where is his degree, his certificate, his scroll, which proves that he has authority to preach to the people? How can he claim to be in their club, their association, without having gone through the proper channels or the proper education or the proper kind of training or whatever? Jesus is an outsider; yet, he is trying to undermine the structures they have been trained to uphold. From their perspective, Jesus has no training to do what he is doing. When they ask for his credentials, they challenge him to lay out the information and experience he has which they do not have. They are earthbound, paralyzed by their own analogies and limited vision.

The same kind of misunderstanding characterizes even those who see Jesus' miracles. We need to keep in mind the activity going on outside the story of Jesus itself. The extent of his powers is surely being gossiped about, John's arrest must be known, the displeasure of the Pharisees must be common knowledge. Misunderstanding of Jesus, then, may be in part provoked by fear. The lack of understanding becomes most striking for us, and most exasperating to Jesus, in 8:11: "The Pharisees came and began to argue with him, seeking from him a sign from heaven, to test him. And he sighed deeply in his spirit, and said, 'Why does this generation seek a sign? Truly, I say to you, no sign shall be given to this generation.'" Why, Jesus must wonder, does *this* generation ask for a sign when he himself, the Son of God, is among them? No sign is needed since, as he tells the high priest (14:62), he is the Christ. The people, too, constantly seek more evidence even though, from our perpective as readers, the evidence is overwhelming that Jesus the character is being depicted as the Son of God. If Jesus could come down from the cross, the chief priests say, then they would believe.

A seventh theme, analogous in part to the lack of understanding of the people, is of the development of the disciples. We see, on one level, an expansion in the narrative of the disciples' various duties and powers—they are called by Jesus, formed into a band, given names, various assignments, and missions. But more interesting from a literary point of view is the disciples' increasing lack of understanding, which leads them, as it does most other people in the narrative, to misconceive and then to deny Jesus. It is clear from the beginning that the disciples, however much the narrative tells us that Jesus explained to them in private the secret of the kingdom of God, fail to understand the parables and the miracles of Jesus. Their response when Jesus walks on the sea (6:48-51) is to be "terrified . . . astounded, for they did not understand about the loaves," the text explains, "Their hearts were hardened." Indeed they did not understand about the loaves, as we will see below, but they have been present at numerous other miracles performed by Jesus. Their response, of course, is perfectly human and reasonable, but they never seem to comprehend who Jesus is. The difficulty of understanding among the disciples, those chosen by Jesus to be his special missionaries, suggests how difficult it is for those who are not so chosen to understand. Not only do the disciples fail to understand Jesus and ultimately deny him, but they also consistently fail to heed his advice.

When they reach Capernaum with Jesus (9:33) he asks them, "What were you discussing on the way?" They are silent, for "on the way," the text informs us, "they had discussed with one another who was the greatest." And yet, a week earlier Jesus had said, "If any man would come after me, let him deny himself." He has told them explicitly and in a number of more subtle ways that they are to think less of themselves, more of others; less of power and glory, more of kindness and mercy; yet they argue about who is the "greatest" among them. Jesus is again angry with the disciples when they rebuke the people for bringing children to him (10:13-14). "When Jesus saw it he was indignant, and said to them, 'Let the children come to me, do not hinder them; for to such belongs the kingdom of God.'" His anger is surely due in part to his having told them a short time before (9:37), "Whoever receives one such child in my name receives me; and whoever receives me, receives not me but him who sent me." The disciples cannot understand Jesus' parables, they forget his advice and requests, they lack faith in prayer (9:17-29), they are not even confident when events repeat themselves.

Jesus tells them (8:2-4) that he has compassion on the crowd because they have nothing to eat. "How can one feed these men with bread here in the desert?" they ask. A short time before (6:37-44), they had fed five thousand men from five loaves and two fish. Are their memories so short? We see the disciples envious of others. Shortly after Jesus has told them, "If any one would be first, he must be last of all and servant of all" (9:35), they drive away a man who is casting out demons because, they explain to Jesus, "he was not following us" (9:38). Jesus tells them why this is wrong, and urges them to "be at peace with one another." But instead, they become envious of one another. James and John ask a favor of Jesus (10:35-37), "Grant us to sit, one at your right

317

hand and one at your left, in your glory." "And when the ten heard it," the narrative informs us, "they began to be indignant at James and John." They are envious and jealous because James and John almost got something that they did not. Jesus patiently tries once more to explain to them: "You know that those who are supposed to rule over the Gentiles lord it over them, and their great men exercise authority over them. But it shall not be so among you; but whoever would be great among you must be your servant, and whoever would be first among you must be slave of all." Jesus tells four of the disciples to be alert (13:33-37), ostensibly because the kingdom of God could come at any time, more practically perhaps because Jesus knows his trial and execution are soon to occur: "Take heed, watch; for you do not know when the time will come. It is like a man going on a journey, when he leaves home and puts his servants in charge, each with his work, and commands the doorkeeper to be on the watch. Watch therefore—for you do not know when the master of the house will come, in the evening, or at midnight, or at cockcrow, or in the morning—lest he come suddenly and find you asleep. And what I say to you I say to all: Watch." Shortly after this advice, in Gethsemane, Jesus asks them to sit while he prays. He returns to find them asleep: "Simon, are you asleep? Could you not watch one hour? Watch and pray that you may not enter into temptation." Once more, Jesus prays. On his return he finds them again asleep, "their eyes were very heavy; and they did not know what to answer him." He comes a third time; they still sleep. "It is enough," says Jesus, "the hour has come . . . . My betrayer is at hand." And in their final act of disloyalty and faithlessness, the disciples all forsake him and flee.

The theme of the disciples' lack of understanding and faith is fully developed. Supposedly they are closest to Jesus and are getting much information from him. Yet, they cannot follow his advice to deny themselves, to receive children; they are envious of others, of one another; they fail Jesus when he asks them to be watchful; they desert him when he is arrested. While the disciples should know better, their actions are similar to those of the people who crowd around Jesus to watch his miraculous cures. It is difficult, however, to be critical of the disciples. They are men of good will, presumably, who do carry out many of Jesus' instructions. Given their perspective in the narrative, they perhaps have reasons to fear and to be puzzled. John has been arrested and executed; the scribes and Herodians are scheming to bring charges against Jesus. The disciples are asked to accept a triumph which involves a crucifixion, a kingdom of God which is like a mustard seed, a promise of being first if they are last, a leader who refuses to defend himself. This is much to ask of average men.

Peter in many ways epitomizes the disciples in his earnestness, his willingness to help, his eagerness to believe, and also, in his inability to stay with Jesus at the end. A simple fisherman, he follows Jesus on the promise of becoming a fisher of men and comes to believe that Jesus is "the Christ" (8:29). Given his sense (and the other disciples') of what "the Christ" should be, a new king of an independent Israel, he rebukes Jesus when Jesus first tells the disciples about his suffering and death (8:32). Who Jesus is and what is going to happen to him seem contradictory to Peter. He is, as a loyal follower, willing to fight for Jesus. He can never move beyond his very human responses and feelings, and there is no reason why we should expect him to. He sees Jesus transfigured (9:2), in conversation with Elijah and Moses, and asks: "Master, it is well that we are here; let us make three booths, one for you and one for Moses and one for Elijah." It is a clumsy, useless statement under the circumstances, but he does not know what else to say (and what else is there to say?). His sense of wonder and amazement never connects with the actuality of his situation. He wants to be helpful, to be approved of. Jesus tells the disciples that a rich man will have great difficulty entering the kingdom of God (10:29). "Lo," says Peter, drawing attention to his contrast to the rich men, "we have left everything and followed you." Jesus curses a fig tree (11:14) and Peter, as if surprised to see the curse work, points out to him, "Master, look! The fig tree which you cursed has withered" (11:21). Jesus tells the disciples they will all fall away (14:27); but Peter insists, "Even though they all fall away, I will not . . . . If I must die with you, I will not deny you." "Before the cock crows twice," Jesus tells him, "You will deny me three times." And Peter, having denied Jesus three times, hearing the cock crow a second time (14:66-72), "broke down and wept." Like the other disciples, Peter is not able to understand how he fits into the unfolding of Jesus' story, or into the unfolding explanation of the kingdom of God. Like the other disciples, the import of the events in which he participates eludes him, the frailty of man in the face of "new teaching" overwhelms him. And he weeps.

III

The development of these themes in the narrative is greatly enhanced by the parables and by the careful juxtaposition of scenes. Jesus' parables, as he implies to us, are "secret" because they are meant to be brought into the light (4:22). The parables are, in fact, brought into the light in a surprising way; they are worked out or explained in narrative form elsewhere in the gospel. What Jesus says in parable form, in other words, is exemplified in the narrative itself. Similarly, the relationship among scenes is carefully controlled. Our understanding of the significance of a particular scene, for example, is frequently clarified when we consider the scenes which precede and follow it. This may not always be the case, of course, with the parables or with individual scenes, but if we look for conscious literary artistry in a work as complex as the gospel, we are likely to find it.

Consider first the parables. We saw above how Jesus' parable in 2:22 reverberates throughout the narrative. "No one puts new wine into old wineskins," Jesus had said. "If he does, the wine will burst the skins, and the wine is lost, and so are the skins; but new wine is for fresh skins." The suggestion is that a total change is about to take place. What Jesus brings is not new ideas for old structures or new structures for old ideas. Both the ideas and the structure are to be "new" and "fresh." Jesus' "new teaching" that amazes and often baffles the people and his disciples contains many paradoxes. Unlike those of the scribes and high priests, his answers are not neat, his rules are not easy to comprehend. The new structure for man is indeed "fresh": it opposes the authorities, conventions, and traditions of Jesus' time. That new teaching, however, may not be complete without Jesus' sacrifice which ransoms man from the unclean spirits: "The Son of man . . . came not to be served but to serve, and to give his life as a ransom for many" (10:45). Jesus' giving of his blood, the "new wine," may represent the essence of his teaching, the denial of self which forms its foundation.

Other parables are worked out in the narrative in more specific ways. The parable of the sower and the seed (4:3-9), for example, is explained by Jesus to those about him, and his didactic clarification is then concretely illustrated in the gospel. "The sower sows the word," says Jesus, "and these [the seeds] are the ones along the path, where the word is sown; when they hear, Satan immediately comes and takes away the word which is sown in them." This first type in the parable appears in 6:5: "And he could do no mighty work there, except that he laid his hands upon a few sick people and healed them. And he marveled because of their unbelief." These people who do not believe are from Jesus' "own country"; he is among them, but they ignore him. The second kind of people in the parable "hear the word, immediately receive it with joy; and they have no root in themselves, but endure for a while; then, when tribulation or persecution arises . . . they fall away." This type is illustrated by the disciples. They accept Jesus' words immediately (following him at his invitation), but when trouble and persecution come, they deny him, Peter three times. A third type hear the word "among thorns; they are those who hear the word, but the cares of the world, and the delight in riches, and the desire for other things, enter in and choke the word, and it proves unfruitful." This type is illustrated in the narrative by both Herod and Pilate. They are fascinated by rebels; Herod by John the Baptist, Pilate by Jesus. Neither of them, it seems, is anxious to have John or Jesus executed. But they are "among thorns"; worldly cares, riches, desires overcome their reluctance. Herod is hosting his birthday feast when Herodias' daughter asks for John's head. He was "exceedingly sorry; but because of his oaths and his guests he did not want to break his word to her." He wants to please his guests in the same way that Pilate later wants to satisfy the crowd in giving them Barabbas instead of Jesus. The fourth type in the parable "hear the word and accept it and bear fruit, thirtyfold and sixtyfold and a hundredfold." The only characters in the narrative who illustrate this type are those who do not deny him, Joseph of Arimathea and the women at Jesus' crucifixion, "looking on from afar" (15:40). There may be other examples of these four types in the narrative. The important point is that Jesus' interpretation of the sower parable is not unrelated to the text; indeed, Mark is providing us with a kind of foreshadowing of the range of human responses to Jesus and his new teaching.

We have already seen in other contexts how brief parables—of the bridegroom (2:19-20) and the mustard seed (4:30-32)—are opened up and developed in the gospel. One of the later parables (12:1-9) seems to summarize the entire life of Jesus. "A man planted a vineyard," Jesus says, "and set a hedge around it, and dug a pit for the wine press, and built a tower, then let it out to tenants, and went into another country. When the time came, he sent a servant to the tenants, to get from them some of the fruit of the vineyard. And they took him and beat him, and sent him away empty-handed. Again he sent to them another servant, and they wounded him in the head, and treated him shamefully. And he sent another, and him they killed; and so with many others, some they beat and some they killed. He had still one other, a beloved son; finally, he sent him to them, saying, 'They will respect my son.' But those tenants said to one another, 'This is the heir; come, let us kill him, and the inheritance will be ours.' And they took him and killed him, and cast him out of the vineyard. What will the owner of the vineyard do? He will come and destroy the tenants, and give the vineyard to others." The parable not only reverberates through the gospel, but back through the preparations which preceded it: Isaiah prophesied the coming of John, John prepared for the coming of Jesus, Jesus seeks to prepare the people for the coming of the new kingdom. God sent his prophet John to his tenants, man; John was arrested and beheaded. God has sent his son, his only heir, Jesus, who will be crucified. The tenants, Jesus promises, will be destroyed (13:5-37).

The enormous care with which the parables are related to events in the narrative, worked out or explained, is complemented by a similar care in the placement of scenes. In any narrative, scene placement is a matter of choice and selection; an event can be described in chapter one, say, or told as a flashback in chapter ten, or placed for emphasis between two similar or contrasting events. Once the incidents which will make up a narrative have been determined, they can be included in any number of places in the text. A good question to ask, then, about events and incidents in a narrative, in the gospel, for example, is why they are set in a particular place.

In 5:25-34, for instance, a woman who has been hemorrhaging for twelve years touches Jesus' cloak and is cured. The incident seems self-contained; it might have been related anywhere in the gospel. Immediately before this, a man had fallen at Jesus' feet and begged him to come to his house to save his daughter who was "at the point of death." Jesus is walking towards this man's house, presumably, when we are given the interruptive account, a kind of digression, of the woman who suffers from hemorrhaging. Jesus pauses to ask who touched his garment—he, then, is *also* interrupted—and because of the interruption, he does not reach the house in time. "Your daughter is dead," some people tell the father. "Why trouble the Teacher any further?" "Do not fear," says Jesus, "only believe." He enters the house, takes the girl by the hand: "'Little girl, I say to you, arise.' And immediately the girl got up and walked." What are we to make of the order of these events? We notice that up to this time, Jesus has either cured by touching the sick or driven out unclean spirits by commanding them to depart. He has been face to face with the person to be cured. In this incident, he is asked to go to a man's house to do the same kind of thing again. On the way there, however, a woman touches *him* and is cured; and the girl in the house, even in his *absence*, will be saved because of faith. The order of events, in other words, enlarges our sense of the power of faith. The interruption of Jesus, and of the narrative, takes us to this conclusion by degrees. He cures with a touch, he can cure if he *is* touched, he can cure when he is absent. It is not Jesus himself, but faith in Jesus, that cures.

The account of John the Baptist's death is another self-contained incident. It might have been described in a number of places in the narrative; indeed, it need not have been described at all—the text could simply have indicated that John was beheaded. What relationship is there between the story of John the Baptist and the story of Jesus? We recognized that John's arrest foreshadowed the arrest of Jesus. Does the foreshadowing extend further? King Herod, we are told (6:14), has heard that Jesus' disciples are casting out demons and preaching to the people. His court is also gossiping about Jesus, some saying he is John the Baptist raised from the dead, others that he is Elijah, still others that he is a prophet, "like one of the prophets of old." "But when Herod heard of it [Jesus' actions] he said, 'John, whom I beheaded, has been raised.'" This is for us the first news of John since his arrest, and we are told that he is dead. From a narrative point of view, we are given the end of the story first. But the past, from Herod's point of view, is the present: John has been raised. We soon recognize, however, that Herod's thought of the present moment foreshadows what will happen in the future: Jesus will die, and rise from the dead. In a sense, then, the account of John is a synopsis of the account of Jesus: the end of the story *should* come first because it is really the beginning—John's death the beginning of Jesus' public mission (he has sent out his disciples), Jesus' death the beginning of the kingdom of God. ("The Son of man . . . came . . . to give his life as a ransom for many.")

We are then told, somewhat to our surprise, that Herod had arrested John "for the sake of Herodias, his brother Philip's wife; because he had married her. For John said to Herod, 'It is not lawful for you to have your brother's wife.' " Earlier, we had assumed that John was arrested because he was a follower of Jesus. We were not, of course, entirely wrong. That Herod is unlawfully married recalls Jesus' words about himself as the bridegroom, foreshadows his criticism of divorce (10:2-12), and most importantly, foreshadows his own arrest, an arrest in part due to his attacks on the authorities because they have followed the wrong beliefs. Herod, like Pilate with Jesus later, fears and is fascinated by John, "When he heard him, he was much perplexed; and yet he heard him gladly." Herodias, however, like the scribes we have seen scheming and grumbling, maintains her grudge against John and wants him killed. Herod gives a banquet in honor of his birthday—it is a festive and gay occasion. During the banquet, Herodias' daughter dances so well that Herod says to her: "Ask me for whatever you wish, and I will grant it." And, prodded by her mother, she asks for the head of John the Baptist. Similarly, Jesus' final sentencing comes during a festive occasion (15:6-15). It was customary at the feast of the Passover for Pilate to release for the people "one prisoner for whom they asked." The crowd, then, like Herodias' daughter, is granted one wish, one favor. Pilate ask them if they want Jesus, but the chief priests, like Herodias' mother, "stirred up the crowd to have him release for them Barabbas instead." Pilate is not comfortable with the request: " 'Then what shall I do with the man whom you call the King of the Jews?' And they cried out again, 'Crucify him.' And Pilate said to them, 'Why, what evil has he done?' " Herod, like Pilate, is equally uncomfortable with Herodias' daughter's request. He is "exceedingly sorry"; he knows that John is "a righteous and holy man." But, we are told, "because of his oaths and his guests he did not want to break his word to her." So, too, Pilate, "wishing to satisfy the crowd, released . . . Barabbas; and having scourged Jesus, he delivered him to be crucified." Soldiers lead Jesus away and crucify him as the chief priests and scribes jeer. His body is taken by Joseph and laid in a tomb. A soldier of the guard executes John and brings his head on a platter to Herodias' daughter, "and the girl gave it to her mother." Her grudge, like that of the high priests and scribes, has been satisfied. John's disciples take his body and lay it in a tomb. And we reach the end, the "beginning," of each story: the foreshadowing, "John, whom I beheaded, has been raised"; and the event foreshadowed, "Do not be amazed; you seek Jesus of Nazareth, who was crucified. He is risen, he is not here" (16.6). The parallels are so striking that it becomes clear why the account of John's death is included in the narrative. If we wonder why it is placed where it is, we might notice that it is framed by the disciples' first major mission. The flashback interrupts the mission. They have gone out to preach (7:12), we are told of John's death, and they return (7:30). The implication of the flashback—told while the disciples are preaching to the people—is that John's persecution and death may foreshadow the fate of all the disciples because of their preaching, as indeed Jesus later confirms.

In 6:35-44, Jesus feeds five thousand people with five loaves and two fish. Curiously, the same miracle is repeated in 8:2-9. Even more curiously, the disciples, having seen both miracles, express concern (8:16) because they "have no bread." Why does the narrative repeat the miracle? And why is it recalled by the disciples in a concern which annoys Jesus? For one thing, the second miracle of the loaves and fishes provides emphasis to Jesus' enormous powers. And yet, following the repeat performance, the Pharisees ask Jesus for a sign ("Why does *this* generation seek a sign?" asks Jesus), and the disciples are upset because they have no bread. The emphasis has worked for us perhaps, but not for those in the narrative. Why? "Do you not yet perceive or understand?" Jesus asks the disciples. "Having eyes do you not see, and having ears do you not hear?" The incidents which provide the frame for the second miracle and for the discussion between Jesus and his disciples perhaps underline the most important point of the repetition. In the incident which precedes, Jesus cures a man who is deaf; in the incident which follows, he cures a man who is blind. He gives hearing and sight to these afflicted people; they now have ears to hear and eyes to see. They are, of course, joyful; the people are astonished. But we recognize, because of the conversation with the disciples, that sight and hearing alone are not sufficient for man to be able to understand Jesus and his teaching. The amazement and joy which accompany the miracles is only a beginning: "They may indeed see," Jesus has said, "but not perceive"; they "may indeed hear but not understand" (4:12).

Another self-contained incident is the transfiguration of Jesus (9:2-3). It might have been placed anywhere in the narrative. What precedes the event which enables us to understand the importance of its occurring when it does in the narrative? Shortly before (8:31), Jesus has told the disciples (and us) for the first time that he will suffer, be rejected and killed (earlier he had only hinted that he would be taken away). For the disciples, in the light of Jesus' many miracles, this is stunning news; indeed, Peter, we recall, rebukes Jesus for it. Their sense of Jesus and of the kingdom of God must be somewhat deflated. They may need, therefore, the reconfirmation of Jesus' power which the transfiguration provides; Jesus, who might have gone to the mountain alone, takes Peter, James, and John with him.

We may ask similar questions of other scenes and incidents in the Gospel. Why are they described in this particular place? What events precede and follow them? What do they foreshadow in the narrative? What do they explain which was not entirely clear before? What other scenes do they parallel? Knowing the right questions to ask about a literary text, particularly one as familiar as the Gospel of Mark, is often more important than knowing the right answers. I have attempted to suggest many of these questions and to offer some answers concerning the major themes as they are established in the first four chapters, the function of parables, and the placement of scenes.

IV

Still, we are in the third quarter of the twentieth century, at a time when the study of literature, indeed the study of all the arts, is being closely scrutinized; sharply criticized; openly harassed by legislators, school boards, and the general public. And, we must acknowledge, many of those leading the attacks are our former students. The dazzling achievement of the creation of a literary world seems not to be enough. There are larger issues affecting society, and to some of those we need to address ourselves. Of what utility is the Gospel of Mark, aside from any religious considerations, as a literary achievement? What does the Gospel invite us to contemplate about ourselves and the lives we lead?

The Gospel asks us to consider the allegorical, even symbolic nature of human existence. It suggests that we are, in a sense, surrounded by parables, by events and circumstances, by placements of scenes, which, properly analyzed, properly interconnected, can open up our understanding of life, as the parables are opened up for us in the Gospel, as minor incidents take on larger implications in context. Our lives are not spots in time, but part of a continuum. From this, the Gospel asks us to note the potential value of each individual, of each incident in the creation of human history. What happens to us *means* something, even if that meaning is puzzling, even if the meaning, as for Peter, is not immediately apparent. Our lives do have patterns of significance. We may even be, without realizing it, like Peter who does not realize it, at the very center of history. But one of our difficulties, the Gospel suggests, is our lack of faith in simplicity, in charity, in passive response to outward aggression. We thrive on confrontation. We cannot, as does Jesus with his tormentors, ignore the minor rebukes and the injuries done to us. Even the men chosen by Jesus as his disciples are envious of others, envious finally, of one another. And that concern for self, a concern which Jesus abandons to the puzzlement of those around him, makes us fear, as Jesus is feared, those who do not conform to our notions of proper behavior, our notions of human standards, human conventions, human laws, human mores. We drive ourselves, as most of those in the Gospel drive themselves, to rebuke and condemn those who challenge our traditions and beliefs. We might even drive ourselves so far that we are able to join in the cry, "crucify him," "execute him," "lynch him," the point at which, with our eyes blind to injustice, our ears cannot hear the simple question, "Why, what evil has he done?"

XVII Revelation

KENNETH R. R. GROS LOUIS

The very title of the final book of the New Testament, the Revelation to John, suggests that in reading it we should learn something that we did not know clearly before. Something is to be unveiled, something is to be disclosed which previously had been concealed. For most readers of Revelation, however, the veil is not pulled off far enough. Most modern readers in particular tend to be confused by the narrative, unable to separate the seen from the unseen, the revelation from the commentary on it. The work is full of symbols which are no longer familiar to a modern sensibility, allusions and passages from the Old Testament which only a biblical scholar can track down, references, perhaps, to contemporary events in John's time for which he provides no easy interpretation. We are dazzled by occasional passages, but the work as a whole leaves us befuddled and confused. There are numerous scholarly books we can read which will explain most of the puzzles, answer our questions, interpret the symbols, place John's revelation in the apocalyptic tradition. Such books are filled with diagrams, charts, and tables which link John's Revelation to the historical circumstances of his time, the Old Testament background, the seven days of the week, various festivals in the Jewish calendar, ancient numerological schemes, and so on. The books are all interesting in themselves, but it is difficult to know what to do with them when we come to teach Revelation as literature. It may be that Revelation is not teachable as literature. We may teach it as an example of a visionary experience and look closely at the quality, sharpness, and clarity of the visions. But that is not the same thing as teaching it as literature. We

may teach it with very modern terminology and discuss St.
John's trip and what he saw on his trip. Certainly, the work
as a whole does have a kaleidoscopic effect not unlike that
produced by the rhythms and frames of contemporary music
and film. There is nothing wrong with teaching Revelation in
terms of twentieth-century art forms so long as we do not
delude ourselves into thinking we are teaching the book as
literature. Revelation is perhaps too long and complex, then,
to teach in its entirety. At the same time, it is a carefully and
consciously wrought statement which offers challenges to
careful, conscientious readers and which contains passages of
striking, not to say mind-expanding, imaginative energy.
The opening three chapters illustrate its careful artistry,
certain thematic links in succeeding chapters substantiate
this artistry, and the closing chapters finally confirm what
we should have seen at the beginning—that Revelation is not
a patchwork of ineffable, unrelated mystical visions, but a
highly wrought and controlled work of art.

"The revelation of Jesus Christ, which God gave him to
show to his servants what must soon take place; and he made
it known by sending his angel to his servant John, who bore
witness to the word of God and to the testimony of Jesus
Christ." We are told that the theme of the narrative is to be
"what must soon take place." We are also told the particular
way in which this information has been revealed: from God to
Jesus Christ to John. The triadic method of revelation is
imitated in the verses which follow. John will bear witness to
God and the testimony of Christ; those who read aloud, who
hear, and who keep what is written will be blessed; the
message comes from "him who is and who was and who is to
come"; from Christ "the faithful witness, the first-born of the
dead, and the ruler of kings on earth." The tripling of phrases
and verbs is not accidental, mirroring as it does in language
the relationship among God, Jesus Christ, and John, the
servant who represents all of God's servants. The structural
importance of the triad for the narrative will become clearer
later when we are introduced to the dragon, beast, and false
prophet in parody of God, Christ, and John. We are not at

this point, of course, aware of the author's plan, but the foreshadowing underlines the conscious artistry of the book. Even the characterization of God as "him who is and who was and who is to come" will be parodied in the characterization of the beast (17:8) who "was and is not and is to come." In the climactic battle between good and evil which ends the revelation, the world of God triumphs over a parody of the world of God—God's enemies are, of course, dangerous, but they are also mocked because of their presumptions. What seems a conventional description of Christ also is a result of careful artistry. Christ is the "faithful witness," a phrase confirmed by the events which follow; he is "first-born of the dead," a phrase suggesting that others will be reborn as indeed they are with the triumph of the new kingdom; he is "ruler of kings on earth," a phrase substantiated by the establishment of the new Jerusalem; he "loves us and has freed us from our sins by his blood," a phrase we recall when the Lamb appears in 5:6, "as though it had been slain"; he "made us a kingdom," the kingdom described in chapter 21; he "is coming with the clouds," a phrase which expands on "what must soon take place," the apocalypse. The text is well planned. Revelation is no mystic's incoherent outburst. The introductory foreshadowing is concluded by words put in the mouth of the Lord God, "I am the Alpha and the Omega," and framed by a repetition of the phrase "who is and who was and who is to come."

At this point, the narrator John takes over. He tells us he is our brother who shares with us "the tribulation and the kingdom and the patient endurance" (a linguistic triad again). What he shares will be elaborated on in his revelation —suffering as God's prophet, endurance under duress, the kingdom of wicked men. John will also come to share, however, in the kingdom of the new Jerusalem. He was on an island called Patmos, preaching on the sabbath, when suddenly he was "in the Spirit" and heard a voice "like a trumpet" telling him to write down what he is about to see and send it to seven churches. On first reading, we might pass by the phrase "in the Spirit," assuming that it is meant to suggest a state of intense concentration or meditation. But on a second reading, we notice that the phrase appears three more times in Revelation. At the opening of chapter 4, for example, a voice calls to John: "Come up hither, and I will show you what must take place after this," and John is "at once . . . in the Spirit." The phrase appears again in chapter 17, verse 3. An angel says, "Come, I will show you the judgment of the great harlot who is seated upon many waters," and in a few moments, "in the Spirit," John is carried away into a wilderness. It appears finally in chapter 21, verse 10, when an angel says, "Come, I will show you the Bride, the wife of the Lamb," and John, "in the Spirit," is carried away to a great, high mountain. The phrase, we begin to realize, announces what are essentially the four major visions of Revelation: the vision which leads to the letters to the seven churches, the vision of heaven following the opening of chapter 4, the vision of the fall of Babylon, and the vision of the new Jerusalem. The phrase marks not only a physical movement on the part of John—turning to see Christ, soaring to heaven, being carried to a wilderness, then to a mountain—but also a spiritual movement, a new moment of consciousness. What is striking about the progression is that John finds it increasingly difficult to describe what he sees. The final vision, as we will see, can be described only in terms of what it is not.

John turns to see who sounded the trumpet and whose voice spoke to him. He is confronted by a stunning sight: "I saw seven golden lampstands, and in the midst of the lampstands one like a son of man, clothed with a long robe and with a golden girdle round his breast; his head and his hair were white as white wool, white as snow; his eyes were like a flame of fire, his feet were like burnished bronze, refined as in a furnace, and his voice was like the sound of many waters; in his right hand he held seven stars, from his mouth issued a sharp two-edged sword, and his face was like the sun shining in full strength." John, understandably, falls at the feet of this figure "as though dead."

The portrait, obviously of Jesus Christ, is the first of four major portraits of Christ in Revelation which, augmented by numerous allusions, especially in the songs throughout the narrative, will produce for us a very full portrait by the end of the book. This first portrait is also another indicator of the artistic unity of the revelations, for the characteristics of Christ enumerated here will reappear in the seven letters. John emphasizes Christ's hair, eyes, feet, and voice. The hair, he tells us, is white as white wool, white as snow. The connotations we have for whiteness, presumably shared by John, help characterize Christ—he is pure, innocent, perhaps old in some sense. His eyes are like a flame of fire, eyes that can penetrate, pierce, burn to the heart of things, to the secrets of the seven churches, their strengths and their weaknesses. John has noted his details carefully. Our initial impressions of the figure before him involve whiteness and redness, snow and fire. We recognize the paradoxical nature of the figure—he seems innocent (white), yet passionate (red), cool (snow), yet hot (fire). He might be, and John seems to me to be conscious of this, a force not only of mercy and forgiveness, but also of anger and punishment. From our perspective as readers of a literary narrative, we don't even know yet who the figure is; what we do know results in a seeming paradox. His feet, John tells us, are like burnished bronze. Several details might spark our imaginations. We may think of feet trampling on something, as Christ will soon trample on the dragon and the beast and the false prophet; we may think of the artificiality of these particular feet, burnished like bronze. But if we do, John offers us another paradox, for the voice of the figure is like the sound of waters, a very natural, though perhaps fearful sound. This is not only a figure who projects heat and cold, whiteness and redness, with all the connotations those words have, but also one who is both artificial, other than natural—in the sense of permanent perhaps—and natural. More striking about the description as a whole is the fact that what seem to be carefully stated details are not specific at all. The figure before John cannot, finally, be described except in a series of similes: he is *like* a son of man, his hair is white *as* wool and snow, his eyes flame *like* fire, his feet are *like* burnished bronze, his voice is *like* the sound of many waters. John *sees* and *hears* someone, but language can only approximate his appearance. The sight is inexpressible, as the New Jerusalem at the end of Revelation will be inexpressible. At least John knows precisely what the figure is carrying —seven stars—and what he holds in his mouth—a two-edged sword, but in summary, he must resort to another simile, "his face was like the sun," an appropriate simile for one whose eyes flame like fire, for one who is a compassionate judge.

John, falling at the feet of this figure, begins to become a real narrator in a visionary world. He responds to what he sees, as he will respond to other events as they are presented to him. Like other narrators of journeys, especially Dante the pilgrim in *The Divine Comedy*, John's attitudes will alter, his fears will diminish as he gains confidence and knowledge about "what must soon take place." We recall that when Dante begins his journey, he is very distressed by the suffering of the sinners, so much so that he weeps and falls unconscious at the contrived story of the pity-seeking Francesca. Increasingly during his journey, however, Dante the pilgrim hardens to the punishments, so that eventually he can angrily (and with Vergil's approval) kick in the head a sinner who is already buried in ice up to his neck. This transformation of Dante the pilgrim is analogous to the transformation of John the prophet in Revelation. Dante swoons after Francesca's story; John falls "as though dead" before the vision of Christ.

The figure comforts John, identifying himself in language we have already heard, "I am the first and the last, and the living one," and with information about which we will hear more at the end of Revelation, "I have the keys of Death and Hades." The author suggests to us a link between this figure and the Lord God who spoke in 1:8, and also plants details which will become central to the end of the narrative. John, as we were told at the very beginning, is to be the agent who will explain "what must soon take place"; and we see him here receiving his instructions: "Write what you see, what is and what is to take place hereafter." Using customary triadic phrases, the text warns us that this is going to be a difficult work to follow if we are expecting a chronological narrative, because it will combine what is past, what is present, and what is future. The figure explains that the seven stars he carries are the angels of the seven churches, a symbolically appropriate association for both are heavenly and bright and both provide illumination. The seven lampstands are the seven churches, again an appropriate analogy since the churches, like the lampstands, do not give light, but contain it. Presumably the seven letters are necessary because the churches have not held their light well; and the danger for the churches (the "lampstands") is that the light could be put out. Whether John's directions to write what he sees pertains to all of Revelation or only to the letters seems to me an irrelevant question. The important point is that he has been assigned the job of scribe (of artist?) who will be shown wonders which he is supposed to describe to others.

The seven letters are stunningly conceived and organized. Any lingering doubt about the book's artistic craftsmanship is surely ended when we recognize the careful and conscious structure of the letters. The structure is not, however, mechanical; patterns are occasionally broken, and a progression is clear from letter to letter. Each letter begins with a characterization of the letter-writer: (1) "of him who holds the seven stars . . . , who walks among the seven golden lampstands"; (2) "of the first and the last, who died and came to life"; (3) "of him who has the sharp two-edged sword"; (4) "who has eyes like a flame of fire, and whose feet are like burnished bronze"; (5) "of him who has the seven spirits of God and the seven stars"; (6) "who has the key of David, who opens and no one shall shut, who shuts and no one opens"; (7) "of the Amen, the faithful and true witness, the beginning of God's creation." We recognize immediately that these characteristics come directly from the portrait of the figure John has just seen. This is not in itself surprising perhaps; what is surprising, as we will see, is that the characteristic selected by the author is also directly related to the content of each letter. The characteristics which open the letters, in other words, are not casually selected. Following the characterization, there follows in five of the letters a statement of praise. In the other two letters, the praise is deleted, not replaced by something else, and the letter-writer goes immediately on to the third part of the pattern. The church of Ephesus is praised for its patient endurance; Smyrna for its firmness under tribulation, poverty, and slander; Pergamum for its loyalty to Christ; Thyatira for its patient endurance; Philadelphia for its loyalty. The praise is basically the same. These five churches have suffered and been sorely tempted, but they have remained loyal and firm, they have endured patiently. We surely recall John's opening words in which he tells us he is our brother who shares "the tribulation . . . and the patient endurance," phrases which suddenly take on new meaning for John's audience. Part three of the letters contains a criticism, although again the pattern is occasionally altered. Ephesus has abandoned its initial love, Pergamum has accepted the teaching of other gods, Thyatira has tolerated the false prophetess Jezebel. The churches who received no praise—Sardis and Laodicea—are criticized for having "the name of being alive," but being dead, and for being "neither cold nor hot." Two churches receive no criticism at all. We should again be struck by the interconnecting links between the letters and the opening chapter of Revelation. The churches are in trouble generally because they have forgotten that there is only one who is, who was, and who is to come; and they are in trouble specifically because they are dead, but seem to live (Christ seems dead but then lives) or because they are neither hot nor cold (we recall the fire of Christ's eyes, the white snow of his hair). The fourth part of the letters is a call to repentance. Again, this element is deleted from two of the letters (to Smyrna and Philadelphia which were not criticized), and altered in the fourth or central letter to Thyatira, in which the call to repent is delivered specifically to Jezebel, presumably as the arch representative of all those in the churches who have forgotten the Lord

God. The fifth part of the letters is a warning of what will happen if there is not repentance. The artistry of the letters is strongly revealed in that the punishment is linked directly to the opening characterization of each letter. If Ephesus does not repent, the Christ who walks among the seven lampstands "will come . . . and remove [its] lampstand from its place"; if Pergamum does not repent, the Christ with the two-edged sword in his mouth, "will come . . . and war against [it] with the sword of [his] mouth"; if Jezebel does not repent, the Christ of fire and trampling bronze feet will "throw her on a sickbed," and her followers "into great tribulation"; if Sardis does not repent, the Christ who has the seven stars (night) "will come like a thief." The sixth and seventh parts of the letters (the order varies) consists of the sentence: "He who has an ear, let him hear what the Spirit says to the churches" (repeated in every letter) and a promised reward to those who are loyal and who endure. The call to hear brings attention not only to the promises, but also to the entire Revelation which is to follow. The rewards, like the warnings, underline the conscious artistry so evident in the narrative. Each promise is related to the portrait of Christ which preceded the letters, and more strikingly, is specifically fulfilled in the new Jerusalem described at the end of Revelation. The book demonstrates close control not only of the letters, but of the entire narrative. Those who remain faithful are promised the tree of life, the crown of life, hidden manna and a white stone, power over nations to rule with an iron rod, white garments and eternal enrollment in the book of life, a pillar in the temple of God, a place on God's throne. The details will return, from our perspective as readers, as revelations in the New Jerusalem.

The letters also suggest progression to the new vision which opens chapter 4. We know from 1:1 that we are to be told "what must soon take place." John then says in 1:7: "Behold, he is coming with the clouds." Shortly after, Christ appears to John in a vision, and finally, he speaks as he dictates the letters. "I will come to you," he says in the first letter; in the third letter, "I will come to you soon"; "hold fast," he says in the fourth letter implying he will come for the present generation, "until I come"; "You will not know at what hour I will come," he says in the fifth letter, suggesting now a definite, measurable time; and in the seventh letter, "Behold, I stand at the door and knock." Christ seems ready to come, the end seems upon the world, but then, instead of our opening the door for him, he opens the door for *us*. John looks up and "Lo, in heaven an open door!" And a voice calls to John, "Come up hither." We are not ready for the New Jerusalem. There is more for us, and for John, to see and understand.

I have touched on only the major elements of unity among the seven letters, between the letters and the opening characterizations of Christ, and between the letters and the New Jerusalem. The more we read the letters, the more we realize how few words are wasted. Even the seemingly casual allusion to the slaying of the prophet Antipas in the letter to Pergamum reminds us of the dangerous time John is living in. The balance between threat and promise in the letters recalls to us the paradoxical nature of Christ, who is fire and snow, red and white, natural and artificial. Overall, the letters reveal to us three details of what is to come which we did not know—judgment is coming, redemption, and the kingdom of God. This is the thematic pattern of each letter. The pattern is in turn linked to what John has told us about Christ in the opening. He is judge, redeemer, and king.

Chapters 4 through 16 describe John's second vision. These chapters are not as tightly organized as the opening three or the closing six chapters of Revelation, but they contain unifying links and a thematic progression leading to the confrontation between good and evil, represented by Jerusalem and Babylon. They are difficult chapters, better suited from a teacher's perspective for essay projects or class reports than for class discussion and analysis. It is perhaps more profitable to isolate certain specific aspects and trace them through the chapters.

Before doing so, we might consider the general progression, which is thematic rather than chronological, as the author mingles past, present and future events. Chapters four and five describe the scene in heaven. We should be aware of John's responses to the remarkable things he sees, and we might also ask in what ways the scene approaches and departs from our expectations. How would we, or one of our students, describe a heavenly scene? The effects of the breaking of the seven seals is the subject of chapters six and seven. Again, we should notice John's involvement and responses (a question is directed to him by one of the elders). Are his attitudes changing or his knowledge increasing? We should also consider the objects, characters, and images which carry over from the preceding two chapters, and which link the seemingly unrelated scene in heaven with the events on earth. Chapters eight to eleven describe the catastrophes which result when the seven trumpets are sounded. As with the scene in heaven, we might ask about the nature of the catastrophes. Who is affected? Do the catastrophes occur in any identifiable order? Would we add to them? John is even more involved during these events: he is ordered not to write down something he has just seen (10:4); he is given a scroll and ordered to eat it (10:8-10); he is told to measure the temple of God with a measuring rod (11:1). Do we get any sense of how he is responding to these commands? Chapters twelve to sixteen contain a series of portents and signs foreshadowing the coming war between Satan and God and also foreshadowing the war's outcome. God's enemies are introduced in a triadic parody of the opening triad of God, Jesus Christ, and John. The dragon with seven heads and ten horns gives the beast with ten horns and seven heads "his power and his throne and great authority," as God gave the same to Christ. One of the beast's heads seems to have a mortal wound (like Christ), but it heals and the people worship the beast, saying, as they might of Christ, "Who is like the beast, and who can fight against it?" John, of course, has already given us the answer to that question. The parody is completed when a second beast rises out of the earth and becomes the spokesman and advocate for the first beast, as John is the prophet of Christ. The beast's followers are marked "on the right hand or the forehead," as the Lamb's followers at the opening of chapter fourteen have "his name and his Father's name written on their foreheads." We know that the dragon and two beasts are a sham triad because they have no ultimate authority. We scorn their pretensions at the same time that we recognize the seriousness of the battle to come. The carefully drawn sides, parodic and mirror images of each other, suggest further the difficulty of describing God and Christ. As the earlier portrait of Christ was sketched through similes, and as the New Jerusalem will be depicted by negatives, the power and authority of God and Christ are more concretely presented by their parodic opposites. The end of chapter sixteen sets the stage for the final battle as the dragon, beast, and false prophet send out "three foul spirits like frogs" to assemble their forces. The battle, by the way, is over before it begins, when the seventh angel pours his bowl into the air and a loud voice from the temple and throne calls out: "It is done!"

As I mentioned above, there are several specific aspects of chapters 4 to 16 which might be isolated by themselves and analyzed irrespective of the thematic progression of the chapters as a whole. One I have already touched on is the change in John's attitude and involvement. He is experiencing this vision, this kind of journey; and we would expect his responses and understanding to progress in some way, as indeed they do. There are several objects which appear throughout these chapters—seals, trumpets, thrones, bowls—and we might concentrate on their function, the similarities and differences among them, their role in providing unity. There are a number of songs of praise in the chapters, and beyond, which contain a progression of their own: 4:8, 4:11, 5:9-10, 5:12, 5:13, 7:10, 7:12, 11:15, 11:17-18, 15:3-4, 19:1-8. The early songs elaborate on the nature of the God "who was and is and is to come" and confirm his right to "honor and power and might" by identifying his authority to create, redeem, and judge. The transition in the songs occurs in 11:15 when voices in heaven announce that "the kingdom of the world has become the kingdom of our Lord and of his

Christ." That God has the authority to assume power has been established; the songs now describe the beginning of the new kingdom and explain how it came to be (19:1-8). The last song, interrupted four times by prose sentences, offers a summary of the narrative from chapter four to the end. The multitude cries out that God has judged the great harlot; John interrupts to say "once more they cried" and the voices then allude to the smoke rising from Babylon. The interruption marks the shift of setting from God's judgment to the destroyed city. In another interruption, John tells us the elders and creatures fall down to worship God. The scene then shifts to heaven, and a voice urges all God's servants to praise him. The final interruption again announces a shift in setting. John hears a great multitude of voices which announce that the time of the marriage of the Lamb has come, "and his Bride has made herself ready." We are prepared for the description of the New Jerusalem.

Chapters four through sixteen are indeed difficult, but we can make them less difficult either by isolating and analyzing certain aspects or else by looking at the larger narrative patterns without worrying about the details, the import of most of which is lost to us anyway and can be recovered only by diligent research.

Chapters 17 through 21 are unified primarily through the narrative device of comparison and contrast. At the opening of 17, John is carried "in the Spirit" into a wilderness and shown a vision of Babylon, representing all the cities of pagan civilization, personified as a woman "arrayed in purple and scarlet, and bedecked with gold and jewels." She is riding on the beast with seven heads and ten horns, a fact which astonishes John because he thought the beast was dead. The angel explains, extending the parody of Christ, that the beast "was and is not and is to come." The angel also outlines for John the forces which will take part in the coming battle. Clearly, the harlot (Babylon) is in contrast to the Bride of chapter 21 (Jerusalem). Further, the Bride and Bridegroom of 21 will marry; the harlot, on the other hand, will fall out of favor with the beast, will come to be hated by it. The obvious contrast underlines the order which is coming in Christ, symbolized by the marriage, as opposed to the disorder and chaos which leads to the destruction of Babylon, of pagan civilization. Babylon forgot the ultimate power of God which John told us about at the opening of Revelation and which the songs of praise have emphasized throughout: "She glorified herself and played the wanton"; in her heart she said, "A queen I sit, I am no widow, mourning I shall never see."

There follows in chapter 18 a series of dirges which contrast to the song announcing the New Jerusalem in chapter 19, as kings, merchants, sea captains, voyagers, and tradesmen bewail the fall of Babylon. The dirges suggest their mistaken sense of power and greatness, of the ends of human society. The mourners concentrate on the luxuries and dainties they will miss, the splendor that will be no more, the fine clothes and jewels being destroyed. Their distorted values are strikingly suggested by the order of the items in the list of lost cargo: "gold, silver, jewels and pearls, fine linen, purple, silk and scarlet, all kinds of scented wood, all articles of ivory, all articles of costly wood, bronze, iron and marble, cinnamon, spice, incense, myrrh, frankincense, wine, oil, fine flour and wheat, cattle and sheep, horses and chariots, and slaves, that is human souls." A mighty angel announces the final end of Babylon in a series of phrases which contain the Poe-like repetition "no more." Such total obliteration cannot itself be described. We can only imagine what will no longer exist—no music, no crafts, no mills, no light, no marriages. Words cannot describe the void, the empty space that was once Babylon.

The scene shifts at the opening of chapter 19 from earth to heaven as the multitudes announce the marriage of Christ and the New Jerusalem. The defeat of the dragon, beast, and false prophet is described and John sees "a new heaven and a new earth," and hears a voice proclaiming the end of tears and death and pain. The contrasts are completed: human rebellion and the fulfillment of God's purpose, Babylon and Jerusalem, the dragon-beast and God-Christ, the faithful prophet and the false prophet, the mourning and the rejoicing, the death of the old world and the birth of the new, the defeat of evil and the triumph of good.

And in chapter 19, we begin to hear of the fulfillment of the specific promises made to the churches in the seven letters. In 19:15, John sees a sharp sword in Christ's mouth "with which to smite the nations, and . . . rule them with a rod of iron" (the letter to Thyatira); in 20:6 we are told that the second death has no power over those who share in the first resurrection (the letter to Smyrna); in 20:12, we see the last judgment being made according to what is written in the book of life (the letter to Sardis); in 21:22, we are told that the temple of Jerusalem is the Lord God (the letter to Philadelphia); in 22:2, we see the tree of life with its twelve kinds of fruit (the letter to Ephesus); and in 22:3-4, we are told that the servants of God will see him face to face, sitting on his throne (the letter to Laodicea). With the promises fulfilled, the revelation is ended. John's fourth and final vision, when "in the Spirit" he is carried to a high mountain, is of the New Jerusalem itself.

It seems clear that Revelation is a carefully wrought work, as the opening and closing chapters indicate, and as the themes and images which unify chapters four through sixteen further support. At the same time, this is an unusual apocalyptic work. There is the *bang* which we associate with apocalypse, "the first heaven and the first earth had passed away, and the sea was no more," but this is not the end of Revelation in the way such bangs end modern apocalyptic works. Chapter 21 and the opening of chapter 22 describe a kind of utopia which follows the apocalypse, the ultimate utopia from the perspective of the author, but from a literary perspective a utopia nonetheless. What is unusual about this utopia is that it does not reform reality, it stands reality on its head. The New Jerusalem has no temple, no sun, no moon, no night, nothing unclean or accursed, and no lamp. We recall the similes which described the vision of Christ, the negatives which described the end of Babylon, the parody of God and Jesus Christ and John. Somehow, John cannot directly describe what his inspiration, his visions "in the Spirit," have revealed to him. The similes, negatives, parodies, and analogies suggest the limits of language. What this finally implies about Revelation as a literary work is that, while it is a stunningly imaginative creation, it contains, in that very imaginative thrust, an enormously important theme in the history of art—of painting, literature, sculpture, music—and that is, the limits of the human imagination. Some things in the universe are inexpressible and will remain inexpressible: imagination and language can only approximate them.

NOTES

Chapter I

1. For traditional Judaism, reading the Bible as mere *belles-lettres* is anathema. It does not deny that the Bible employs literary devices or that the Bible is not literature too. The devices however are only the means to an end, the end being the teaching of Jewish virtues—moral, theoretical, and practical. Hence the approach here is inspired by classical teachings, but it does not reproduce them. Neither does it fairly represent them. My debt to the scholarship of Y. Heinemann and A. A. Halevi is obvious on every page.
2. We shall use Torah, Scripture, and Bible as synonyms for the so-called Pentateuch.
3. From Spiegel's masterful introduction to Louis Ginzberg, *Legends of the Jews* (New York: Simon & Schuster, 1956). The introduction and the *Legends* themselves are a valuable resource book. A word of caution: Ginzberg paraphrases only the "pearls" or the "answers" or the legends. Neither the primary sources nor Ginzberg identifies the "signals" or the "irritants" or the questions. That remains the task of the reader. Another text which is provocative and helpful is the approach to literature taken by William Empson in his *Seven Types of Ambiguity*. Maurice Samuel's *Certain People of the Book* is excellent. Thomas Mann's books on Joseph should also be read, as should the commentaries of Cassuto.

Chapter II

1. For practical criticism that illustrates all of the theoretic points that I make in this essay, see my book *The Literature of the Bible* (Grand Rapids: Zondervan Publishing Company, 1974).
2. For an elaboration of this and other points made in my discussion on the definition of literature, see the chapter entitled "The Nature of Literature," by Rene Wellek and Austin Warren, *Theory of Literature*, 3rd ed. (New York: Harcourt, Brace and World, 1956), pp. 20-28.
3. *The Growth of the Biblical Tradition: The Form-Critical Method* (New York: Charles Scribner's Sons, 1969), pp. 69-70.
4. *Early Christian Rhetoric: The Language of the Gospel* (Cambridge: Harvard University Press, 1971), p. xxii.
5. "Literary Criticism," in *The Aims and Methods of Scholarship in Modern Languages and Literatures*, ed. James Thorpe (New York: Modern Language Association of America, 1963), p. 63.

6. *The Business of Criticism* (London: Oxford University Press, 1959), pp. 23-24.

7. Wilder, *Early Christian Rhetoric*, pp. 35-36.

8. *Anatomy of Criticism: Four Essays* (Princeton: Princeton University Press, 1957), p. 316.

9. *The Bible As Literature* (New York: Oxford University Press, 1970), p. 258.

10. By an "archetype" I mean simply an image, symbol, plot motif, or character type that has recurred throughout literature. Leslie Fiedler speaks of archetypes as "any of the immemorial patterns of response to the human situation in its permanent aspects." ("Archetype and Signature: A Study of the Relationship between Biography and Poetry," in *An Introduction to Literary Criticism*, ed. Marlies K. Danziger and W. Stacy Johnson [Boston: D. C. Heath and Company, 1961], p. 268.)

11. *Fables of Identity: Studies in Poetic Mythology* (New York: Harcourt, Brace and World, 1963), p. 12.

12. For a particularly excellent discussion of the unique importance of dialogue and story in New Testament literature (and by extension in the Bible as a whole), see Wilder, *Early Christian Rhetoric*, pp. 40-70. The classic study of the unembellished style of biblical narrative, along with comments on several other items on my list of distinctive features of biblical literature, is Erich Auerbach's essay entitled "Odysseus' Scar," in *Mimesis: The Representation of Reality in Western Literature*, trans. W. R. Trask (Princeton: Princeton University Press, 1946), pp. 3-23. The avoidance of visual detail in the Bible is discussed by Dom Aelred Baker, "Visual Imagination and the Bible," *Downside Review*, 84 (1966), 349-360.

13. Philadelphia: Fortress Press, 1971.

14. "Introduction" to *The Bible: Selections from the King James Version for Study as Literature* (Boston: Houghton Mifflin Company, 1965), p. xv.

15. In speaking of the literary unity of the Bible it is, of course, appropriate to raise the question, Whose Bible—Jewish or Christian? Because the New Testament builds on the Old Testament, the unity that I claim for the Bible is generally applicable also to the Old Testament as a self-contained unit.

16. Toronto: University of Toronto Press, 1972.

17. Koch, *Growth of the Biblical Tradition*, p. 58.

18. Gardner, *The Business of Criticism*, pp. 107, 120.

19. *Anatomy of Criticism*, p. 315.

20. "Modern Theology and Biblical Criticism," in *Christian Reflections*, ed. Walter Hooper (Grand Rapids: William B. Erdmans Publishing Company, 1967), pp. 152-166.

21. *Unpopular Opinions* (New York: Harcourt, Brace and Company, 1947), pp. 167-221. In the "Foreword" to the book Sayers states that her aim in the four essays was to show that by using the methods of biblical scholarship "one could disintegrate a modern classic as speciously as a certain school of critics have endeavoured to disintegrate the Bible."

22. *On the Composition of Paradise Lost: A Study of the Ordering and Insertion of Material* (Chapel Hill: University of North Carolina Press, 1947). Gilbert's failure to see the unity of Satan's characterization is a good example of how a critic's preoccupation with different sources can lead him to violate the unity of a literary text.

23. Ralph L. Tweedale, *Wasn't Shakespeare Someone Else?* (Southfield, Michigan: Verity Press, 1971).
24. Peter Bracher, "The Bible *and* Literature," *English Journal*, 61 (1972), 1171, 1175.
25. *A Fresh Approach to the New Testament and Early Christian Literature* (New York: Charles Scribner's Sons, 1936), pp. 16-17.
26. J. Coert Rylaarsdam, "Foreword" to *Literary Criticism of the Old Testament*, by Norman Habel (Philadelphia: Fortress Press, 1971), p. ix.

Chapter III

1. I am deeply indebted to my colleague, Professor Roy W. Battenhouse, for suggesting many of the structural patterns I discuss throughout this essay.

Chapter IV

1. *A Preface to Paradise Lost* (New York: Oxford University Press, 1942).
2. I am indebted to Professor Kalman Bland for some of these suggestions concerning Eve.

Chapter V

1. For a discussion of early Hebrew literary style, see Erich Auerbach, *Mimesis* (Princeton: University Press, 1946), Chap. 1.
2. For a full discussion of exogamy and endogamy, see Edmund Leach, "The Legitimacy of Solomon: Some Structural Aspects of Old Testament History," in *Introduction to Structuralism*, ed. Michael Lane (New York: Basic Books, Inc., 1970), pp. 248-92.

Chapter VI

1. The three most helpful literary analyses of Exodus 1–2 are: M. Greenberg, *Understanding Exodus*, Heritage of Biblical Israel, vol. 2, pt. 1 (New York: Melton Research Center of the Jewish Theological Seminary of America, Behrman House, 1969); B. D. Napier, *The Book of Exodus*, Layman's Bible Commentary, vol. 3 (Richmond: John Knox Press, 1959); and Umberto Cassuto, *A Commentary on the Book of Exodus*, trans. Israel Abrahams (Jerusalem: Magnes Press, 1967).
2. Gen. 17:6-8, 28:3-4, 35:11-12, 48:3-4.
3. Greenberg, *Exodus*, p. 21.
4. Cassuto, *Commentary*, p. 8.
5. B. S. Childs, "The Birth of Moses," *Journal of Biblical Literature*, 84(1965): 120.
6. Greenberg, *Exodus*, p. 20.
7. The Hebrew text recording the location of Hebrew bondage at Pithom and Raamses is problematical. See D. B. Redford, "Exodus 1:11," *Vetus Testamentum*, 13(1963): 401-18.
8. Cassuto, *Commentary*, p. 11.
9. *Ibid.*, p. 12.
10. Greenberg, *Exodus*, p. 29.
11. *Ibid.*

12. Gen. 27, 38; Josh. 2, 9; Judg. 3:15-30, 4:17-22; I Sam. 19:11-17; II Sam. 12:1-15; I Kings 20:35-43.
13. See Charles H. Nichols, *Many Thousand Gone* (Leiden: E. J. Brill, 1963), pp. 36-38.
14. The sly triumphs of Brer Rabbit and the later "John the Trickster" stories are in this vein. Nichols, *Many Thousand*, p. 91f. See also J. Mason Brewer, *American Negro Folklore* (Chicago: Quadrangle Books, 1968), p. 28; and Gilbert Osofsky, ed., *Puttin' on Ole Massa* (New York: Harper and Row, 1969), pp. 21, 46f.
15. See D. B. Redford, "The Literary Motif of the Exposed Child," *Numen*, 14(1967): 209-28.
16. Greenberg, *Exodus*, p. 37f. For another example of narrative focus, compare I Chron. 3:5 and II Sam. 12:24f.
17. Childs, "Birth of Moses," 115-18.
18. Cassuto, *Commentary*, p. 17f.
19. See Gen. 12:3; Exod. 19:4-6.
20. Greenberg, *Exodus*, p. 40.
21. Cassuto, *Commentary*, p. 19.
22. Greenberg, *Exodus*, p. 41f.
23. Cassuto, *Commentary*, p. 20 suggests that the smothered "go" connotes deep emotion on the princess' part, and this is a possible alternate interpretation.
24. Childs, "Birth of Moses," 110-15.
25. From the Midrash, as cited in Greenberg, *Exodus*, p. 43f.
26. I Sam. 4:6-9 is another example of the biblical writer mocking the faulty understanding of Israelite reality which existed among outsiders.
27. Exod. 14:11f, 16:2f, 17:2,7; Num. 14:22-45, 16:13f, 20:4, 21:5, 25.
28. Exod. 19:12f.
29. Exod. 3:5, 33:17-23.
30. Exod. 34:29-35.
31. Deut. 34:6.
32. Exod. 7-12, 14:13f, 17:8-13, 20, 32:19f.
33. Childs, "Birth of Moses," 115-18 (who cites S. Freud, *Moses and Monotheism*).
34. See also Gen. 15:14; Exod. 12:41, 14:8.
35. See also Gen. 15:7; Exod. 6:6f, 13, 27; 7:5; 12:42, 51; 13:3, 9, 14.
36. Greenberg, *Exodus*, p. 45.
37. *Ibid.*, p. 42.
38. The text of verse 15 is rough and unusual, making it difficult to determine where one literary unit ends and the next one begins. Some translations end the preceding paragraph with verse 14, where Moses becomes fearful that his murdering the Egyptian has become known; but such an ending is penultimate, closing it off before we discover Pharaoh's response. Other translations begin the next episode with verse 16, but both the well and Moses' presence nearby, crucial to the development of verses 16-22 and presupposed by it, are mentioned in verse 15. The break must come somewhere in the middle of verse 15, and this can sometimes happen, since the Bible was divided into chapters and verses at a much later time.

In ancient times the Hebrew Bible was translated into other languages which had become more familiar to the Jewish community. In most cases the Hebrew text still preserves the more original reading, but sometimes a translation will help restore an earlier form, preserving a less corrupted stage of the Hebrew text. The Greek translation of verse 15 reads: "But Pharaoh heard this thing, and he sought to kill Moses; so Moses fled from before Pharaoh, and he dwelt in the land of Midian. *And when he had come unto the land of Midian,* he sat down by the well." Note that the italicized clause does not exist in any of the modern translations because it no longer exists in the Hebrew text. But we can see what probably happened: someone copying the Hebrew text jumped from one "land of Midian" phrase to the next, and thus a whole clause was omitted from the Hebrew text. This omitted clause (designated 2:15e), incidentally, introduces the episode we are about to examine.

39. Judg. 6:14f, 10:1; I Sam. 11:3f.
40. James Plastaras, *The God of Exodus* (Milwaukee: Bruce, 1966), pp. 46-48.
41. B. D. Napier, *Book of Exodus*, p. 23f.
42. Greenberg, *Exodus*, p. 55.
43. *Ibid.*, p. 54.
44. Exod. 12:29; Jer. 37-38.
45. Isa. 38:18; Ezek. 26:20, 31:14,16f; 32:18, 24f, 29f; Ps. 28:1, 30:3, 88:6, 143:7; Prov. 1:12.
46. Gen. 37:19-24.
47. Ezek. 29:3f; Ps. 74:12-17; Isa. 51:9-11.
48. II Sam. 22:17 (cf. Ps. 18:16); Ps. 29:3, 69, 77:16-20, 93; Isa. 43:2; Lam. 3:52-55; Ezek. 31:15f; Hab. 3:10-15.
49. Deut. 1:19, 8:15, 32:10; Ps. 29:8; Isa. 14:17, 27:10, 32:15; Jer. 2:31, 22:6; Hos. 2:3; Ezek. 6:14; and especially Lev. 16:1-10.

Chapter VII

1. Baruch Kurzweil, "Job and the Possibility of Biblical Tragedy," and "Tragic Elements in the Book of Job," in *Be-Ma'avak al Erkhei ha-Yahadut* (Jerusalem and Tel Aviv: Schocken, 1970), pp. 3-38. The first essay has appeared in English translation as "Is There such a Thing as Biblical Tragedy?" in *Anthology of Hebrew Essays*, ed. Israel Cohen and B. Y. Michaoi (Tel Aviv: Massada, 1966), I, 97-115.
2. There exists an English translation of Franz Rosenzweig's *Der Stern der Erlösung* entitled *Star of Redemption*.
3. Northrop Frye, *Anatomy of Criticism: Four Essays* (New York: Atheneum, 1967), p. 54.
4. The story of Saul, considered *in toto*, together with its moments of success also fits into an overall pattern of rise and fall. At first Saul's deeds are crowned with success, later come his failures.
5. Others besides Moses are said to have beheld God. "And they saw the God of Israel; and there was under his feet as it were a pavement of sapphire stone, like the very heaven for clearness. And he did not lay his hand on the chief men of the people of Israel; they beheld God, and ate and drank" (Ex. 24:10-11). Also, "The LORD spoke with you [plural] face to face at the mountain, out of the midst of the fire" (Deut. 5:4). But these two instances do not refer to beholding God at an absolute proximity. Such a

beholding is impossible, as Moses' rebuttal proves when his request is denied.

6. At one point, it is true, Moses refers to his old age: "And he said to them, 'I am a hundred and twenty years old this day; I am no longer able to go out and come in'" (Deut. 31:2). But he follows this immediately with the decisive reason: "The LORD has said to me, 'You shall not go over this Jordan.'"

7. Franz Kafka, diary entry for October 19, 1921. The English is taken from his *Diaries 1914-1923*, ed. Max Brod, trans. Martin Greenberg, with the cooperation of Hannah Arendt (New York: Schocken, 1965), pp. 195-196.

8. The fable "Before the Gates of the Law" appears in Kafka's *The Trial* in the chapter "In the Cathedral" and also as an independent story in his first book of short stories.

9. In Politzer's opinion, the expression "an inhabitant of thereabouts" (in German: "ein Mann vom Lande") is to be understood as coming from the Yiddish *am ha-aretz*, meaning a simple, uneducated man. See Heinz Politzer, *Franz Kafka: Parable and Paradox* (Ithaca: Cornell University Press, 1962), pp. 176-177.

10. The poem is rendered in a simple and literal translation.

11. "Could you ever discover anything sublime, in our sense of the term, in the classical Greek literature? I never could. Sublimity is Hebrew by birth." *Specimens of the Table Talk of the Late Samuel Taylor Coleridge* (New York: Harper, 1935), vol. 2, p. 41 (July 25, 1832).

12. *The Poetical Works of William Wordsworth* (Edinburgh: Paterson, 1931), p. 323.

13. A. C. Bradley, "The Sublime," in *Oxford Lectures on Poetry* (London: Macmillan, 1965), pp. 37-63.

14. Immanuel Kant, "Kritik der Ästhetischen Urteilskraft, Allgemeine Anmerkung," in *Werke* (Wiesbaden: Insel Verlag, 1960), vol. 5, p. 365.

15. "Das Erhabene muss jederzeit gross, das Schöne kann auch klein sein." Immanuel Kant, "Beobachtungen über das Gefühl des Schönen und Erhabenen," *ibid.*, vol. 1, p. 828.

16. Bradley, "The Sublime."

17. Hayyim Nachman Bialik, *Complete Poetic Works*, ed. Israel Efros (New York: Histadruth Ivrith of America, 1948), vol. 1, pp. 27-28. This particular poem was translated by L. V. Snowman.

18. The translation of the title of this poem does not follow the original, in which Bialik talks about "Har-El"—the Mountain of God—but not about Mount Sinai by name.

19. Heinrich Heine, "Geständnisse, Memoiren, Kleinere biographische Dokumente," in *Werke*, ed. Raimund Pissin and Veit Valentin (Berlin: Bong, n.d.), vol. 15, p. 50.

20. On this point see Fry, *Anatomy of Criticism*, pp. 190-191.

Chapter IX

1. S. R. Driver, *An Introduction to the Literature of the Old Testament* (Cleveland: World, Meridian Books, 1891, 9th ed. [1913], p. 453; M. E. Chase, *The Bible and the Common Reader* (New York: Macmillan, 1955), pp. 193-96.

2. All Biblical quotations are from the AV, though I have checked them

against *The Jerusalem Bible*. Throughout italics are mine for purposes of emphasis.

3. G. Fohrer, *Introduction to the Old Testament*, David E. Green, tr. (Nashville: Abingdon Press, 1968), p. 251.

Chapter XI

1. Erich Fromm, *The Forgotten Language* (New York: Grove Press, 1957), Chap. 2. His very brief passage on Jonah is one of his many comments on literature.

2. Edwin Good, *Irony in the Old Testament* (Philadelphia: Westminster Press, 1965), Chap. 2. Much of the following discussion of Jonah as an object of ridicule is based on this book; see also Ackerman, Jenks, et al., *Teaching the Old Testament in English Classes* (Bloomington: Indiana University Press, 1973), Chap. 13, and D. F. Rauber, "Jonah—the Prophet as Shlemiel," *The Bible Today* (October, 1970), which emphasizes the story's prototypical Yiddish humor rather than its irony.

3. Most of the commentators' explanations mentioned in this section and the next one come from Elias Bickerman, *Four Strange Books of the Bible* (New York: Schocken Books, 1967), Chap. 1. A very readable book, it does not always indicate scholarly justifications for the various hypotheses, but they do exist.

4. Rauber, "Jonah." See also Leo Rosten's *The Joys of Yiddish* for definitions of these two terms. Briefly, a *mensh* is a man of character and a *shlemiel* is a bungler.

5. Fromm, *The Forgotten Language*, p. 23.

6. Bickerman, *Four Strange Books*, p. 45.

7. *Ibid.*, p. 4.